MYTH AND HISTORY IN ANCIENT GREECE

MYTH AND HISTORY IN ANCIENT GREECE

THE SYMBOLIC CREATION OF A COLONY

Claude Calame

Translated by Daniel W. Berman

PRINCETON UNIVERSITY PRESS   PRINCETON AND OXFORD

First published in France under the title *Mythe et histoire dans l'Antiquité grecque: La création symbolique d'une colonie* © Editions Payot Lausanne, Nadir s.a., 1996

English translation © 2003 by Princeton University Press
Published by Princeton University Press, 41 William Street,
Princeton, New Jersey 08540
In the United Kingdom: Princeton University Press, 3 Market Place,
Woodstock, Oxfordshire OX20 1SY

LIBRARY OF CONGRESS CATALOGING-IN-PUBLICATION DATA

Calame, Claude.
[Mythe et histoire dans l'antiquité grecque. English]
Myth and history in ancient Greece : the symbolic creation of a colony / Claude Calame; translated by Daniel W. Berman.
p.   cm.
Includes bibliographical references and index.
ISBN 0-691-11458-7 (alk. paper)
1. Mythology, Greek.   2. Cyrene (Extinct City)   I. Title.
BL783 .C3513 2003
292.1'3 — dc21   2002030257

British Library Cataloging-in-Publication Data is available

This book has been composed in Sabon

Printed on acid-free paper. ∞

www.pupress.princeton.edu

Printed in the United States of America

10 9 8 7 6 5 4 3 2 1

Contents

Preface

THE practical study in method presented here, an exploration of one of the countless narrative and fictional constellations of the Greeks, is born of a feeling of malaise.

Malaise aroused first by the inadequacy of many of the categories sustaining the modern field of cultural and social anthropology: of the "mask" reduced to an object for the museum; of the "Other" opposed to the "Self" by means of the reductive schematics of binary interaction; of "ritual" detached from the phenomenon of symbolic speculation; and — the interest of this study — of "myth" considered as a universal category of "savage thought." The impression of confusion is accentuated when the anthropologist takes ancient Greek culture as his terrain, because in addition to spatial distance, there is the additional problem of exoticism brought about by the passage of time.

Malaise, as well, concerning the epistemological colorlessness brought about by the infiltration of a neoliberal ideology into the humanities. The polish of appearances and superficiality supports claims made for the sake of competition and immediate profit. To the omnipresence of thought marked only by the slogan "may the best man win" (in the masculine . . .), must be opposed, even in the quite reserved fields of the humanities, a resistance based upon a reflective and critical asceticism. This function will be assigned here to traditional scholarship, although its pedantry may be an object for reproach, and also to the semionarrative approach, the technical character of which may be considered disagreeable. The first has, nonetheless, the advantage of incorporating the research of those who have passed over this terrain before; as for the second, it should, at least, guarantee the respect due to a certain methodological coherence.

We should not, however, impose schemas constructed in a structuralist mode on a culture that appears to us in texts that are often of a poetic nature. This is to say that we must take into account the production and the function of these symbolic manifestations within their historical, social, and ideological contexts. It is also to say that, in order to avoid the dogmatic ponderousness of strict structural semiotics, we should abandon the principle of immanence which closes the text on itself independently of the situation of its production; we should recover, in the manifestations of the symbolic process, the practical categories that are particular to them. We shall thus be interested in the dynamism of discourse production, with its capacity to construct a fictional world based on a reference to an ecological and cultural given, and with its power to act, in return, upon this reality, in a precise historical context.

Particularly in the domain of the creation and writing of history, a discursive and enunciative perspective is able to demonstrate how discourse production, through processes that are far from being uniquely narrative, reformulates events considered to be foundational in order to restore to the community practices of ideological and pragmatic bearing. These re-creations (often speculative) of spaces, narrative reformulations of chronologies, and reasoned configurations of actions create active representations within the culture from which they stem. In order to be accepted within the community of belief in which the symbolic manifestation is to be inserted, the fictional is combined with the plausible. Moreover, the culture concerned will see these symbolic particularities vary with the historical changes that animate it, according to its own historicity. We, as modern readers, can only take note, admiring the constant creativity of this crafting of meaning, of this constant movement and resemanticization of symbolic productions as they vary with the cultural transformations of the society in question.

From this perspective, the narratives of the foundation of Cyrene, the great Greek colony in Libya, are exemplary. The historical event of the colony's foundation undergoes the most varied transformations in the mouths and by the pens of historiographers and poets. Shaped by narrative structures, enriched by different types of metaphors, modalized by enunciative processes, and expressed in the most diverse discursive and literary genres, these symbolic constructions are filled out with multiple textual and extradiscursive functions. In addition, their study reveals the inadequacy of the anthropological category of "myth": we should always prefer indigenous notions to taxonomies with universal pretensions. Thus the study presented here is a diptych, an attempt at critical anthropology of ancient Greek culture.[1]

This double essay was not conceived through a solitary confrontation with the texts. The reflections in the introductory section were incorporated into one of the interdisciplinary seminars entitled "Anthropologie des cultures, anthropologie des discours," held at the University of Lausanne for the past ten years despite lack of institutional recognition. Concerning the category of myth and its use in the field of anthropology, my discussions with M. Kilani and P.-Y. Jacopin were lively and profitable. These were extended in correspondences with F. Affergan (Collège de Philosophie, Paris) and R. Pottier (University of Lille I), before taking a provisional written form in an exchange with M. Coquet, P. Ellinger, and F. Lissarrague (Centre Louis Gernet, Paris).[2] In addition, many parts of this study were presented on different occasions under various titles; in the United States at Bryn Mawr College (R. Hamilton), Harvard (G. Nagy), Princeton (F. I. Zeitlin), Yale (H. von Staden), and Columbia (S. Saïd); at various universities and institutions in Italy, including Cagliari (V. Citti), Cosenza (A. Gostoli), Macerata (I. Chirassi), Perugia (M. Rossi Cittadini), Pisa (G. Nenci), and Venice (C. Brillante); also in France at the universities of Besançon (P. Levêque), Grenoble II (M.-L. Desclos), and Lille III (J. Boulogne), in Germany at the University of Konstanz (W. Rösler), and in Switzerland at the University of Geneva (P. Borgeaud), and at the Cantonal Library of Lugano (G. Reggi). The different studies of which this work is composed benefited from the comments of many in attendance at these talks; I am only able here to cite the names of my hosts. I express my gratitude collectively to all these friends, along with students in courses drawn from the material of this study, who have offered suggestions and comments.[3]

The manuscript benefited in its final stages from a sabbatical leave of a semester that the University of Lausanne grants professors after eight years of service, which I extended at my own expense for a second semester. Its publication has been aided by the financial support of the Commission des Publications of the University of Lausanne, whose generosity and efficacy have proven invaluable; for the composition of the index I have benefited from the collaboration of Pierre Voelke. I have discovered in Jacques Scherrer, director of Editions Payot Lausanne, an attentive and comprehensive interlocutor, in contrast with the Parisian editors, who so often claim that there is no longer a "market" for studies in the humanities. Elaborated by Daniel Berman at Yale University, with whom it has been a constant and rewarding pleasure to collaborate, the present American translation has been made possible by a subsidy from the Fondation du 450[e] Anniversaire at the University of Lausanne, and through a new grant by the Commission des Publications of the same university.

I was about to send the French manuscript to the editor when there came to my desk the remarkable commentary on the *Pythian Odes* of Pindar produced by a group of scholars of the Instituto de Filologia Classica at Urbino, edited by Bruno Gentili.[4] It was unfortunately too late to take this work into account for the original edition of the present study, in which the three *Pythian* odes dedicated to the celebration of Cyrene by the Theban poet occupy a central place. A brief look nonetheless reassured me of the numerous convergences between this work of commentary and my own ideas, no doubt brought about by the influence of the group in Urbino. Now the tireless organizer of this commentary on Pindar's *Pythian Odes* should find here the expression of my gratitude, and I have taken advantage of the present American translation not only to point out explicitly these convergences but also to update the French original at many points in other ways. These improvements were made possible not lastly through the accurate reading of the anonymous reader of the Press, whom I would like to thank for a very useful evaluation. Thus the present book can be considered a second, updated, and enlarged edition of *Mythe et histoire*.

C.C.

Introduction to the English Edition ⸻

DANIEL W. BERMAN

THE French version of this book, *Mythe et histoire dans l'Antiquité grecque*, first appeared in 1996. At that time, several of Claude Calame's works had already been translated into English, most recently *The Craft of Poetic Speech in Ancient Greece* (1995). That book, a translation of *Le récit en Grèce ancienne: Enonciations et représentations de poètes* (1986, 2nd ed. 2000), has become almost required reading for scholars and students of the Greek narrative tradition. It is a collection of essays, treating a broad range of genres and periods of Greek material, connected by the author's signature theoretical model, the "semionarrative approach." While it may be the most recognized of his works on this side of the Atlantic, Calame's studies had been known many years previous by specialists interested in Greek lyric poetry; a version of his doctoral thesis, *Les chœurs de jeunes filles en Grèce archaïque* in two volumes (1977, 2nd ed. in Engl. trans. 1997, rev. 2001),[1] and his magisterial text and commentary on the surviving fragments of Alcman (1983) established his position as an authority on Greek melic poetry and the cultural contexts surrounding its composition and performance. In these works, he was already beginning to apply the theoretical approach for which he is now known. In the years following the original publication of *Le récit*, especially in those leading up to the emergence of the French version of the present work, Calame has focused more and more on the importance of adherence to a theoretical model capable of avoiding the interpretative pitfalls that come with observing the mechanisms at work in the production and consumption of narratives in ancient Greece, a culture so removed from ourselves in time and even space. But from the beginning his work has shown a keen and balanced awareness of the benefits and dangers of a rigorously theoretical approach. Whereas *Craft* can be seen as a collection of discrete studies based on a theoretical model, *Myth and History* is, in effect, a single in-depth examination of a set of narratives describing the same event, spanning genres, geographies, and chronologies. It is, more than any of Calame's other works to date, a thorough and exacting example of theory in practice.

It will be a useful point of departure, especially for those readers unfamiliar with Calame's many studies, to place the present volume in the context of his other works (they are numerous, and not all will be mentioned here). His first studies, as mentioned above, were primarily concerned with archaic Greek poetry, most specifically choral lyric. *Chœurs* appeared in 1977, and the edition of Alcman in 1983. This was followed by *Le récit* in 1986 and the magisterial *Thésée et l'imaginaire athénien: Légende et culte en Grèce antique* in 1990 (2nd ed. 1996). *Thésée* marks a departure of sorts for Calame, since it treats a body of material organized according to a thematic principle. A more thorough survey of the traditional Greek narratives concerning Theseus is not to be found, but the work accomplishes more than just this. In a sweeping first chapter, Calame elucidates the bases for his "semionarrative" approach, his method for understanding what he terms the "symbolic process."[2] The chapter is a landmark, for it expresses with a new clarity and authority both Calame's anthropological perspective and the theoretical model he has developed to approach Greek narrative material, in the case of *Thésée* material that includes literary, ritual, and visual manifestations of the symbolic process. It serves, as well, as a clear model for the first chapter of the present volume, which also consists primarily of methodological exposition, in this case specifically pertaining to "discourse production" in a primarily literary mode.

Thésée was the first monograph Calame dedicated to a body of narratives on a single subject, the figure of Theseus and his adventures. The thematic approach was productive and appealing; he has also written a study on the figure of Eros, first published in Italy in 1992 and entitled *I Greci e l'eros. Simboli, pratiche, luoghi*. A French translation appeared in 1996, and an English one in 1999.[3] *The Poetics of Eros* seeks to create, in essence, an anthropology of the concept of Eros, or love, in the ancient Greek world through close examination of how the narrative tradition treats it. The book, while significantly less methodological than many of Calame's other works, clearly shows how flexible the semionarrative approach can be when coupled with an anthropological perspective: the narratives considered need not be concerned with the same protagonists, the same setting, or have the same location of composition. The common thread of Eros remains throughout, but the specific points of reference to the various (and varying) conceptions of love, as they are portrayed over time and space, constantly change. The theory creates a space for comparison (a term, in fact, Calame himself uses quite frequently in reference to the "comparative" methods he employs) that is, in certain ways, a point of objectivity from which to observe and compare multiple narrative entities.

"Theory," in the case of Calame's work, is, as it should be, a means, not an end. Calame's semionarrative theory, based on the fundamental works of Greimas,[4] is not intended to be obfuscatory or rebarbative. As the author himself states in his preface to this volume, it is formulated as a means of bringing what scientific or empirical objectivism might be possible to bear on a subject that by its nature eschews such objectivism. The material's inherent subjectivity, of course, is readily admitted. But the theoretical model offers a common ground from which to begin an examination of the narratives in question, and a common point of reference from which to observe the different ways narratives affect and are affected by their cultural and physical environments.

The complex relationship of a given narrative to its historical and cultural environment — broadly including aspects of performance, composition, and reception, along with details of political and social milieu and even ecological and geographical setting — is at the heart of Calame's approach. A narrative, by nature, bears the distinct marks of the culture (understood as a set of symbolic practices and representations in use at a certain time, in a certain place) in which it is created. In addition, a traditional narrative itself becomes an instrument for change within its cultural context. This change, Calame's "pragmatic effect," can manifest itself as a development or shift in interpretation of a "historical" event[5] or even as a physical change to the traditional space of a given community. However this pragmatic effect is expressed, it is an integral feature of the narratives Calame examines, and indeed of any narrative with "collective importance," the nebulous phrase so often associated with defining the nature of "myth" in the Greek tradition as well as others.[6] Thus when Calame speaks of "discourse production," he uses the term to describe the complex process by which narratives are produced, performed, and experienced, a process that always involves communication between author, speaker, actor (if appropriate) on one side and hearer/audience on the other, and inevitably produces change in the environment in which it acts.

Before examining some of the specifics of Calame's approach, we should dwell a moment on the term "myth." The term itself, of course, presents grave difficulties of interpretation. There is no need to reiterate in any detail here what is treated in the first chapter of this book. But to discuss Calame's semionarrative approach is also to be forced to consider its implications for the august concept of "myth" itself. Calame began questioning the usefulness of the term long ago. He edited a valuable collection of essays in 1988 entitled *Métamorphoses du mythe en Grèce antique* (Geneva) in which the changing faces of Greek "myths" are examined from a variety of perspectives. A culmination of his ideas can already be seen in his 1991 article entitled "'Mythe' et 'rite' en Grèce. Des catégories indigènes?"[7] in which he questions and problematizes the terms "myth" and "rite/ritual" from an anthropological perspective. Calame maintains that Hellenists should not employ the concept of "myth" as it has come to be used, because the concept implies several characteristics that are inapplicable to the Greek narrative tradition. First, "myth," and use of the term "mythology" to describe the science of studying "myths," presupposes the possibility of categorizing and organizing narratives that have been removed from the time and place of their composition and performance. This, within the framework of Calame's approach, is impossible. Second, and related, the term as it has been used since Heyne[8] inherently defines particular narratives in contradistinction to and comparison with a canonical, or "original," version. While this presents critics with a useful tool for the comparison of departing versions that treat similar characters, locations, or themes, it impedes the same critics' ability to understand the relevance of a particular narrative for those for whom it was intended and by whom it was composed. When Calame states that "there is simply no ontology of myth,"[9] he is calling into question the value of classifying a body of narratives, extremely heterogeneous in composition, subject matter, and goals, under a single heading, or as a single entity. Classicists and cultural anthropologists (Calame, of course, is both) interested in the world of ancient Greece must beware of foisting a modern taxonomy on a complex system that is quite distant in time from their own. Thus, in the first section of the present volume, Calame discusses the unsuitability of the terms "myth," "legend," and "folktale" to the Greek material in question, terms that have formed a triad canonized most famously by James Frazer.[10] Modern taxonomies fall away upon close comparison with both ancient and even contemporary comparative material, such as narratives of the tribes of Papua New Guinea or the Himalayas.

The denial of the ontology of "myth" is a direct result of the semionarrative approach Calame employs here and elsewhere. The method itself is both innovative and grounded in long-standing approaches to narrative and traditional mythic discourse. Calame is most indebted to the semiotic methodology developed by Greimas, which itself has roots in the classic structuralism of Lévi-Strauss.[11] His readings are based on the identification of three levels of "semionarrative structures" within a particular discourse. These structures together contribute to the aforementioned process of discourse production. It will be useful here to discuss briefly the three levels, with the particular goal of introducing the reader to what can at times seem a formidable amount of technical language. In this discussion and throughout the translation much care has been taken to use terminology consistent both internally and with other translations of Calame's work in English, especially the 1995 *Craft*. In addition, the bilingual (French and English) semiotic dictionary of Greimas and Courtès has been used when applicable.[12]

The first level consists of what Calame calls "discursive structures." These are the practical elements of narrative production: characters (also termed "actorial/actantial figures"), setting, time. Thus this first structure involves the processes of actorialization, spatialization, and temporalization. For discursive structures to be effective (in a social and cultural sense) they must be anchored to the natural and social world in certain ways; in other words, they must have social, cultural, and/or physical reference. In the case of the Greek material under discussion here, there are certain ways we can further specify this referencing. Traditional narratives in Greece almost always have actors that are either super- or infrahuman (rarely subhuman, with the notable exception of the fables of Aesop), and they almost always take place in a recognizable geographical space. For Calame, an understanding of the nature of these references to the natural and cultural world allows comparisons between narratives that may otherwise be quite distinct in scale or even subject matter. We can also note here that the way a narrative maintains these references with its cultural and natural environment has provided critics with an almost standard set of criteria for the categorization of narratives as "myth," "legend," or "folktale."[13] We mentioned above that these categories present a flawed taxonomy. This can be attributed at least in part to the fact that the terms are based on an incomplete understanding of the discursive process and, related to this, of the relationships narratives maintain with the world at large. The second and third levels serve to fill out this understanding.

The second level of structures Calame terms "semionarrative surface structures." On this level, narratives with actors, in space and time (functions of the discursive structures) reorganize figures and values of the natural world. This is achieved through the organization and reorganization of the actorial figures in relation to each other and in space and time. Calame employs semiotic terminology (Sender, Subject, Antisubject, Receiver) in order to arrange actorial figures according to their changing roles ("actantial positions") within a narrative. These organizations and reorganizations take place according to a "syntactic plan" of discourse called the "narrative schema." This schema defines the stages necessary for a narrative to exist at all: a phase of *manipulation* (that is, an initial action, often of a Sender, that sets the narrative in motion, often creating or created by a situation of *lack*), a phase of *competence* (valorization of the actantial Subject that leads to his/her/ their ability to perform the necessary task presented by the phase of *manipulation*), *performance* (the action itself, performed by an actantial Subject with the necessary *competence*), and *sanction* (the result of the *performance*, often a return to a narrative equilibrium parallel to that previous to the Sender's *manipulation*). Of course, every narrative does not exhibit these phases in the same way; one of the central activities of the semionarrative method as employed here is the recognition of the variations possible in the schema and how they can exert a practical, or "pragmatic," effect on the society for which they are produced. This effect can be identified as a reorganization of the values, psychologies, or ecology of a given social system, or the organization or disruption of cultural taxonomies within the community.

The semionarrative approach is perhaps most dynamic in this second level of semionarrative surface structures. It is here that the close connection between narrative and its context, so important for this approach, is decisively forged. Calame is at his best when he is identifying relationships between narratives based on the narrative schema, and uncovering ways that individual narratives subtly but consistently alter values and perceptions among their listeners. In observing this process, he recognizes that narratives often make use of *isotopies*, which are defined as repeating semantic or figural elements that recur both within specific narratives and across narratives treating the same theme or subject. These isotopies (such as "matrimonial union" or "cultivation," to choose two that are prominent in this book) serve to organize a complex narrative according to a semantic plan larger than what can be achieved simply by the processes of actorialization, spatialization, and temporalization. They can organize (either paratactically or hypotactically) whole narratives out of series of narrative schemata, often in quite complex ways. Isotopies thus both reflect and aid in the reorganization of the culture in which the discourse takes place.

An integral final level is that of "deep semionarrative structures," in which two or three often contradictory terms are asserted simultaneously. The "themes" identified on this level form the basis of the isotopies discussed above. Figures and concepts from the natural world, expressed most clearly on the level of discursive structures, and modified and reorganized on the level of semionarrative surface structures, are determined here. At the very foundational level of discourse, we find contradiction. Students of myth and myth theory will note that in this level there is acknowledgment of the presence of binary oppositions, a central tenet of structuralist approaches to myth and literature. Calame's method is in most ways quite distinct from classic structuralism, especially in its insistence on the relevance of social and cultural context for the understanding of a given discourse. While the recognition that at this final level there is often the assertion of contradictory terms should not be perceived as a concession to structuralist readings on the whole, it is indeed an acknowledgment that there is some validity in this aspect of the method. Calame is not "antistructuralist" per se but "poststructuralist" in the truest sense of the term. The recognition that at the foundation of the isotopies organizing the narrative discourse there exists contradiction creates the possibility of interpreting mythic discourse on its own terms, without the hindrance of the need for strict rationality or logical consistency in the modern sense.[14] This is the aim of classic structuralism, as well, but it is achieved by that method at the expense of the social and ideological context of specific narratives. Calame's semionarrative approach has the advantage of recovering this context while retaining the undeniable force of the structuralist's oppositions.

This theoretical model is brought to bear in the present study on the narratives treating the foundation of Cyrene, the famous colony on the north shore of Africa. Cyrene's narrative tradition is extremely rich, and leads Calame from Pindar, who describes aspects of the founding of the city in three odes, through Herodotus, to the Alexandrian poets Callimachus and Apollonius. The journey makes a single observation abundantly clear. The distinction between two modern poles — what we would term "myth" and "history" — is extremely difficult to define for the Greek material. When Pindar speaks in *Pythian* 4 of Euphemus, the Argonaut and ancestor of the future founder of Cyrene, or Herodotus theorizes on the meaning of the stammerer Battus' name, the interaction of the discourse on the several semionarrative levels Calame identifies shows that both texts are engaged in the same process. They moderate and modify the traditional material they interact with for specific purposes — the very reorganization Calame insists upon. The bulk of this book consists of analyses of these reorganizations: how they operate, upon what they act, and why they do so. These discussions should be left in the capable hands of the author. It remains only to say that throughout the fascinating guided tour, the conclusion becomes easy to anticipate. For the Greeks, there is no "history" as distinct from the narrative (and, until a relatively late date, poetic) tradition, and no "myth" that is not implicated in the process of discourse production. "Myth" and "history," as defined in their modern senses, cannot be separated.

This book should have a wide appeal. This English edition perhaps has as its primary audience American undergraduates and graduate students who will find it easier to access Calame's ideas in translation than in the original French. But the book has been updated in the course of the translation, making it useful also, one hopes, to the professional. In the notes and bibliography, reference to books and articles that have been translated into English has been made where possible. Still, the citations make clear Calame's academic genealogy, and a limited effort has been made to "Americanize" the bibliography further. Thus this book will serve another purpose, perhaps, in introducing those unfamiliar with recent European scholarship on ancient Greek myth and literature to progress being made on the Continent.

MYTH AND HISTORY IN ANCIENT GREECE

I

Illusions of Mythology

Is it appropriate once again to question that privileged object of the study of cultural anthropology that has evolved through the course of more than a century as "myth"? Is it prudent to apply this concept and category to ancient Greece? Do we not situate the ancients' thought itself precisely at the origin of our predicament when faced with this ambiguous category? Greece offers to us its garden of myths, in all its fertility; but it seems as if the Greeks, through the criticism they exercised on narratives within their own tradition, originated the very category that defines for us the stories we are accustomed to call "myths." Herein lies the paradox: we attribute to the Greeks the origin of a critical concept of which they themselves would supply, in return, the most brilliant and exemplary specimens.

Indeed, on closer examination, the Greeks never elaborated a singular concept or definition of the mythic, nor recognized a group within the abundance of their own narratives as fitting in an exact manner within the confines of such a category.[1] If they had developed such a distinction, Aristotle, that master of nomenclature, would not have failed to acknowledge it; however, in reading his *Poetics*, we see that the term *mûthos* is limited to the technical meaning of the plot of a story, particularly of a tragedy. Thus a Greek term is used in modern times to designate a different set of meanings from those that the term covered in its native sense. If "the existence of myths" is supposed to be "attested in all societies studied, or even simply approached, by ethnologists,"[2] and if a myth found in a particular culture is now placed within a universal category, it is because this type of narrative has been situated at a distance essential to the claim of objectivity that modern anthropology has instituted between "primitive" societies and our own. Fabula, then myth, "that particular type of story that takes as its subject the history of the gods of ancient Greece" represents the point of differentiation that is supposed to delineate Western society, in constant progress, from traditional societies. Myth, then, achieves the status of a mode of human thought, itself significant of the "otherness" of cultures not yet having reached the privileged stage of development that their occidental observers inevitably have achieved. For myth to return to a critical sociology dedicated to the culture of the "same," we must wait for Barthes.

But the Greeks, for their part, always adopted this approach of internal criticism toward their own narratives. We see that for Herodotus, the first historian-anthropologist, or still for Pausanias, ethnologist of his own culture, the stories of foreigners are no more readily labeled "mythic" than those told in Greek, by Greeks.

Here, perhaps, is the focal point of most misunderstandings. Even if the countless definitions of myth that have been put forward a posteriori are centered upon elements of content, one can easily find stories that at first glance appear to be mythic but do not fit within that category defined as such. The implicit but regular application of a standard of narrative verisimilitude coincides with the anthropological nature of the concept of myth; a critical and distant perspective on cultures geographically or chronologically far removed is needed in order to classify as "myth" those stories actually situated at the heart of these exotic communities' traditions.[3] A brief foray through the history of these concepts will be, in certain respects, instructive. Throughout the eighteenth century the term "myth" was applied not only to the stories of the Greeks and Romans; it also came to include little by little the Indian, Nordic, and African traditions, and likewise to oppose the biblical tradition, alone considered worthy of belief. Among the French, however, where *"mythe"* did not establish itself outside the *Encyclopédie*, the term *"fable"* has been preferred![4] Already in the sixteenth century, one who quenched his thirst for allegorical figures at the source of the "mythological" patrimony of the Greeks and Romans could rely on an abundance of ancient mythographic handbooks; he was also persuaded that the narratives of those people newly found in the great period of discovery, along with the stories of the ancients themselves, were only distortions of the traditional biblical narrative.[5] Myth is very much the domain of the unfamiliar, of the pagan, who, living in another time or under different skies, does not have the benefit of the lights of Truth. In his ignorance of the revealed biblical narratives, he can construct only irrational fictions.

Perhaps the best mode of questioning a category in order to avoid the vagueness of its definition and its Eurocentric partiality is simply to follow the development of a few Greek narratives: those that find themselves, more than the term *mûthos* itself, at the origin of the Western concept of "myth"; those that remain surprisingly lively, independent of the generic category to which they are now forced to be a part; and those that constitute a (true) history of a community and are therefore able to highlight certain paradoxes within our own conceptions. The anthropological and narrative approach that shall be proposed here can only lead to reflections on our own ways of narrating. To study the stories of other people is inherently to examine our own stories, and ourselves.

1. The Substance of Myth and Mythology

This rereading of a few Greek stories is aimed at rethinking certain of our generic classifications, along with the pertinence of the categories of "myth," "mythology," and "mythic thought," concerning both ancient Greece and our own modern anthropological approaches. It requires certain additional general arguments, apart from the historical inquiries already offered with excellent results by others.

1.1. Common Sense and Scientific Effort

Encyclopedias, those anthologies of received ideas, for their part present a summarizing shortcut for such a chronological inquiry. A comparative reading of corresponding articles in the works supposed to have amassed the received knowledge of Europe suffices in filling the lacunae left by the majority of historical studies. It is quite rare to find posed the questions of the communal representation underlying the notion of myth, of the shared knowledge implied, or indeed of an acknowledged norm concerning this concept as it is employed throughout the extent of Western culture. The parameters running through the different encyclopedic definitions of myth, given in the form of indubitable assertion, are three: first, whether *Aussage, account, histoire,* or *racconto,* myth is presented as a form of enunciation and narrative. Second, it presents a transcendent time, peopled by superhuman characters, such as the gods. Lastly, and in consequence, as a product of the imagination, myth lacks the value of truth, even if, together with its readily allowed function as foundational narrative, it gains authority for the community that produced it.[6] Thus for the establishment and attribution of the qualification of the "mythic," the definition of a point of view external to the indigenous perspective is also necessary.

Attempts at definition proposed recently by cultural anthropologists or historians of religion, which are undoubtedly — indeed, inevitably — influenced by this encyclopedic tradition, restate in turn these underlying principles. Now, certainly, elaborate precautions are taken. We now know that the nomenclatures of narratives are relative to each individual culture; that they resort to a certain number of terms that define a specific segmentation within the indigenous narrative corpus; but also that these can be constructed by the anthropologist himself on the basis of a stylistic criterion or different contexts of enunciation (we shall return to this point later). From the scientific and academic point of view of cultural and social anthropology, myth is nonetheless understood as a narrative concerning the gods or divine beings, a narrative to which one could easily attach Eliade's foundational function: the primary character attributed to mythic temporality would have, as a universal corollary, a formative impact on the *hic et nunc* of the social life of those listening to a particular narration. Myth then becomes, for the historian of ancient religion, an "applied narrative," one that is a "primary verbalization of supra-individual concerns and of matters of collective importance in real life."[7]

Classicists, anthropologists, and folklorists apply the same rhetorical tools, creating scientific understanding through encyclopedic knowledge. Starting with an inquiry concerning a single culture, a description is proposed based on four criteria: form, content, function, and context. Myth is then defined again as a narration, recited or dramatized. It essentially gives a report of the sacred origins of the world and of the indigenous community by narrating the events of creation that took place in primordial times. The cosmogonical and foundational acts attributed to the gods or heroes of myth thus assume an exemplary function that attests to their supposed ontological nature. In the end, myth most frequently has a ritual context, a "form of behavior sanctioned by usage" to which it imparts its ideological content.[8]

In the eyes of the scholar, however, the historical point of view, inevitably involving the need to set myth in perspective vis-à-vis our own culture, quickly reappears: myth belongs originally to primitive cultures; it reveals itself there as not only a fundamental but also a chronologically primary form of communication. To treat a problem so fundamental as the time and actions of origins seems thus to require a form of enunciation associated with that actual time . . .

1.2. Myth as a Mode of Thought

One cannot criticize the Hellenist for adopting a historical perspective. But this very perspective, characteristic of nineteenth-century thinkers who were happy to have found a tool for explication, has contributed to the formation of myth as a substance. Through the passage from ancient societies to exotic ones, myth has come to transcend its status as narrative and has assumed the rank of a mode of human thought.

The historical and evolutionary approach invites us, all the same, on a brief foray through the past. In Italian and German scholarship, at least, in order to transform myth into a mode of thought, historicism and anthropology have been fostered by pre-Romantic conceptions. Consider Vico singing the praises of mythology: he shows us, by the light of his allegorical readings, that the stories of the first poets present a reflection of the still-rough character of their authors, but also their first attempts to understand human form and to express, through the intermediary of language, the forces of nature. Like the Greeks, the civilized nations knew a Jupiter and a Hercules, seminal figures of civil truth. Already for Bacon, these fabulous narratives recounted the actions of divinities who were merely the allegorical and anthropomorphic incarnations of moral and philosophical principles — before the argument comes the parable. In this manner, one can notice in myth the first traces of civilized thought.[9] Heyne, precisely through the use of the term *mythus*, or more precisely, *sermo mythicus*, intended to return dignity and serious study to what his contemporaries had denounced as the nonsense of "fables." For Heyne, myth, as an explanation of nature or as historical recollection, represented man's first attempt, through poetic and symbolic productions, to explain and express his sensory impressions. It is the first steps of man, in a childhood attached to sense and to the concrete, moving toward maturity of thought, and eventually metaphysics![10] This understanding of myth distinguishes itself clearly from the definition of mythology given by the corresponding article in the *Encyclopédie*. There, myth is still "the fabulous history of the gods, demigods, and heroes of antiquity, as its very name indicates"; still "the confused *mélange* of imaginary visions, philosophical daydreams, and the debris of ancient history." Its conclusion: "analysis of these fables is impossible"![11]

The course of this progressive linear development, from the empirical babblings of myth to the enlightenment of abstract reason, marked all anthropological thought of the nineteenth century. The "prelogical" character attributed to myth conferred on it, at the beginning of the twentieth century, a reinforced position within the notions of primitive thought and "*pensée participante*" developed by Lévy-Bruhl. The use that Cassirer proposed at this time as well, through its outline of the different symbolic forms and their required coexistence, falls definitively within the same evolutionary and idealizing context: "At first the world of language, like that of myth in which it seems as it were embedded, preserves a complete equivalence of word and thing, of 'signifier' and 'signified.' It grows away from this equivalence as its independent spiritual form, the characteristic force of the logos, comes to the fore." Organized in accordance with the forms of "pure intuition," mythic thought knows no causal analysis, nor any distinction between the whole and the part, since it is attached only to objects through their immediate presence.[12] Myth would thus have its own logic.

This being the case, is there not a paradox in noting that the very founder of modern structuralism devoted himself to transmitting, through contemporary anthropological reflection, a concept of myth constructed as a substance and thus as a mode of human thought? True, through the appeal to synchrony (but to the detriment of a diachronic development), mythic thought is here no longer considered representative of a first stage, primary in the linear evolution and progression of civilization. But the very essence of the structural perspective, which seeks to restore the meaning of myth through the arrangement of narrative and logical units that transcend their linguistic manifestations, leads to the existence of a "substance of myth." The organization of this substance would be brought about by the intellectual patchwork that constitutes precisely the distinctive feature of mythic thought. A genuine "science of the concrete," mythic reflection would thus operate in a specific manner, situating itself "between the *percept* and the *concept*." Beyond the linguistic surface of mythic narratives and their modes of communication, one discovers in this way the organization of the elements of sense and the employment of a logic that, though not inevitably revelatory of the first babblings of mankind, are still characteristic of exotic cultures, the societies without history or writing that anthropologists attempt to save from disappearance or oblivion.[13] We should not forget the paradoxical declaration that concludes *Du miel aux cendres*:

> If myths belonging to the most backward cultures of the New World bring us to this decisive threshold of the human consciousness which, in Western Europe, marks the accession to philosophy and then to science, whereas nothing similar appears to have happened among savage peoples, we must conclude from the difference that in neither case was the transition necessary, and that interlocking states of thought do not succeed each other spontaneously and through the workings of some inevitable causality.

It is not surprising to find this propensity for creating a substance and thus a mode of thought out of myth in the work of Hellenists concerned with traditional Greek narratives. For proponents of the historicist perspective, substantialized myth allows the tracing of a direct line for the development of Greek thought; advancing from *mûthos* to *lógos*, the formation has from here become a paradigm for the evolution of human thought in general. It is a persistent paradigm, at its foundation difficult to disprove, and is implicit in several recent critical approaches. On the one hand, connected with the transition of an oral culture to a civilization of writing, the development of a type of thought that progressively becomes clearer is supposed to lead the Greeks from the dramatic actions animated by the divine powers of myth toward the demonstration concerning abstract entities that constitutes philosophy, from "the logic of ambiguity, of equivocality, of polarity" inherent in myth, with the shiftings and tensions organizing its polysemy, to the logic of noncontradiction and the effort of categorization championed by Aristotle. On the other hand, by adopting a resolutely nonhistorical point of view, one can propose, beyond the different forms of expression of myths, "mythology as a frame of mind"; one can delimit in this way, with the aid of all the various versions and narrative forms of Greek myths, the practical domain of a unitary mode of thought, a system of symbolic representations spanning, without chronological distinction, the entire history of Greek culture. At once incorporating and incorporated, the narrative realization of myths, their verbalization, then their written form — simply put, "mythology as learning" — would be looked upon simply as ways of thinking about myth that become, through their repertoire, mythology.[14] This progression of myth into mythology is, moreover, rather insidious: even when postulation of a form of thought beyond the multiplicity of narratives is avoided, the temptation to agglomerate persists. In this way, the corpus of Greek myths comes to be elevated once more to the level of "Greek Mythology." The capital letters have the function of designating the existence of an "intertext" or, better yet, a system. The famous *Bibliotheke* attributed to Apollodorus becomes the standard, that late collection of local and Panhellenic stories concerning the gods and heroes from the primordial union of Earth and Sky to the return of Odysseus from the Trojan War.[15] But let us not jump ahead!

Whether through historical time or from a synchronic perspective, the question always remains one of contacting a reality of thought transcendent of individual narratives which are seen as simple linguistic manifestations; "mythic" narratives are thus considered the manifestations of a substance defined by a specific mode of contemplating the cosmos or culture. Myths are thus in some way "naturalized."

1.3. Double Mythology

From myths we can move to the second meaning of the word, mythology: from texts and the thought that produced them to an analysis of what they have been subjected to for the past five centuries. Indeed, according to the definition established by the Aristotelian classificatory efforts of the nineteenth century, mythology is as much "the fabulous history of the gods, demigods, and heroes of antiquity" as it is "the science and explanation of the mysteries and fables of the pagans." Both a scientific approach and composite material for that approach, mythology coincides with the corpus of myths of exotic and pagan societies existing isolated from the truth while also indicating the activity that these myths incite on the part of Western scholars.[16] This ambivalence is inherent, no doubt, in the very use of the term *mythology*. For the deist Andrew Ramsay, mythology consisted of the Greek and Roman narratives treating the succession of the ages and the battles of the gods, standing in opposition to a philosophical conception of the cosmos and the soul, such as Plato's. At precisely the same time, however, the abbot Antoine Bannier had already described mythology as the mythologist's knowledge of the stories and gods of the ancients. As such, and because he states as its goal research into the historical backgrounds of these poetic inventions, he judged the study worthy of the name "*Belles-Lettres*."[17] Here we are present, without a doubt, at the moment of the birth of "Mythologiques"!

In this way the mythic tradition of every people who have become the object of anthropological reflection is merged and confused little by little with the approach exercised upon it. One suspects that this type of reductionism has itself contributed to making myth both an invariant and an inherent aspect of every exotic culture, even before it becomes a universal product of human thought. But does it suffice merely to acknowledge the existence of this agreement about the permanence of what is mythic, based both on the Eurocentrism of our predecessors and on the application of common sense? If a counterproof is required, one must find it through good semantic methods, in the two bases of the study of distinctive traits: comparative and contrastive analysis. The examples which follow will demonstrate these procedures.

2. Contrasts and Comparisons

Before any comparative discussion about exotic taxonomies, however, there is our own contrastive taxonomy, which we have not failed to project (as ethnocentrism is inevitable) on different groups of narratives of other cultures. . . .

2.1. Folktale, Legend, Myth

The contrastive triad that has become canonical in our European tradition was formulated quite some time ago by researchers on narrative in the field of folklore. Following the lead of the Romantic classification of poetry into the three genres of epic, lyric, and tragedy, the triad "folktale/legend/myth" was put in practice in the reasoned collection of European narrative heritage by the brothers Grimm; the two volumes of *Kinder- und Hausmärchen* of 1812–15 were followed by *Deutsche Sagen* (in two volumes, 1816–18), leading to, at the top of the hierarchy, *Deutsche Mythologie* (two volumes, 1835). And who better than Frazer was able to ensure the establishment of this reciprocal and contrastive definition? Myths: the erroneous explanations of fundamental phenomena relating to man or to nature; they thus represent a first philosophy, a first science, but one marked by ignorance and error. Legends: traditions, oral or written, narrating the fortunes of people who actually existed or of natural events having occurred in real places; they are situated between truth and falsehood. Folktales: anonymous and purely fictitious stories that, although pretending to narrate actual events, serve only a diversionary function.[18] But this contrastive analysis cannot be understood as distinct from historicism. Drawing their origin from reason, memory, and imagination, respectively, myth, legend, and folktale are here merely the nascent forms of science, history, and romance respectively!

The triad received a modern interpretation in the 1960s through the definition, for each of the constitutive categories, of distinctive traits determined in a consistent manner. These have been expressed in tabular form:[19]

"Form"	Belief	Time	Place	Attitude	Principal Characters
MYTH	Fact	Remote past	Different world: other or earlier	Sacred	Nonhuman
LEGEND	Fact	Recent past	World of today	Secular or sacred	Human
FOLKTALE	Fiction	Any time	Any place	Secular	Human or nonhuman

We notice that the "formal" question of the modes of manifestation and enunciation of these three categories is immediately eliminated, since the forms of all three—prose narrative—are concealed by the adopted perspective! Perhaps this is no coincidence, if we owe it to a classicist to have upheld the academic character of this terminology, even if it has not kept him from making myth a form of primitive philosophy, legend a type of proto-history, and folktale pure diversion. And yet the Greek narrative tradition is precisely the sort that offers the most convincing examples for those who would strive to demonstrate the absence of relevance, or at the very least the fluidity, of these truly academic categories.[20]

Let us apply the distinctive criteria defined by this more modern contrastive analysis to a Greek narrative. Is the story of Troy, as it is recounted in the *Iliad*, myth or legend? The incontestable presence of belief in the Homeric heroes even among listeners in the age of Plato, the integration of the chronology of the Trojan War with contemporary chronography in a document such as the *Marmor Parium*, the undeniable correspondence between Iliadic geography and places known in Classical Greece, the festivals associated with recitation of the Homeric poems from the end of the Archaic period, and the psychological reactions attributed to both heroes and gods, all place the *Iliad* in the domain of legend. But the retreat of the gods to a largely fictive Aithiopia, the determinant role of their will, the anger of the anthropomorphized Scamander and his cosmological combat with fire tilt the narrative toward myth, while the divine voice ascribed to the horse of Achilles invokes the category of folktale. Furthermore, through its political and military causality, the organization of the narrative approximates what we would expect from factual history!

Alternately, if it has been possible to show that the greater portion of the episodes of the return of Odysseus in the *Odyssey* find in other cultures parallels which we consider to be folktales, it nonetheless remains that in the eyes of the Greeks, Odysseus is as real, as historical, as Agamemnon; the time of the voyages of the many-wiled hero fits within a calculated chronology, even as the will of the gods falls with all its weight on the development of the action and the focus of Odysseus' story is constituted precisely in an exploration and definition of the limits of humanity and, by consequence, of Greek civilization. Folktale, legend, or myth? Perhaps even history?

One who intends to resort to the terminology established by more than a century of anthropological tradition well risks finding himself in a position as uncomfortable as it is inevitable. In addition, it is all the more delicate because the taxonomy stemming from European academic effort is itself subject to temporal and, above all, cultural variations. Among German speakers, for instance, who have had some influence in this classificatory effort, "legend" corresponds to *Sage* but also to *Legende*; the first term covers in part the semantic field attributed to myth when it is applied specifically to accounts of German culture, while the second essentially refers to hagiographic narratives of the Christian tradition.[21] Even when subject to scientific scrutiny, the terminology of narrative, with its culturally determined variations, seems an ever-changing spectrum of colors.

2.2. Indigenous Taxonomies

Clearly the classifications of narratives are themselves as numerous as taxonomies of animals or of manufactured objects, as variable as the cultures which produce them, and as changeable as the destinies of each of these cultures. The Hellenist who has left his library of Greek texts for Papua New Guinea and who arrives in an Iatmul village after a tortuous voyage along the meanders of the Sepik, sees — from his first invitation to a narrative recital — one of his best-anchored and most precious operative concepts shattered. At Palimbei, there are two forms of rhythmic recitation, which are distinguished neither by their content nor by whether they are believed, but which are nonetheless separate in their enunciation. On the one hand, the *sagi*, limited to a small circle of hearers, refer only to themselves, narrating a plot sustained by an unchanging actor and by a set literary form; on the other, on the occasion of great debates about the property of the clan that take place in the house of elders, are the *pabu*, argumentative and endless narratives that are continually exhausted and redirected by the development of dialogue between the protagonists of the dispute.[22] The two forms together recount the general history of the clan; the distinction between them hinges on the manner of their enunciation, conditioned by the occasion and the social function of the narration. We thus have a complete split from our own system of classification.

The Pahari culture of the central Himalaya offers another good example. The European ethnologist who attempts to approach without prejudices this culture, which has known several political divisions, manages to distinguish within its vast oral literature a rather expansive category of "sung narratives," defined according to the mode of execution of the stories concerned. But desiring to refine his analysis, he may realize that the Indian folklorists who have preceded him in some of the regions marked by Pahari civilization have proposed for the same narratives no fewer than five different categories: some motivated by the subjects of the narratives in question, some distinguishing one from another by meter when their authors have in general striven to correspond to the categories of their Sanskrit originals, some in accordance with the heterogeneous criteria applied to them by the culture itself. Reduced to our own concepts, this multiform list might lead to a distinction between religious ballads (narratives of divinities), heroic ballads (narratives of heroes), and ballads of love. A glance at the indigenous taxonomy, however, shows five types of sung narratives, completely different even from the five categories proposed by local folklorists. An analysis of the terms defining these categories in fact shows that they correspond to criteria of a heterogeneous classificatory system, relative either to the circumstances of execution of the narratives or to qualities of their protagonists. Only the simultaneous grasp of a complex nexus of parameters finally allows the elaboration of a homogenous system of classification for the use of the European academic public.[23]

In pressing the comparative inquiry further, we would notice, for example, that among neighboring cultures, the same names are used for different types of narratives. Thus in Burundi, the *umugani* correspond both to legend and to historical or etiological narratives, while nearby in Rwanda, the term *umugani* is reserved for the first category while *igitéenerezo* designates the other two. It is only here that we recognize the beginning of a long continuation of variations which, influencing as much the signifiers as what is signified, can be correlated with differences of hierarchy expressed in the social structures of the two respective neighboring regions. When the ethnologist reaches the marginal areas of Rwandan civilization, where it merges with other cultures, it is the European categories given as equivalents that disintegrate, in need of new translations.[24]

Certainly it has been possible to believe that confirmation of the triadic European *doxa* can be found in certain exotic terminologies of narrative, but these equivalencies are established either through clear violence to the evidence or after a series of rhetorical precautions concerning the fluidity regularly marking the definition of indigenous categories. Thus Malinowski himself, who claimed to be guided by indigenous classifications in his celebrated study of myth, quickly leads the reader to note that the *kukwanebu, libwogwo*, and *liliu* of the Trobrianders correspond exactly to the folktales, legends, and myths of the anthropologist. In reading through his work, one notices nevertheless that the *kukwanebu* represent a category more specific than folktales, that in the category of *libwogwo*, one must include in addition to legends the historical narratives based on oracular testimony and the fantastic "folktales" transmitted through an oral tradition, and that the *liliu* are limited to myths having the function of justification for a ritual or an ethical norm. Owing to this absence of intercultural homogeneity, the interpreter finds himself at a complete loss, unless he is reduced to the interposition of categories such as "Other" and "Self" and to presenting a negative rebuttal to one of the fashionable preoccupations of anthropology: the quest of "Otherness."[25]

3. Greek Nomenclature?

What of Greek categories? Thought to be situated at the origin of our own, would they not participate more willingly in the play of cross-cultural translation? Once again, we shall be limited to some topical examples.

3.1. The "Myth" of the Philosophers

We begin with Aristotle, a specialist in the art of categorization. This master of literary genres presents us with an initial disappointment, for he reserves for the term *mûthos* a meaning both specific and technical. We observe that Aristotelian "myth" in the *Poetics* is nothing more than the story told, the plot of a narrative, in particular that of the dramatic narrative of a tragedy. To compose from "myths" (*mûthoi*) and from *lógoi* reveals itself in the end to constitute the basis of poetic activity. There do exist *mûthoi paradedoménoi*, traditional "histories," but even if they contain implausibilities, we cannot change them; it is in general that which is situated outside the bounds of *mútheuma* which is qualified as *álogos*, as irrational.[26] In those narratives where one can tolerate a certain amount of implausibility, *lógos* only includes *mûthos*, and fictitiousness is not a criterion of distinction. It comes as no surprise, then, to see Aristotle use the compound verb *muthologéo* in his definition of both the act and the product of narration: "to recount," as in to place a *mûthos* in *lógos*; "to recount," as in putting a plot to words. In this way, the traditional narrative (*tò hupò tôn arkhaíon memuthologeménon*) of the invention of the flute by the artisan Athena, just as that of the loves of Ares and Aphrodite, have in them some "reason" (*eulógos*); in this way also the legend of the Argonauts (*muthologeîtai*) can attest to the historical practice of ostracism.[27]

In the *Metaphysics*, Aristotle walks a fine line as he strives to distinguish the foundations of the corruptible essences of eternal entities. There is, on the one hand, the theological explanation, such as Hesiod presents, but this involves the subtle realm of the mythologue (*muthikôs sophizómena*); on the other hand, there are those who proceed through demonstration (*di' apodeíxeos légontes*). But the thought of philosophers such as Empedocles can also lead to *aporia*. Besides, in those ancient traditions (*arkhaîa kaì pampálaia*) which have come down to us in the form of "myth" (*en múthou skhémati*), not everything is to be rejected. Even if they present nature in the form of divinities, these traditional narratives were formulated "to serve the laws and interest of the community" (*tò sumphéron*), and their "mythic" form (*muthikôs*) is explained by the need to persuade the masses. With a tone that seems to anticipate the voice of Vico or Heyne, Aristotle adds that these stories are to be considered relics of a former philosophy; as such, they constitute a part of traditional knowledge (*pátrios dóxa*). We find here, potentially, the seed of the definition of the philosopher that opens the *Metaphysics*. Through his capacity to marvel at and question the world, the *philómuthos* is an early *philósophos*.[28]

Plato, to whom tradition attributes the definitive rejection of myth as fictional, ought to supply us with a less fluid definition. We can look to the famous passage of the *Protagoras* that contrasts two procedures for demonstration: narration of one of the myths (*mûthon légon*) the very old recount to the very young (in this case the myth of Prometheus and

Epimetheus), or explanatory discourse (*lógoi diexéltho*), the tool of the philosopher. But, as in *Gorgias* or *Timaeus*, when there is a strong contrast between the fiction of *mûthos* and the truth of *lógos* (*plastheìs mûthos/alethinòs lógos*), the choice is for myth. Since the myths of the Underworld or of Atlantis are instruments of philosophical demonstration, *mûthos*, as a result, becomes *lógos*![29]

If the protagonists of the *Republic* are to be believed, *mûthoi* represent a particular set of narratives, but only a subset of the more inclusive category of *lógoi*. In fact, besides the true stories, *mûthoi* constitute a subset of untrue stories. These narratives nonetheless find their place in early musical education through the recitation of poets such as Hesiod and Homer, learned by children even before the gymnastic arts. The stories are consequently attached to mimetic and illusory forms of poetry. Yet on the expressed condition that they do not present morally reprehensible acts such as the castration of Ouranos or the murder of Cronos, they may remain included in the repertoire of the ideal city. Thus only the most beautiful legends (*memuthologeména*), those involving valor, deserve to be heard.[30]

If we might extend a first glance to the territory we generally reserve for historians — we will return to it again below — we can recall that Thucydides does not hesitate to refer, at the beginning of his work, to what for us would constitute the legendary history of Greece. His reservations in relating the ancient deeds (*tà palaiá*) are due as much to their temporal distance, which deprives him in part of the signs and proofs necessary to establish their validity, as to their transmission by poets and logographers who exaggerate the facts in order to please their audiences. That which is *muthôdes* is thus situated as much on the side of provoking pleasure through poetry as in the domain of an unverifiable past. From this moment on, the matter of poetry's power to charm, which can exert itself even on the writer of history, comes to animate reflection by Greek historians on their craft. This is the case up to the rhetorician Lucian, who, in his work dedicated to the writing of history, clearly sets the historian's occupation in opposition to the activity of the poet. To poetry belongs the striking *mûthos*, the flattering praise, the exaggerations; to history, what is useful. But (remember the Second Sophistic) even well-conceived history can be accompanied by the pleasantries of praise . . .[31]

Returning to the field of philosophy, let us progress from the end of the second century A.D. to the fourth. The emperor Julian, as the last defender of polytheism, makes himself the advocate, in opposition to the Cynic Heracleius, of narratives falling into the category defined in the singular by the term *mûthos*; they are the object of a specific activity, *muthographía*. Before rushing to a "genealogy" of myth through research of its "invention," Julian attempts a definition: myth is a composition of falsehoods, but one which through its plausibility aims at utility and the seduction (*psukhagogía*) of its hearers! Julian certainly was an attentive reader of the *Republic*, and his definition exhibits the two criteria traditional from that time on, the charm of stories meant to enchant the ear, and fiction aiming at verisimilitude. But, by the same measure, fiction can also assume the role assigned to history, which is dedicated to utility! In effect, to fabricate myths (*múthous pláttein*) is also to educate. The pedagogical function of myth is apparent in its genealogy. Anticipating also Vico or Heyne, Julian sees in *mûthoi* an invention of common men, similar to charming musical instruments. They are thus like images (*eídola*) and shadows of true science (*alethès epistéme*); they express themselves in a figurative manner (*di' ainigmáton*). Having left behind the childhood of humanity, the good philosopher can gain instruction from myth, in learning to read the hidden sense (*tò lánthanon/lelethós*) behind its language. And so implausibility becomes useful![32]

Is it necessary to go back to the time of Xenophanes, the first assailant of the Greek legendary tradition? But while the Presocratic poet from Colophon condemns the fictions of the ancients (*plásmata tôn protéron*) such as the battles of the Titans, Giants, and Centaurs, he does so not because of the implausibility of these traditional narratives. The determining, and typically Greek, criterion is that of utility. Since the beginning of the so-called Archaic age and the birth of the city, every poet presents himself as an educator of citizens gathered at the banquet. From the point of view of the signifier, the narratives condemned by Xenophanes are not designated by a particular term delimiting a single narrative category. Certainly, in the same poem, the matter is of *mûthoi*, but in accordance with the meaning of efficiency assumed by this term in all Archaic poetry, such "performative" words have here to be addressed to the gods, spoken in the benevolent spirit of pure narratives (*lógoi*).[33] One can condemn as fictions only the stories that do not correspond to the ethics defended by the poet/pedagogue and his patron in front of a public consisting of the circle of their political allies. A bit later, the condemnation will focus more precisely on those stories with a narrative form that can, through the charm it exhibits, maintain the illusion of an image that is fabricated; consequently it is less fictional than "fictionalizing" (*fictionnelle*). The discursive connection with truth is a question of ethics, and, secondarily, of literary expression.

3.2. Historiographical Narratives

The first historians, like the first poet "moralists" of Greece, do not judge narratives according to the criterion of their empirical truth. Or, more exactly, the narrative rejected as fiction does not correspond to a specific category or denomination. When Hecataeus, in writing his work, programmatically opposes what he presents in writing (*grápho*) to common views held by Greeks, he not only claims to present what is simply likely (*hôs moi dokeî alethéa eînai*, "how it seems to me to be true") in lieu of claiming responsibility directly for the truth, but overall he defines his own activity of discursive presentation paradoxically with the verb *mutheîsthai* in order to reserve the term *lógoi* for the risible narratives of his countrypeople!

Even if Herodotus places in doubt the reality of an event in a story he himself recounts, the "father of history" does not then attempt to restore the truth. Instead, by expressing his own opinion he exposes the consequences that the event in question would have had if it had indeed been real. He is content to express his own reservations concerning the truth of a story he has told, and he invites his readers/auditors to suspend their judgment, as he has done. Even if the visual evidence seems to support and confirm the received oral and aural account, truth (*aletheia*) is not the privilege of the historian-investigator, nor is it his claim. Truth, in fact, is the domain only of the gods, who alone are omniscient; man must be content with what is plausible.[34] But whether the story is true, plausible, or false, with Herodotus we regularly find ourselves in the domain of *lógos* and *légein*. There are only two exceptions, where *mûthos* is used to designate an implausible narrative. In both cases, however, the naiveté of the legend concerned requires complementary qualification by means of an intermediary adjective. Whether the protagonist is Ocean or Heracles, the story is the object of the act of *légein*. It is surprising that Herodotus uses the term *lógos* to describe his own *History*, using the term in a sense near to that of "plot."[35]

Just as for Hecataeus, there exists for Herodotus neither a word nor a category reserved for fictive stories; he does not regularly employ the term *mûthos* at all. This is an essential observation for reflection centered on designation and qualification in one's own culture of the narratives of exotic civilizations. Herodotus, the historian and ethnographer, reserves neither a specific concept nor a term for defining the narratives of his foreign sources. For the story of Cyrus, Herodotus has at his disposal four different versions told by the Persians; these stories of others are all presented as *lógoi*. Among them, the historian only recounts the *lógos* that avoids exaggerated praise of the Great King. A foreign version is even occasionally preferred to a Greek one, especially when the source is an Egyptian priest.[36] No myth here, especially not myth exclusively attributed to the (depreciated) culture of an illusory Other.

Perhaps the most paradoxical use of the term *mûthos* in the Classical

age is found in a celebrated passage of the *Wasps* of Aristophanes. In
the course of the exchange between the sensible enemy of Cleon and the
ridiculous heliast, his friend, the endless misunderstandings finally end
with recourse to the narration of histories (*lógous légein*). To a demand
made by the first to pronounce serious (*semnoî*) discourse meant for an
educated and advised public, the second responds with scatological an-
ecdotes and fables in the manner of Aesop; the cultivated man replies to
the boor that he has spoken nothing but *mûthoi*. While this passage
seems clearly to oppose the terms *lógos* and *mûthos*, the significance
attributed to each of them does not correspond at all to what we might
attribute to them implicitly. In speaking of *lógoi* drawn from everyday
life, the enemy of Cleon expected histories relating to a political career
or ephebic exploits, while *mûthoi*, on the other hand, are for him ram-
bling drivel, certainly, but they have nothing to do with the history
of the gods or heroes! In contrast, in the *Phoenician Women* of Euripides, the story Polynices tells about his dispute with his brother following the curse of Oedipus on his two sons is conceived as a *mûthos*.
In its simplicity, it is presented as a speech of truth.[37]

We must look to the fourth century, in particular to the orators, to
find the term *mûthos* overlapping with certain usages our modern concept of myth. Demosthenes, for example, employs *mûthoi* in the plural
in two quite distinct senses: first, to designate those discourses which,
like those told by the friend of Cleon, are mere rubbish, that is to say
groundless stories (defined in parallel by the term *lógoi*!); second, to
refer to narratives relating to the "heroic order," in other words to a
legendary past, the truth-value of which is never in doubt. In a funerary
speech, there is no reason to question the veracity of the battles undertaken by the Athenians against the Amazons or against Eumolpus, king
of Eleusis. One never finds *mûthos* used to refer to the legendary past
joined with an assertion of the fictional nature of the story defined as
such. This holds true for Isocrates, as well, who classifies as *mûthoi* just
as easily narratives of the Trojan War as those of the Persian Wars; both
are exemplary of the hatred felt by the Greeks for the Persians.[38] These
sorts of *mûthoi*, because of their exemplary nature, can only be considered historical narrative. Clearly, the line of division between what we
would call legend and history for the Greeks is defined by a criterion
other than fictionality.

To return to the domain of historical and ethnographic inquiry, let us
look forward five centuries and return to Pausanias, the domestic ethnologist, surveying continental Greece and researching the foundations
of a culture that had become almost foreign to him. And yet, in spite of
the critical distance one would expect of an author composing in a civilization and for a public that in that time was entirely dedicated to

writing and reading, he strangely embraces the position of Herodotus. This consists of a twin method: a prudent attitude of neutrality concerning the narratives he reports in writing, and also a refusal to place in any particular category stories he considers fictional. One does indeed find in the writing of Pausanias the word *mûthos*, but with the general sense of "story," without pejorative connotations or judgment on the truth-value of its contents.[39]

3.3. From History to Allegory

Even so, is not the Second Sophistic precisely where we finally find the question posed of the historical value of the traditional legends? Does not Philostratus in the end voice his incredulity concerning what is *muthôdes*, in claiming to represent the unreality of the histories that recount myths? Compared with what observations of nature (*phúsis*) can teach us, all heroic legends come to nothing; how, then, is it possible to give credit to a "mythology" with heroes ten cubits tall?[40] Pausanias shows himself to be more cautious. Having reached the heart of Arcadia, the country of the origins of civilization and the object of his travels, he finally understands. He hears the Arcadian story (*légetai*) describing the rescue of Poseidon by his mother Rhea, who hides the newborn in a flock of sheep and substitutes a foal in his stead in order to satisfy the voracity of her husband Cronos. At the beginning of the writing of his work (*suggraphé*), Pausanias had rejected such narratives (*lógoi*), even Greek ones, because of their frivolity (*euethía*). But he now understands that these *lógoi* should not be read literally, but rather *di' ainigmáton*, in an allegorical manner. His conclusion: when they concern divinities, those things spoken (*tà eireména*) by the Greeks must be recounted as they are.[41] Here there surfaces again the inescapable argument from utility. The stories the Greeks tell cannot but offer some sort of wisdom.

Thus in the second century A.D. there is still no modern category of myth, but instead an attitude of caution, if not of respect, toward the *lógoi* of the indigenous tradition, in spite of the physical or historical implausibilities found within them. Ethical and religious criteria once again prevail over those of empirical truth-value. It would show bias, however, in considering this same period, not to include the cutting distinction presented by Sextus Empiricus: to history (*historía*), which relates facts as true as they are real (*gegonóta*), he opposes myth (*mûthos*) — here we are at last! — which depicts unreal and untrue actions (*pragmáton agenéton kaì pseudôn ékthesis*), but also fiction (*plásma*), which recounts actions as if they really did happen (*homoíos toîs genoménois legómena*). A final definition? In fact, concerning the destinies of certain of the Homeric heroes, the skeptic philosopher only contests the versions of their stories in which they metamorphose into animals. Instead, for Sextus, true history has false history as a complement. While this second category includes *mûthoi* and *plásmata*, true history concerns the actions, places, times, and characters of renowned men, but also those of heroes and gods! From the point of view of content, the division between fictional myth and true history does not correspond to modern criteria.[42] More later . . .

Moreover, three centuries later, when Proclus, commenting on the *Timaeus*, finds himself confronted with the problem of evaluating the plausibility of the story of Atlantis, he rejects the thesis that it is "a myth and a fiction" (*mûthos kaì plásma*), instead preferring an allegorical interpretation.[43] While, for us, this type of reading reaches its apex in the polysemic exegesis Porphyry presents on the cave of the nymphs welcoming Odysseus upon his return to Ithaca in the *Odyssey*, we should not forget that the allegorical interpretation (*allegoreîn*) of the Homeric texts dates back to the sixth century B.C., when Theagenes of Rhegium, the first "grammarian" of Homer, proposed to see incarnations of water in Poseidon and the Scamander, or of intelligence in Athena.[44]

Barely recognizable in its modern meaning, myth recovers through the secondary meaning which is attributed to it through the allegorical reading. Only the more skeptical philosophers can, without pause, permit themselves to reject as fictions those narratives which, in Greece, are always of the civilization of the Self.

3.4. Rewriting the Past

No doubt the caution with which the Greek historians have always treated legendary narratives stems from this. The critical approach certain philosophers could allow themselves to take in the name of a naturalistic, physical, or even an ethical perspective was followed to a great extent by historians, especially concerning *lógoi* relating events of Greece's more distant past. For while some have been able to affirm that Herodotus distinguishes between a "time of the gods" and a "time of men" by allowing only the second into his historical inquiry, we must not forget that this second category extends equally to a "time of heroes." Thus the occupation of the first historiographers is truly to reach back to beginnings in order to combine both "legendary" past events and more recent events into the continuity of a homogenous chronology. Thus, like Acousilaus of Argos, one can trace a unique line, focalized on Argos, that begins with a cosmogony as its point of departure and follows with a theogony, in order to record the heroic deeds of Heracles, the Trojan War, and the returns of the heroes in terms of the Argive genealogy founded by Phoroneus, the first man; son of the river Inachos, he is a sort of local Prometheus. Or again, one can follow the example of Pherecydes of Athens, who is content to synchronize the different heroic genealogies beginning with the birth of an offspring of a god who leads the historiographer through to his own contemporaries and patrons.[45]

The result of such an effort of rationalization of the legendary past of one's own culture is not consignment of that material to the category of the fictive, nor the development of a class of myth, but the formulation of a continual temporal succession that makes the heroes of legend the real founders of the present. Thus the inscription known as the *Marmor Parium*, mentioned earlier, traces (in a unique chronological line supported by actual figures of years counting from when the inscription was produced in 264/263 B.C.) the judgment by the Athenians in the dispute between Ares and Poseidon, Deucalion and the flood, the foundation of Thebes by Cadmus, the ordeals of the Danaids, the rule of Minos, the arrival of Demeter at Athens, the rape of Kore and the foundation of the Mysteries of Eleusis, the Trojan War, the birth of Homer, the journey of Sappho to Sicily, the capture of Sardis by Cyrus, the murder of Hipparchus by Harmodius and Aristogeiton, the battle of Marathon, the first victory of Aeschylus, the sea battle at Salamis, the death of Sophocles, that of Philip II of Macedon, and the rise to power of Alexander the Great![46]

The same is true in the Roman period. After having surveyed at the beginning of his work the ancient histories of Egypt, Assyria, Scythia, and other peripheral regions, Diodorus of Sicily, upon reaching the history of Greece, cannot help imparting a certain discomfort in the modern reader. Where do the ancient mythologies (*palaiaì muthologíai*) cease? Where does history begin? The narratives from times past that constitute the "mythologies" seem to be distinguished by the distant periods to which they refer and which prohibit the citation of complete proof because of the multiplicity of heroes, demigods, and men that make up their genealogies. Overall, they are also distinguished by the discord produced by multiple versions of actions from the more distant past (*arkhaiótatai práxeis te kaì muthologíai*). There remains no other solution for this late-Republican historian than to retreat to the methods outlined by his predecessors, authors of Greek histories from the fourth century. Like Callisthenes and Theopompus, Ephorus, a student of Isocrates, had made a distinction between what Diodorus three centuries later calls the "ancient mythologies" and "more recent events." The consequence: the universal history of Ephorus begins with the return of the Heraclids. The time of the gods thus belongs to "mythology," while that of heroes and men, to history.[47]

But, surprisingly, Diodorus himself (hemeîs dé) intends to include deeds of the gods in his history. "Mythology" becomes in this case "archaeology." He sees, in fact, no reason to deny to the "discourse of history" the most conspicuous actions of heroes and demigods who have accomplished great feats of war or who, in times of peace, have contributed in a substantial way to the good of society. His universal history of the Greeks will thus begin with the birth of Dionysus: although belonging to the distant past (tò palaión), this god is the source of numerous benefits for mankind. According to this perspective, the battles between the Greeks and the Amazons belong to the "archaeology" and the courage shown by Penthesilea during the Trojan War fully deserves its place in memorial history. This is so even if the "paradoxes" of these episodes have led certain predecessors to consider these stories "fictional myths," or more exactly, fabricated narratives (mûthoi peplasménoi). What is mythic is thus a question of point of view. As in Xenophanes, the determining criterion for integration into history of actions of the gods or heroes is not their empirical truth, but instead a matter of social utility, even of piety. We can now better understand Diodorus' opening statement of intention: never mind if the "mythological" stories like those of Hades have a fabricated content (hupóthesis peplasméne); they contribute to the arousal of piety and justice among men. The same holds true — even more so still — for history, that "prophetess of truth." Its "divine mouth" has a memorial function, in recounting, for example, the heroic deeds of Heracles. This exempts it, when legendary narratives are involved, from focusing with a more particular gaze on the truth![48]

The conception of Dionysius of Halicarnassus, compiling his Roman Antiquities at the same time, is not very different. Of the struggle between Heracles and Cacus to civilize Latium, the historian recounts both the lógos muthikós and the more truthful lógos alethinós. From case to case, the allegorizing or historicizing interpretation can reduce the heroic deed to its human motivations, but often utility (sumphéron) comes to override truth.[49] Likewise in the Byzantine period, when Photius, following the Alexandrian geographer Agatharchides, condemns a series of mûthoi, it is because they bring injury to the gods, whom they present as "adulterers, victims of the thunderbolt, lame, thieves, more feeble than men, quick to insult, unjust, and plaintive." But if it is not possible to condemn en masse all the producers of stories (muthopoioí) filled with impossibilities, it is because among them are poets such as Homer, Hesiod, Aeschylus, or Euripides, and poets are more concerned with seduction (psukhagogía) than with truth.[50]

Yes, Thucydides himself claims that the work of time, but also that of the poets and logographers dedicated to charming their listeners, has caused the most ancient events to move to the side of what is *muthôdes* regardless of whether one believes in them. He affirms in grand fashion, as well, that the work of writing, confronting signs and proofs, comes to substitute for that of memory, and thus the oral tradition. He does not, however, place in doubt the existence of the reign of Minos (known by *akoé*, by the oral tradition!), the historicity of the Trojan War and the ancestors of Agamemnon (whose actions have been transmitted by a memory capable of retaining *tà saphéstata*, the most secure facts), or the reality of the intelligence of Theseus (*súnesis*: a quality the historian attributes equally to a person as "historical" as Themistocles). This procedure is all the more paradoxical because Herodotus, as attached as he is to oral/aural testimony, does not hesitate to situate the thalassocracy of Minos beyond the human sphere when he compares it with that of the tyrant Polycrates of Samos. Behold Minos consigned to the "time of the gods," beyond the "time of men," which includes also the age of heroes and which is the subject of Herodotus' *Histories*.[51]

The facts of legendary history can be established by the same indications and the same proofs as the actual development of the Peloponnesian War. For Thucydides, the concentration of temples on the Acropolis is proof (*tekmérion*) of the state of the city before the intervention of Thesean synoecism. But the limited dimensions of Mycenae in the fifth century should never be used as a determining sign (*akribès semeîon*) by which to doubt the size of the expedition of the Greeks against Troy; in this case, one must trust in the priests and tradition (*lógos!*). The same advice holds for the Cyclopes and the Laestrygonians, aboriginal inhabitants of Sicily. There is thus in Thucydides no "radical rupture" between the marvelous fictions of myth and the lights of rational history, which one could recognize as precursory to the position of a Fontenelle.[52] In contrast, we can detect in him a certain suspicion of poetic narrative forms, forms meant more to charm the ears of the public than to serve the city. The offensive aspect of what is *muthôdes* is its poetic character, and thus its "fictionalizing" nature. But once again, it is unthinkable to eliminate from the progression of events through time the constitutive episodes in the past of one's own culture — even more so, of one's own city.

3.5. Archaeologies

Since perhaps the Alexandrian period and certainly the nineteenth century, the philological tradition has tended to call the history Thucydides traces of the city of Athens, from its origins to the beginnings of the war with the Persians, by the name *archaeology*, not *mythology*. Certainly this is not entirely the result of chance. Thucydides himself, in describing these "ancient," but no less historical, events, makes use of the term *palaiá*: formerly (*pálai*), Greece was not inhabited by a stable population; Minos is the earliest man (*palaítatos*) to have gained mastery of the sea; ancient Hellas (*tò palaiòn Hellenikón*) knew the same level of development as that of the barbarian world contemporary with the historian. In a word, this period, which extends to the time of the constitution of the Athenian empire—to the eve of the Peloponnesian War—is called *tà palaiá*, "remote times," or alternatively, *tà arkhaîa*, "ancient times."[53] What distinguishes the events of this ancient time from the reality of present actions (*autà tà érga*) is less their truth than their traditionality. Attempting to pacify the Lacedaemonians in order to avoid a declaration of war, the Athenians in Thucydides' account do not forget to mention the services they rendered to the Greeks as a whole during the Persian Wars. The invocation of these directly experienced events, still present in visible memory (*ópsis*) by one and all, would have a greater effect on the hearer than the recalling of *palaiá*, past events transmitted by the oral tradition (*lógoi*) and apprehended through audition (*akoé*).[54] This distinction further reveals the mobility of the chronological boundary between legendary past and historical present. Depending upon context, the Persian Wars may be included in both!

It is no different among the Athenians of Herodotus, if not for Herodotus himself. Not content in principle to prefer visual evidence for a narrative meant to rely more upon the eyes than upon the ears, Herodotus clearly presents it as advantageous for the Athenians participating in the battle of Plataea to refer not only to past events (*tà palaià érga*) but also to more recent exploits (*tà kainá*). To the Tegeans, who have just cited the legendary deeds of their king Echemos against the Heraclid Hyllos in order to claim a position of strategic importance in the battle of Plataea, the Athenians counter by recounting their hospitality toward the Heraclids, their piety toward the Argives killed in the battle of the seven against Thebes, and their victory against the Amazons. But that is all for the distant past. What is more important is the recent past, such as the battle of Marathon, where the Athenians repulsed the Persians in a kind of single combat. To prove, in another discourse of this type, the need for the Athenians to possess a fleet, Demosthenes proceeds no differently, citing both past and more recent events (*kaì palaià kaì kainá*). In this case, the *arkhaîa kaì palaiá* correspond to the retreat of the Athenians to the island of Salamis and to the decisive battle that followed in 480. As for *kainá*, they begin with the expedition conducted in Euboea that ended with the capitulation of the Thebans; it took place in 357, only a year before the composition of

Demosthenes' speech. The first event is left only to memory (*mnéme*), while the second has the benefit of eyewitness confirmation (*hà pántes heorákate*): to the oral tradition of the past is opposed the visual evidence of recent times.[55] This is exactly analogous to what we have seen in Thucydides and Herodotus, with the only difference that, 125 years after the events, the Persian Wars have definitively passed to the side of *arkhaîa*, ancient times.

We noted that Diodorus of Sicily does not hesitate to move the fluid boundary between "mythology" and "history" backward in time; he intends thus to integrate the actions of the gods with what he explicitly calls *arkhaiología*. We know too that from the fifth century these narratives of ancient times aroused a renewed interest. Concealed in poetic forms through which they had been continuously reformulated up to that point, they were more and more entrusted during this time to the prose of those we call historiographers. Is this, then, the birth of mythography? Once again, caution must be used when employing these terms; *mûthos* and myth are not the focus of inquiry in the first attempts at collection and chronological systematization of local "legendary" traditions. The work mentioned above by Acousilaus of Argos, the most ancient of the historians (*historikós*) according to his biography, carried the title *Genealogíai*, as did that of his colleague Hecataeus, and the work of Hecataeus was called also *Heroología* or even simply *Historíai*. On the other hand, the heroic genealogy of Pherecydes of Athens, the first writer of a treatise in prose, was called by the ancients *Historíai* or *Theogonía*. The interest of Asclepiades of Tragilos in the stories dramatized in tragedy in comparison with more ancient versions determined the title of his work in six books, the *Tragoidoúmena*. And Andron of Halicarnassus was able to call the work in which he placed in parallel the genealogies of the great families of Greek cities *Suggeniká* or, more widely still, *Historíai*. These are indeed the first writings of history, but their design and function remain near to the poetic forms that precede them and that continue to be practiced simultaneously.[56]

It goes without saying that this enormous historiographical and "archaeological" work of collection, classification, comparison, and reorganization of the abundant narrative heritage of the Greek cities forms the basis of the compendia and catalogues of "myths" compiled by the Alexandrian antiquarians. If here, however, we are truly witness to the birth of mythography, and thus of mythology in its common meaning, there is still room for abuse of the terms employed. For us, the paragon of these mythological manuals is clearly the *Bibliothéke*, erroneously attributed to Apollodorus of Athens, the author of a long work entitled *On the Gods* in the second century B.C. *Bibliothéke*, not *Mythography*, is the title adopted for this work, which Photius had read long ago.

About this handbook, the erudite Byzantine tells us that it contains the most ancient stories (*tà palaítata*) of the Greeks and that it compiles all that is known of the gods, the heroes, and those people who lived in ancient times (*arkhaîon*), before the Trojan War.[57]

True, the Greeks of the imperial age would have known of "mythographers" and "mythography." But to them the term *muthográphos* simply meant, like the *muthológos* of Plato, a teller of stories about ancient times. According to Diodorus of Sicily, we owe these stories, among which one finds, for example, the varying versions of the genealogy of the Muses, *certainly* to the "mythographers," but also to celebrated poets such as Homer, Hesiod, or Alcman. In addition, when Dionysius of Halicarnassus compares divergent tales describing the native populations of Italy, he cites both "mythographers" and poets. Among the first we find not only Cato, author of the *Origines*, but also two Greek historians from the Classical age, authors of regional histories whose chronologies reach back to primordial times: Antiochos of Syracuse and the above-mentioned Pherecydes of Athens, cited by Dionysius as a specialist on genealogies.[58]

Strabo classifies "mythography" as a historical form (*en historías skhémati*) in prose, in opposition to poetry, which for him can be expressed in a "mythic" form (*en múthou skhémati*). The height of paradox: to insert narratives defined as *mûthoi* (*muthographía*) into historiography is, according to Strabo, to surrender to a taste for marvelous invention and the desire to please. But when he is confronted with a poet such as Homer, the *mûthos* is not only valorized inasmuch as it is a narration adapted to the poetic form, but above all it can appear as the formal presentation of the results of an inquiry (*historoúmena* opposed to *plásma*, fiction!). In this case, Strabo suggests, one might as well follow the historian Theopompus, who appears to have confessed that in his histories he also recounted *mûthoi* pertaining to obscure and unknown topics. Postalexandrian mythography is thus a close relative of the mythology accepted by Plato. We shouldn't forget that an inscription from Amorgos attests to an Apollo and Muses who are mythographers![59]

Let us return to the *Bibliotheke* attributed to Apollodorus, specifically to the epigram that opens the work as we have it. This text defines the work as an erudite manual of *mûthoi*, narratives conceived at an early date (*palaigeneîs*), a manual meant to be used as a substitute for the poetic forms in which these narrations are dispersed: the Homeric poems, elegiac verses, tragedies, melic poetry, cyclic poems. In effect, these narratives of the gods and heroes of times passed are henceforth reduced to their plots, arranged, catalogued, and above all stripped of their poetic vestments. They have become what we now call "myths." Their only function is to satisfy the antiquarian interests of the erudite readers of the imperial age. Before plunging into the *Bibliotheke*, Photius informs us in his own *Bibliotheca* that he had glanced at another mythographic work written in the Augustan age, a compendium by Conon. It appears to have been a collection of fifty local legends, called simply *Diegéseis*, *Stories*.[60]

We can recognize this Alexandrian taste for rare stories grouped thematically in the *Metamorphoses* of Antoninus Liberalis, the *Katasterismoí* attributed to Eratosthenes, or the *Passiones Amatoriae* of Parthenius. This interest in the collection of exotic narratives centered on a common theme, detached from their context, and reduced to the skeletons of their plot, prefigures the interest of modern scholars in "mythologies."[61] It contributes, in a way, to the construction of a normalized object of myth.

Difference in content forms the division less between myth and history than between historiography and poetry. Regardless of the fact that Thucydides found the Homeric charms in the writings of the logographers who were his predecessors a matter for reproach, we must not forget the sharp distinction made by Aristotle in the *Poetics*. The difference between historian (*historikós*) and poet (*poiétes*) lies less in the contrast between prosaic and poetic form than in content. For the historian, this constitutes narration of events that have taken place (*tà genómena*); for the poet, those of the sort that could take place (*hoîa àn génoito*). The domain of epic and dramatic poetry, which above all are for Aristotle narrative vehicles of *mûthoi*, is that of probability, specifically probability on a general level (*kathólou* as opposed to *kath'hékaston*, which is reserved for historiography). From here arises the exemplary and moral value of the stories recounted in poetry, a value that, in fact, a great many Greek historians do not hesitate to claim equally for themselves. This holds as well for the rhythmical and musical powers of a poetic prose such as the narratives of *arkhaîa* with which Hippias, according to Plato, succeeded in both flattering the ears of his Lacedaemonian public and simultaneously educating them; they were narratives of heroic genealogies and of foundations of cities, constituting an "archaeological" memory that resembles, through its charms, mythology (*muthologêsai*).[62]

Plutarch, situated near the final period of Greek civilization, will provide the conclusion to this discussion, which has aimed to show the constant ambivalence the Greeks demonstrated toward the narratives, and indeed the concept itself, that we, without hesitation, call myth. While discussing the various forms of glorification in the tract he dedicates to the reputation of the Athenians, the moralist takes his definition of poetry from Plato: its essence is *muthopoiía*, the creation of "myths," of stories. And myth is nothing other than a false discourse (*lógos pseudés*), but one that resembles the truth. It is fiction, but plausible fiction, embellished with the pleasing language, rhythms, and melodies of the poetic art; it is not fictional, but rather "fictionalizing." Accordingly, if the *lógos* of the historian is the image and representation of actions that really happened, *mûthos* is only the image of the *lógos*, and thus a mimetic discourse of the second degree. His intention to write a biography of Theseus, however, confronts the author of the *Parallel Lives* with what we would call the problem of myth. In turning to the most distant past, just as when the geographer approaches the extremes of the inhabited world, he in effect leaves behind the period which would allow a basis for plausibility (*eikòs lógos*). The period is not accessible through an inquiry based on facts (*prágmata*) but rather through marvels the poets and mythographers (*poietaì kaì muthográphoi*) recount, which can be granted neither credit nor certitude. Decisive and insurmountable opposition? No, because *lógos* (that is, reason), can greatly purify the mythic (*muthôdes*) and thus confer on it the appearance of historical inquiry (*historía*); when the "archaeology" eludes probability (*tò eikós*), the listener indulgently allows himself to be charmed![63] We can allow Thucydides his rigor, but we must share with him a critical and measured trust in the legendary past of Greece.

To be sure, as conceived and in every case as expressed by the Greeks, *mûthoi* are stories which do not themselves correspond to a narrative type, an ethnocentric concept, or a particular mode of thought. Referring, when used in the plural, to a fluid set of narratives, the term *mûthos* does not define an indigenous category. Conversely, the modern category of myth — traditional and foundational story, but fictive because of its representation of the superhuman — is not recognized in Greece as a specific signifier.

4. The Production of Symbolic Discourse

Myth is not a universal reality, mythology not a kind of cultural substance; consequently, it is not a genre, not some "Idealtyp"; there is simply no ontology of myth. In addition, no more should we speak of mythology as the science of myth.[64]

Should we attempt escape this *aporia* that constrains us from making myth into a relative category proper to contemporary anthropological thought? Certainly, the richness of traditional narratives produced by individual cultures is abundant enough to sustain our interest independently of any generic classification, whether indigenous or universal. Mythic or not, these narratives survive, demanding our attention and sagacity. No one would contest that their exotic character, and also their depth, require translation and explanation. Appealing to our curiosity through their intensity, these objects of culture can be characterized in a global manner by several distinctive traits — understood through a perspective that will be in the present study and from now on both deliberately European or Western and academic. They are the material results of a process of signification, and thus present effects of meaning to those for whom they are intended, and then to us, through the medium of narration.

4.1. Symbolic Manifestations

Should we be forbidden from imagining how this process of the constitution of meaning, carried out through a product of culture, might function? Whether it is manifested materially in the form of oral or written narratives, social rituals, or figural or plastic representations, the symbolic process — we shall call it thus henceforth — seems regularly to be aroused by a singular occasion: decisive modification in the history, lifestyle, or ecology of the society in question, which also affects the emotional state of individuals. This modification provokes the need for reflection, operating in contact with both empirical reality and the conceptual and cultural preconceptions and representations inherent in the society concerned to construct a figurative "response." If one avoids making a distinctive property out of specifically mythic thought and attaching it to an early stage in human development, the process of symbolic construction and elaboration can be imagined in terms that recall those proposed by Heyne two centuries ago. However that may be, this intellectual elaboration, this process of production of thought, is reified in different manifest forms, among which are linguistic and narrative discourse. Particularly among the linguistic productions, the categorization of myth can only produce an artificial segmentation that is biased, and in the end, arbitrary. In the response, in a large part speculative, to a novel or exceptional empirical experience, we can uncover the social function of the products of the symbolic process.[65]

Consider the words of Italo Calvino, summarizing the process of literary creation, in one of the *American Lectures* he was never able to present:

> We say that different elements contribute to forming the visual part of the literary imagination: direct observation of the world, imaginative and dream-like transfiguration, the figurative world transmitted by culture through its different levels of manifestation, and a process of abstraction, of condensation

and interiorization of perceptible experience, which is of as decisive importance in its visualization as in its verbalization of thought.

Where does the difference lie between literature and the manifestation
that anthropologists subsume under the category of myth? As Calvino
notes, a work of literature is par excellence the product of a universal
capacity for symbolic creation. As an imaginative and speculative exercise in language, it constructs a specific universe that, because of the
particular indeterminacies of linguistic expression, each reader and each
listener is induced to reinterpret and re-create out of his own natural
environment and from his own set of cultural references.[66] It is entirely a
product of the symbolic process and thus traversed and determined by
the circumstances of its enunciation: composition, communication, reception, then rereading. It is on these variable circumstances of production and fruition that we must eventually found the boundary between
"myth" and "literature." Meant to be performed on the occasion of a
particular cult for the benefit of an entire community, an epicinian of
Pindar or a tragedy of Aeschylus only becomes a work of literature in
the etymological sense at the moment when, cut off from the circumstances of its original enunciation, it is an object solely for reading. It is
no mere chance that in the writings of Plato, followed by Aristotle, the
notion of the "poetic," the art of creation (*poietikè tékhne*), is born
from the idea of *mímesis*, of representation, both plastic and linguistic.

This is to say that in ancient Greece in particular, these symbolic linguistic manifestations regularly cause the modern categories of "mythic
narrative" and "literary work" to overlap. The narratives we consider
"mythic" exist only as products actualized in the form of their recitation, that is, in the literary forms attached to the clearly defined circumstances of their enunciation. It falls in particular to these forms, which
correspond in general to ritualized events, to present and integrate the
narratives called "mythic" within a community of given beliefs. Only by
abstraction, by bracketing of the ritual situations in which they are represented, by exclusion of the poetic forms that are the medium of their
communication, is one able to constitute a myth of Oedipus or a legend
of the Atreidae. "Greek mythology" only begins with mythography; its
debut is the moment when an Apollodorus, fashioning himself a nar-
ratologue, reduces to their plots those narratives that in fact only exist
in ritual situations and poetical works. "Myths" are not "texts," but
"discourses."[67] Moreover, when we speak of narratives meant for a public defined by fixed conditions of enunciation, we must speak also of the
precise social and cultural function involved. Through the very forms of
enunciation it assumes, the symbolic situation, particularly the linguistic
one, contains a constitutive pragmatic aspect. Speculation on natural

and cultural reality by varying symbolic processes necessarily has in return a practical effect on cultural reality itself.[68]

Only through this approach is it possible to rethink the much-debated
links between "myth" and history. To be sure, we grasp what constitute
for us "historical events" only through a memory itself subject to the
symbolic process. This means that, at once as stimuli and products of
the symbolic process, the events of factual history — its actors, its temporality, its spaces — very much can be reworked through symbolic speculation, in particular in the form of narrative expression. Through the
"fictionalization of history" and the "historicization of fiction" and — as
we shall see — through the discursive activity stemming from an instance
of enunciation that is itself spatially and historically marked, actors,
actions, and the spatial and temporal framework of "real" history undergo transpositions and metamorphoses during the creation of discourse.[69] It is up to us to decode them!

4.2. Semionarrative Readings

In these terms it is no longer possible to represent the process of discourse production, and consequently that of the signification and production of meaning, as a generative course beginning with the most
abstract entities and moving forward, by means of expansion and discursive figurations, to its expression. We should contemplate here particularly some successive revisions that have been proposed to the
famous Jakobsonian schema of communication. The attention is now
focused on empirical elements and cultural constructs that constitute at
once the origin and the object of discourse production and its significant
re-elaboration. What is at stake is no more a message encoded by a
sender to be decoded by a receiver, but a discursive manifestation, resul-
tant of schematizations stemming from an enunciative "ecosystem"
meant to be understood, seen, or read in a situation or psychosocial
setting often different from its production.[70]

It remains to pose the question of how the act of discourse production functions, by means of a semiotics of enunciation conceived as the
study of the process of construction and actualization of meaning. More
precisely, it remains to consider the problem of the form in which it is
possible to represent such functioning. In classic Greimassian semiotics,
phenomena located in different levels of semionarrative and discursive
structures, deriving from figures suggested by the natural and cultural
world, are combined in the process of production of meaning.[71] One
thus does not proceed "vertically" from the more abstract to the more
figural, from the fundamental world to the more superficial, but "hori-

zontally" through the dialectical interlacing of processes operating on different levels.

On the other hand, when an erudite reading places us before the "finished product," nothing prevents us, from the perspective of the receiver, from attempting to "descend" from the discursive manifestation to the more "profound" plans of its organization and schematization. This is a matter of pure reasoning, related to the artificial character of all academic analysis. And since we are here interested essentially in narrative materializations of the symbolic process, classified in general under the rubric "myth," our analysis can borrow its tools particularly from narratology.

This analytic approach will serve, in concluding these abstract reflections, not only to set out the operative procedures for reading we will use in the study of the narratives of the foundation of Cyrene, but also, at each of the phases of this narrative examination, to call to mind what could have led to the definition of the anthropological category of myth.

Focusing on the grammatical and syntactic articulation and on the semantic depth not any more of a single sentence, but of a whole discourse, semionarrative reading in its first stage is sensitive to surface structures, called "discursive structures." In linguistic manifestations, one quite quickly perceives the effects of the production of discourse and enunciation. The text defines in its progression a series of actorial figures; these actors, without having the psychological depth that we are accustomed to attribute to individuals, are inscribed in the space and time that outline the discourse as it develops. These processes of actorialization, spatialization, and temporalization are essentially figurative. Through them, elements and figures drawn from the natural and social world are invested in the discourse. These, in turn, arouse the effect of reference, and thus the impression of reality appropriate for the narration. While in the narratives the anthropological tradition has considered "mythic," actors and times are provided with qualities that define them as either infra- or superhuman, from the point of view of space the locations depicted in these narratives are still readily culturally defined sites; they are endowed with a geographical identity by the community in question.

At a more abstract level, called "semionarrative surface structures," the discourse is used to reorganize figures and values that the elaboration and schematization borrow, in the process of discourse production, from the natural world and the culture in question. In what concerns the narration most particularly, this reorganization operates on a syntactic plan through usage of a plot corresponding to a *schema* that can be defined, in its repetitions, as *canonical*. With its four phases, *manipulation* (engaged by a situation of *lack*), *competence*, *performance*, and *sanction* (which results in a moral, through which the story returns to the narrative equilibrium), this schema is the basis of the syntactic unity and coherence of the narrative discourse; it is the foundation of both plot production and the causal and logical connections that constitute it. The developed narrative can be composed of several *sequences*, each one of which follows the canonical schema. These sequences can be linked together or interwoven into one another. The canonical schema also defines the actantial positions of *Sender* (*Destinateur*), *Subject*, *Antisubject*, and *Predicate*. In the course of the production of a plot, these syntactic positions are occupied by different actors and corresponding (semantic) qualities and values; the interplay of their reciprocal relationships lays out the conflicts within the narration. On the semantic level, the coherence of the narrative configuration and thus of the whole discourse is established by the reiteration of semantic figures and elements that define more or less abstract *isotopies*.[72] We could state that in any narrative we find, in a first phase of manipulation, a Sender which gives to a Subject the competence to act as a hero. Provided with specific semantic qualities (as Predicates) thanks to the phase of competence, the semionarrative Subject is able to face the phase of performance and to realize his qualities being opposed to a narrative Antisubject. The Predicates (and thus semantic values) he has been provided with are confirmed, generally through a second intervention of the Sender in the final phase of sanction.

As concerns narratives placed under the modern appellation of myth, these seem to reorganize, when they are not disrupting, the taxonomies and axiologies, *the social and symbolic classifications of reality and the hierarchies of values* of the community involved. From this comes the primary pragmatic effect of "myth," as understood as a response to an exceptional situation. It is also on this semionarrative surface level that the "mythic" narrative establishes, through its speculative component, metaphorical connections between the various domains of ecology and other general knowledge of the society in question. These, in particular, are the metaphoric procedures that make fruitless all attempts at a great division and strict distinction between logical (or scientific) and symbolic (or savage!) thought.[73]

Finally, the syntactic and semantic dimensions become merged at the most abstract level, that of "deep semionarrative structures." The simultaneous assertion at this level of two or three terms that are contradictory, but affirmed to be true, has come to be a touchstone for what is considered "mythic." As the result of our progressive movement toward abstraction, these terms undoubtedly correspond to themes that form the basis of the figurative isotopies. Precisely these terms seem to determine, through symbolic elaboration and reflection, the selection of figures and concepts borrowed from the natural and social world of the community. These are then represented, through production of discourse and plot, in the form of a narration that we agree to call "mythic." On this level, in every case, the discourse can be seen as the effect of culturally and ideologically determined symbolic construction.

4.3. Symbolic Enunciations

This is all to say that the exploratory or cognitive value of these narratives issues from the symbolic process. Independently of any generic category, what is constructed here is a fiction based on a reality. But — this is perhaps the way a narrative considered "mythic" distinguishes itself from products of modern literary activity — this fiction, this tool of speculation, is meant to have a practical effect. Accordingly, these narratives are in general the object of belief on the part of their addressees. For this reason in particular they cannot be severed from the conditions of their enunciation in order to be reduced to pure objects of observation in the anthropologist's study. The very process of discourse production excludes all immanence of text.

In addition, this means that the character of these narratives can assume the most varied forms of expression, in order to obtain the desired symbolic efficacy. Consequently, it is impossible to classify them within a category more specific than the quite vast one of symbolic or, even more simply, discursive narrative representations.

Finally, this is to say that an ideological effect is brought about by these narratives, founded upon natural and social reality, through speculation on their subjects and the presentation of an original representation of them. Although they find their motivation in history, these symbolic and figurative narrative manifestations should not be considered as reflections (other than deforming ones) of a social and historical reality.

By reason of their fluid position relative to their own past, the Greeks offer to us, as distant readers, narratives that would be situated precisely between "myth" and "history" if they were categorized from our academic perspective. We shall see that the determining criterion is that of fictionality. But the boundaries between truth, plausibility, and falsity vary in both space and time; they vary from one culture to another, and are modified from one period to the next. This is another reason to focus our attention on narratives in which these very limits are blurred, and another reason to be aware of their symbolic and "fictionalizing" effects.

Since the configuration of time plays a determining role in the production of narrative plot, I have chosen here to reread several symbolic creations of discourse centered on the relationships of an enunciator (represented in the text by the figure of the narrator-speaker) with the representation of his past — without forgetting that time is always figured through the intermediary of space! In the end, it will be a question of examining, from the point of view of the functional pragmatics of the symbolic process adopted here and in relation to our own frame of spatial and temporal reference, the connections established by the production of discourse and by the process of schematization between the space/time figured in the symbolic narration and the space/time of its enunciation.

The essential goal for the Greeks was always, in poetic activity as in historiography, to protect in memory that which was precisely most memorable, even if, in time, the faith of the Greek reader, as ours, could wane. We leave — temporarily, at least — the last word to Dionysius of Halicarnassus, who judges the work of the predecessors of Thucydides thus:[74]

> These historians (*suggrapheîs*) all pursue the same goal: to bring to common knowledge all the traditions (*mnêmai*) of peoples and cities conserved in local monuments and writings deposited in sanctuaries or in archives, without adding or subtracting anything. These traditions contain certain narratives (*mûthoi*) in which people believed long ago, and dramatic adventures that appear rather absurd in our day.

II

The Foundation Narrative of Cyrene

CONTEMPORARY archaeologists agree: Cyrene, the Greek colony in Libya, had its beginnings in the second half of the seventh century B.C. The presence of some objects dated to the Late Helladic III A and B periods on the site clearly points to more ancient contacts between Greece and the Mediterranean coast of Africa; nothing, however, before the middle of the Archaic period indicates the development of a city in the Greek sense of the term.[1] Such is the interpretation of archaeologists, readers of signs who start with the ruins left by the work of erosion over the ages. They take their inspiration from Thucydides and his "palaeology," his reconstruction of *palaiá*, of "ancient" history from the "indications" (*semeîa*) to be found and read also in material culture. As archaeologists in the most basic sense of the word, they attempt to insert their findings into a chronology conforming to our sense of history, an arithmetic time with a double orientation implying a point of reference imposed by Christian civilization. By this perspective, the linear accumulation of years is outlined beginning with the date attributed to the birth of the founding hero of our own culture, and also counting back from this same point.[2] Nothing could be more foreign to the Greek manner of temporal organization of the historical past.

The diversity of conceptions the Greeks were able to formulate about their past is clearly shown in the multiplicity of foundation events that a single poet is likely to situate at the origin of a single city in the process of singing the praises of its leaders, his contemporaries. In the case of Cyrene, they include the abduction of the nymph Cyrene by Apollo in Thessaly and celebration on the shores of Libya of his union with the young huntress of lions (events situated in an indeterminate past), the occupation of the same site by the sons of Antenor accompanied by Helen following the destruction of Troy, or the trajectory of the clod of Libyan earth transported by a son of Poseidon to another son of the same god, and finally washing up at Thera (Santorini) in order to regain metaphorically its country of origin through the colonizing expedition of Battus, the founder of Cyrene, seventeen generations later. In this third version we are presented with a chronological calculation, but only through an indication of the ascendancy of Arcesilas IV, the king of Cyrene, specifying the span of time separating the colonizing act of

Battus from the time and circumstances of the narration by means of enumeration of the actual king's ancestors. The different circumstances of transmission to the addressee and audience of these events occurring in an indeterminate past are, however, capable of being quite precisely dated and located. The three legendary versions of the founding of Cyrene mentioned here are known to us through epinician poems composed under the reign of Arcesilas IV; the list above presents, in order, fragments of narratives contained in the ninth, fifth, and fourth *Pythian Odes* of Pindar.

The first of these epinicians celebrates a victory won in the hoplite race by Telesicrates of Cyrene during the twenty-eighth Pythian games in the year 474 B.C. The ode was most probably sung in the Greek city in Libya; as is the case with other victory songs, its ritual performance was an integral part of the festivities marking the return of the athlete to his city. The second celebrates the renowned success in the chariot race by the brother-in-law of the Cyrenaean king Arcesilas IV during the thirty-first Pythian games of 462 B.C. It was sung in honor of the charioteer himself, the parent of the king, near the Garden of Aphrodite, in Cyrene itself, perhaps on the occasion of the celebration of the festival of the Carneia, a Spartan festival we will come to later. The last of the three odes was composed to sing the praises of the same victory. It was most likely performed in the actual palace of the king, probably during a banquet specifically celebrating the victory in the four-horse chariot race, the most prestigious to be won at the games.[3]

But this is not all: in the picture of Libya he paints in describing the expedition launched by Cambyses against a city neighboring Cyrene, Herodotus traces the history of the Greek colony in Libya from its origins (4.145–167). Beginning with the descendants of the Argonauts dwelling on Lemnos, who are chased by the Pelasgians to Lacedaemon, he leads his listeners from these heroic times to the reign of Arcesilas III of Cyrene, who, in 525, had pledged allegiance to the Persian king. Moreover, after having followed the chronological thread of events up to "that moment" (*tóte*, 4.167.1), Herodotus adopts the prospective view the Delphic oracle allows him, making allusion to the reign of Arcesilas IV, the last king of Cyrene, who, ruling from 462, was forced to cede the throne in 440. The history of the colony is thus traced up to the moment of enunciation of Herodotus' narrative.

Two centuries later, the story of the colonization of Cyrene finds new expression in the hands of a poet who tells a new story of foundation of the Greek city in Libya. Perhaps in competition with an episode told in the fourth book of the *Argonautica* by Apollonius of Rhodes, the *Hymn to Apollo* of Callimachus discretely sets the metamorphosed story in relation to the moment and the circumstances of the poem's production.

While the Battiads, sovereigns of Cyrene, are probably the "kings" (68) of the *actual* narrator of the story (that is, Callimachus), Ptolemy II Philadelphus is—as we shall see—just as well the "king" (27) of the same speaker of this strange poem. As for historical documents, a decree of the accord of the citizens of Cyrene with the Therans, promulgated in the fourth century, is the source of another summary of the Cyrenaean foundation legend. In citing the *Agreement of the Founders*, which carries this brief account, this inscription seeks to coincide the time of colonization with the present of the document's dedication.[4] From the poems of Pindar to the founders' stele, all the versions of the symbolic birth of Cyrene place the past of colonial history in relation to the present of their enunciation.

1. Pindar and the Time of Performance

It would be somewhat premature to accept here the equations between ancient and modern chronology proposed by contemporary scholars. Certainly, the odes of Pindar classified as "epinicians" by the Alexandrian editors exhibit references to the occasion of their performance, as is the case in the tradition of Archaic choral poetry in general. This is to say that in addition to the world, internal and textual, they refer to, each of the poems also makes reference to the extradiscursive situation in which it is sung; in other words, the discourse of each poem bears the marks of its enunciation. The procedure of enunciative self-reference, particularly common in the Pindaric *Epinicians*, thus has an internal as well as an external face!

1.1. Performative Self-Reference and Temporal Location

In *Pythian 9*, this poetic procedure of enunciative self-reference is relatively discrete. Opening the poem, the strong affirmation of the narrator-speaker's desire to proclaim the victory of Telesicrates in the hoplite race simply includes the location of the course and the Cyrenaean origin of the victor; one cannot find here reference to the place of performance of the song or to the exact date of the victory, which is immediately inserted into the time of the narrative (*pote*, 5). Without the erudition of the Alexandrian commentators, summarized by a knowledgeable scholiast, we would not know that the victory celebrated by the narrator was gained at the twenty-eighth Pythiad. *Pythian 5*, initially addressed to Arcesilas, is clearly meant for the king of Cyrene, a contemporary of Pindar. The praise of the charioteer of the king "welcomed

near the water of Castalia," along with the brief description of the race
in the hippodrome brings us back to another victory at Delphi, while
mention of praise for the king sung near the Garden of Aphrodite indicates the probable place of the performance of the poem, at Cyrene.
The same victory is celebrated in *Pythian* 4; in addition to the textual
indications locating the chariot race at Delphi, the demand of the narrator that the Muse stand "today" by the king of Cyrene gives a deictic
indication of the time and place of the performance of this long ode.
But here again only the scholiast inserts the moment into an established
chronology, by correlating this *nunc* with the thirty-first Pythiad.

Thus while the three narratives of the foundation of Cyrene presented
by Pindar are placed in relation to the moment and location of the
performance of the epinician odes in which they are situated, this is
effected through a relatively imprecise process of temporal and spatial
localization, in terms of the succession of generations or reigns, or by
geographical connections. This twofold localization gains meaning only
through reference to the enunciative situation of the ode, in the *hic et
nunc* of its performance by a chorus of Cyrenaeans, and in the eyes and
ears of those for whom the poem is intended.[5] Of course, these circumstances of enunciation lost their immediate topicality because the Alexandrian commentators on the *Epinicians*, for their part, felt the need to
insert the odes into their own temporal system, a "chronical" system
corresponding to the traditional forms of temporal computation known
by the Greeks in the Classical age: local lists of priestesses of Hera at
Argos, lists of the annual eponymous archons at Athens, or, from a
more Panhellenic standpoint, lists of the victors at the Olympic games,
held every four years.[6] Without the chronological work of the Hellenistic critics, we would be unable to locate the moments of performance of
these three odes in our own system of historical time, unable to assign the
dates of 474 to the ninth *Pythian* and 462 to the fifth and the fourth!

Does not this projection onto a chronologically indeterminate past of
foundational events, stemming from a known time and place, constitute
precisely one of the criteria of classification of the anthropological category of myth? Do not these events, situated in a transcendent past and
attaching the ephemeral present to an atemporal permanence, provide a
path of privileged access to the essence of mythology? Are these primordial and exemplary acts not precisely capable of asserting the specificity
of the category, if not the essence, of those narratives we have come to
place in doubt?

Three observations concerning the three odes of Pindar suggest that
we be cautious. First, the double temporal localization to which these
poems are subject, between the moment of their performance and that
of their editing by scholars, shows that with the passing of time itself,

their relationship with the past, not simply the outline of their chronol-ogy, is modified. There is thus nothing here of myth per se, only variable perspectives on particular narratives, products of the symbolic process. Second, the three narratives whose development we can follow are so different that it is impossible to consider them variants — genetic or structural — of a unique, ontologically stable, version. Temporal and spatial variations on distinct themes, the stories are so creative and speculative that they tend to efface completely the material and "histori-cal" reality the archaeologists attempt, with great difficulty, to recon-struct. Finally, beyond the fact that no original version stands out among the divergent narratives, we do not know of a story that might have the value of a standard, in relation to which the Pindaric narratives would appear as simple literary creativity.

Certainly the celebrated *Agreement of the Founders*, to which we will return, summarizes in prose a story describing the oracular command given by Apollo to Battus and to the people of Thera to found a colony in Libya, along with the preparations they made. But the text of the fourth-century stele itself gives a slightly different version of the event from what we find in the undatable summary that introduces it. The decree, in fact, indicates that the terms of the *Agreement* were known by the ancestors (*prógonoi; SEG* IX, 3.5) of those who composed the text and that the corresponding oath had been taken "formerly" (*pote*, 1.14–15)! This signifies that the relationship of the Greeks with their past should be understood not as a relationship to myth, in the sense in which we commonly understand this Eurocentric concept, but as a mul-tiform connection to *palaiá*. This connection with a more or less distant past varies not only according to the symbolic and speculative possi-bilities of spatial and socially accepted circumstances, but is also mod-ified with the passage of time.

The present study thus particularly concerns the different forms of configuration of time. It is a matter of understanding how, starting from actual empirical time (present and past), a "textual time" is constructed through different modes of the symbolic process. We shall see that the configuration of this narrated, and by consequence enunciated or spo-ken, time (*erzählte Zeit*) is largely dependent on the "time of speaking" (*Erzählzeit*), and that this time of the utterance depends on the time of the act of enunciation; in the process of inscribing itself in the text through different temporal indications ("uttered enunciation") and through the rhythm of the narration (*Erzählzeit*), this time of the act of enunciation connects us to the production of discourse. It aids in posi-tioning the time narrated, which is not marked by the linear character generally attributed to "chronical" or "calendar" time, in a present place and moment; the main operator of this essential relationship is the "instance of enunciation," the enunciative point of connection between the discourse (the text) and the extradiscursive situation it depends on. That "instance of enunciation" is represented in the discourse by the figure of the "narrator-speaker."[7]

This is to demand a great deal of abnegation from the modern reader, in asking him or her to refrain from referring these attempts to measure the time traversing these utterances of times past to the construction of historical or better, historiographical time. But in the narratives of the foundation of Cyrene, the influence of the time of enunciation on the time narrated, in relation to the configurations stemming from symbolic speculation, is the very thing that makes the marked distinction we have been able to trace between myth and history in fact so very fluid. To construct historical time in the modern meaning of the expression is not the main concern of Greek poets and historians.

1.2. Forms of Historiography

The polymorphic relationship of the Greeks with their *palaiá*, their more — or less — distant historical past, is expressed in Pindar's age in narrative forms in which the form and content of communication are extremely varied. In effect, what we call the legendary history of Greece is passed on through a multitude of narratives that take on diverse poetic forms and that cannot be reduced to completely homogenous categories according to their content: histories of a ruling family in the form of genealogies, narratives of the foundations of cities (*ktíseis*), local histories centered on a particular event, biographies of heroized "historical figures."[8] And still our knowledge of these different "historiographical" genres depends on the fragmentary products that emerge from the attempt, beginning in the fifth century, to impose coherence on this material through rewriting of the "legendary" past. This is how the history of primitive Greece is presented to us in the systematic work of Hecataeus of Miletus in his prose critique of the epic legends; it takes shape in the attempt of Acousilaus of Argos to insert the legends of the Trojan War and Heracles into the perspective of a genealogically unique progression, centered on Argos and stretching back to a theo-cosmogony; it corresponds also to the efforts of Pherecydes of Athens to synchronize various legendary genealogies. All these works, concerned with the rewriting of legendary history, were generally called by the ancients *Genealogíai* or *Historíai*. Closely related in content to the poetic forms from which they partially take their stance, these "archaeologies" in prose trace a line without the solution of continuity, in terms of chronology or authenticity, between the heroic past of *palaiá* and the present.[9]

On the other hand, in moving back from the Classical to the Archaic period and in focusing our attention more precisely on forms of expression, we notice that (legendary) history is not necessarily composed in a specific genre. In general, it merges with literary genres defined by the nature and form of the performance of the corresponding poems. Examples would include a narrative of the wrath of Achilles or of the events leading to the Trojan War in an *Iliad* or *Cypria*, both designated by Herodotus as *épea*, as poems in dactylic meter; a genealogy of Orestes written by the Lacedaemonian poet Cinaethon in the same literary genre, also composed in dactylic hexameters; the struggles of the people of Smyrna against Gyges and the Lydians narrated in elegiac verse in the *Smyrneis* of Mimnermus of Colophon; or a long narration in melic verse on the destruction of the city of Troy in the *Iliou Persis* of Stesichorus. We should also mention the quite numerous legendary narratives presented piecemeal in Archaic melic poetry that illustrate the aim of a poet composing for a specific ritual or social situation. Here are those poets and logographers denounced by Thucydides who, he asserts, seeking to flatter their listeners, confer on *palaiá* and *arkhaîa* a "mythic" dimension.[10]

The fifth century is still largely dependent on these different modes and forms of presentation and creation of history. It is thus impossible to determine whether the Cyrenaean narrative of the foundation of Cyrene the *Agreement of the Founders* presupposes was written in prose or verse, and, if it was in verse, in what meter it was composed. For our purpose, we shall only take notice of this or other narratives in works whose aim is different from that of writing the history of a city, such as the *Epinicians* of Pindar, meant to praise the qualities of a victor in one of the contests in the Panhellenic games, or the *History* of Herodotus, seeking to determine the causes of the great confrontation between the Greeks and barbarians during the Persian Wars. We shall also include the erudite works in epic form — Homeric hymn or narrative — of the Alexandrian poets Callimachus and Apollonius of Rhodes, with their etiological component. Whether in melic verse, *lógos* in prose, or poems in the Homeric style, the foundation narrative of the great Greek colony in Libya exists for us in the most varied literary forms.

A genetic or essentialist hypothesis certainly cannot account for any autonomous narrative of the foundation of Cyrene, which is instead made up of many legends, or fragments of legends, integrated within genres marked by their form and oriented according to certain perspectives and functions. The course taken in the following analysis does not treat the legend of foundation as an abstract narrative entity, but instead follows its development in the principal forms of its realization, beginning with Pindar, then Herodotus, and in contrast with Callimachus or Apollonius of Rhodes. As concerns the scraps of the *Libyca* or the *Cyrenaica*, works generally dated to the Hellenistic era, their fragmentary character forces us to give them a secondary role. The information taken from these narratives with historical pretensions can function to clarify or complete the unavoidable abridgments of the texts we can properly call poetic.[11] If, in order to judge these different narratives, it is still necessary to provide evidence demonstrating the impertinence of our encyclopedic concept of myth, we might consider the following paradox: in Pindar, the more recent the foundational event, the more "mythological" is its appearance, and among the writers of local histories, the more distant the event, the more "rational" it seems!

1.3. Narrative and Figurative Temporality

Perhaps the complexity of the enunciative situations of the foundation narratives of Cyrene justifies the semionarrative approach proposed here. Faced with these quite elaborate texts, it will first be necessary to recover the thread of a constantly interrupted narrative, blurred and twisted by the contingencies and peculiar logic of the genre of praise that transmits the story. This is to say that, in Pindar in particular, the time of enunciation (*temps de l'énonciation*) interferes constantly with the time spoken within the utterance (*temps raconté dans l'énoncé*). Pindar is, in fact, a master of the ruptures, condensations, retrospective reversions, and simple allusive touches that contribute to the construction of his laudatory compositions.[12] But parallel to a reconstruction of the logic of the narrative action and the causality linking the individual acts that compose it, we must contemplate the values that these actions gain by being attached to actors, to spaces, and to an adjusted order of succession, and by being affirmed, denied, and transformed into new values. At the semantic as at the syntactic level, it is a matter of shifting from discursive structures to semionarrative structures, according to the guidelines set out in the first chapter. Reconstruction of the narrative logic by reference to the (semionarrative) *canonical schema* will thus have as a corollary the pursuit of *isotopies* traversing the entire text, ensuring its coherence beyond the more superficial processes of actorialization, spatialization, and temporalization. We can then attempt to determine the *themes* underlying these figural reiterations in the actors, spaces, and time narrated. We should be reminded that the thematic level is the most profound and most abstract semionarrative level, where, in accordance with general themes, the choice of figures from the natural world permitting the discursive and figurative production of the narrative is made. It is at this point of connection between language and the world of reference that the discourse can be considered the product of a process of symbolic construction and interpretation.[13]

Culturally determined, these different expressions of the process of production of meaning have no value in themselves. They can be understood only from the perspective of the production of discourse and thus of the situation of enunciation particular to each text analyzed; there can be no semantic analysis without reference to the conditions of production and reception of meaning, through enunciative marks and instructions for "reading" that the discourse itself bears. Acting independently of the critical community that prescribes for us the tools of interpretation used here, the values that the text sets in play and that the semionarrative analysis attempts to trace are only of pertinence to the world of beliefs of the public for which the narrative was originally intended. We must set aside the supposed independence of the text, and eschew the denial of its depth or its polysemy. Whether epinician, *lógos* of historical inquiry, or erudite epic poem, in each case we have a symbolic representation elaborated in the perspective of a singular situation and a particular community. Historical or legendary, the past constructed by narration is always a function of the present.

2. *Pythian* 4: The Birth of a Land

We shall begin with Pindar, the earliest witness to the existence of narratives of the foundation of Cyrene. We start with the most developed of his texts, *Pythian* 4.

2.1. *Semionarrative Structures and Narrative Time*

The opening of the Pindaric narration is centered on the occasion of its recitation, the celebration of Arcesilas IV, king of Cyrene. Its beginning thus coincides with the time of enunciation (T1, marked by the word *sámeron*, "today," 1). It is also clear at the outset who has been the instigator of the royal action and who thus appears, in an explicitly mentioned phase of narrative *manipulation*, as the Sender (*Destinateur*, as explained in §4.2 of chapter I) of the king (himself the semionarrative *Subject* of the action): Apollo, who, in this final moment of commemoration (and thus of *sanction*) of the agonal exploit, appropriates the role of the Muse as inspiration for the ode. But very quickly as well, beginning with this present moment of celebration and *sanction* of the victorious deed incited by Apollo, Pindar's time machine, so potent a force in his poetry, begins its work.[14] The hymn celebrating the exploits

of Arcesilas evokes the oracular pronouncement addressed in an indeterminate past (*pote*, "once upon a time," 4; T2) to the man destined to
become the founder of Cyrene. Through the intermediary of the Pythia,
Apollo again intervenes; he addresses his prediction to Battus, called at
this moment "the founder of fertile Libya" (*oikistêra karpophórou Li-
búas*, 6). Whether in an ode inspired by the Muse and communicated by
the poet, or through an oracle transmitted by the Pythia in the presence
of Apollo, whether in the present of the song (T1) or in the past (T2),
both are a matter of speech with a divine origin. Spoken by an inspired
mediator, they draw together the human actor and the divinity guiding
his action. Both Arcesilas and Battus, through the voice of a narrator or
through that of a prophetess, benefit from the protection of the god of
Delphi. This enunciative play on different time levels refers us to the
situation of the performance of Pindar's poem.

The victory won by the chariot of Arcesilas thus situates us at the end
of a narrative program, at its moment of *sanction*. This *sanction*, however, has an inverted meaning, since, as incarnated in the poem, it is
conceived as an honor paid to a god as *Sender* of the victorious action.
In contrast, Battus finds himself at the beginning of a trial placed upon
him by the same god; this is the initial phase of *manipulation* of the
narrative program defined by the *canonical schema*. The narrative constructed by Pindar thus seems to make the history of Battus, the founder
of Cyrene, the narrative starting point for that of the actual king of the
city: it constitutes, in itself, the phase of *manipulation* of the basic narrative. In the poem, we thus witness on the one hand the *sanction* of the
victory of Arcesilas (T1), and on the other the *manipulation* of the
foundational act of Battus. At this point of the narration, the act of
foundation seems to represent the *manipulation* of the victory. The narrative, however, is still not fully articulated.

From here, we reach back to a time seventeen generations previous to
the foundational act of Battus (here designated as T4). It is again through
the intermediary of divinely inspired speech that the narration is finally
able truly to develop. No longer in the ode of the poet inspired by the
Muse, no longer through the oracle spoken by the Pythia under the
influence of Apollo, it comes now in a prediction from the immortal
mouth of Medea, overcome by a prophetic delirium (*zamenés*, 10)
seemingly without origin. In this prophecy addressed to the Argonauts
during their stop on the island of Thera, the narrative expands, but still
without yielding to a linear development. Medea's first utterance to the
demigod Argonauts refers to the course of Battus; it is therefore situated, in relation to the time of T4, in the direction of T2, by means of a
prolepsis. But the prediction of Medea places this colonizing course on
a completely distinct figurative level, because it involves actors who are

only partially anthropomorphic. From the insular land that represents Thera, Libya, personification of the land of Libya, will take over a root; from this root Libya is destined to engender future cities through "foundations" (*theméthlia*) consecrated to Zeus Ammon (13–47). Here we learn, through an implicit reference to the agonal occasion of the poem (T1), that the Theran seafaring colonists are destined to become tamers of horses and drivers of chariots.

Medea then finally enunciates the phase of *performance* of this story of colonial foundation, along with the narrative transformation it implies. The prophetess promises to the future founders of Cyrene, along with their metamorphosis, very nearly the same future that Teiresias foresees for Odysseus during his audience with the hero in the Underworld in book 12 of the *Odyssey*. Teiresias prophesies to Odysseus that he will return to his city and restore it to order; he will then have to walk until the moment when the oar he carries is confused for a winnowing fan. A sacrifice to Poseidon will then mark the departure of Odysseus from the domain of the sea and the beginning of a period of earthly abundance for his people. For the descendants of Battus, this passage from roving the sea to fixation on a productive land is expressed by the transition from mastery of the sea to that of horses. Even on land, the colonists will thus remain associated with one of the privileged domains of Poseidon.[15]

This assimilation between the two narrative transformations — the metamorphosis of the land of Thera into Libya and the change of status of the future colonists — must also be achieved on the level of narrated, or spoken, time. Thus the beginning of the chronological reckoning engaged by the mention of the seventeen generations separating, from the point of view of the narrator, the prediction of Medea from the foundational act of Battus is carefully effaced by a double *pote*, "once," at verse 10, and again at verse 14. Both the speech of the inspired daughter of Aietes and the event of foundation that she announces are situated in an indeterminate time. T2 and T4 are superimposed!

*

Entirely indeterminate as it is, this past begins nonetheless to take on the form of a succession of events. Thera the metropolis of a colony? This is the occasion for Medea to recall an essential precedent, not of the action of colonists, but, stretching back in time, one effected by the earth itself. Newly situated in an indeterminate time (*pote*, 20), the narrative action, in referring to this nonanthropomorphic foundation, finally finds its beginning, its phase of *manipulation*; it represents a posteriori an anticipation of the *manipulation* of which the object will be the founder Battus. After the earlier prolepsis and anticipation in the time told, this analeptic movement back in the *erzählte Zeit* situates the start of the narrative action recalled by Medea in a time. more removed still (T5), but one integrated, as an episode in the expedition of the Argonauts, into the same generation.

The Pindaric narrative, however, only follows the canonical schema of the narration in its most formal aspect. First, in place of the situation of semionarrative lack that generally starts a narrative plot by inserting it within a causal sequence, the narrative of Medea presents a paradoxical initial situation. Attempting to return to the Mediterranean from Ocean, the Argonauts are forced to drag their ship for twelve days "on the back of a deserted land" (26). They arrive at the mouth of Lake Triton, a body of water enclosed on all sides by land. There, the "chariot" of Jason, defined by synecdoche on the metaphorical meaning of "beam" (*dóru*, 27), regains its marine sense, as does its "bridle," which recovers its function as an anchor.[16] In this way, the categories of navigation and equitation find themselves mixed, while they neatly mark off the final phase of the narrative, involving the transformation of the seafaring colonists into breeders of horses. At this singular moment, Triton-Poseidon appears to the Argonauts, alone.[17]

In the absence of a true situation of lack, the meaning of the phase of *manipulation* of this first narrative is initially hidden in order to give the narrative action its beginning through a break in its logical balance. In the guise of a mortal, Poseidon gives to Euphemus, the first of the Argonauts to disembark on the shore of Lake Triton, a piece of earth: it is his "gift of hospitality" (*xeínia*, 22; *xénion*, 35; see also 30). Note that the words of hospitality that accompany this gift are explicitly assimilated by Pindar to a banquet one might offer to a stranger (29–31). Arcesilas IV receives the song of Pindar precisely in the framework of a banquet, as well (2). The original *xénion* that Euphemus receives from the hands of Poseidon is thus a prefiguration of the hymn that the king of Cyrene, his descendant, receives from the poet! This implicitly creates a link between the more remote time of the "myth" (T5) and the present (T1) circumstances of enunciation and performance of the poem, through the praise of the actual king of Cyrene. The narrated time (*erzählte Zeit*) is now linked with the time of the narrative (*Erzählzeit*) and with the extradiscursive time of the narration. Does the gift represent a simple act of welcome? Not really, since the gesture is accompanied by a clap of thunder, sent by Zeus himself. Described as *aísios* (23) and thus connected with the force of destiny, the sign from Zeus that accompanies the gift of Libyan earth marks a point of departure for a new narrative direction in the course of the expedition of the Argonauts. The subject of the action will no longer be the Argonauts as a group, but Euphemus, king of the holy city of Taenarum, *ánax* (45) and *héros* (36), the son of Europa and Poseidon, a master of horses (*hípparkhos*, 45), an infant born in the center of continental Greece near the Cephisus, but a sovereign-hero ruling over a portion of the (*liminal*) extremity of the Peloponnese. Poseidon, in taking the form of the mortal Eurypylus, thus speaks to one who is his equal. This Eurypylus, the scholiast informs us, is himself the incarnation of Triton, but more importantly, he is another son of Poseidon, the god who embraces the earth and who has the power to shake it (*gaiáokhos, ennosídas*, 33).[18] The object marking the act of hospitality and placing the two sons of Poseidon in relation to each other is a simple handful of the earth of Libya, destined, as we shall see, for some strange transformations.

Since it is not preceded by a state of lack, and since it is not by consequence the object of a demand, the gift of the miraculous clod is presented as a spontaneous present, without causal determination. While the double divine intervention establishes this gesture of hospitality as a phase of *manipulation* of the narrative action in which Euphemus is destined to be the protagonist, this first stage of the narrative leads to a *competence*, then a *performance*, destined to elude the realization they might have been able to achieve. Foreseen through the intermediary of the visionary prophecy of Medea in the form of a prolepsis, the development of the narrative program engaged in this phase of *manipulation* might have been entrusted to the king Euphemus; he would have thrown the clod, upon his return to Taenarum, into the mouth of Hades, which was said to open near the cape also bearing the name of Taenarum. In the fourth generation (that is, in T3), the descendants of Euphemus of Taenarum, with the Danaans who emigrated from Sparta, Argos, and Mycenae, would have had the Libyan continent in their full possession (*ke . . . lábe*, an unreal condition in the past, 47–48).[19] But things do not come to pass in this manner, and the wait of seventeen generations ensues. The narrative of the foundation of Cyrene constructed by Pindar in *Pythian* 4 thus takes place on no less than five distinct temporal planes:

> T1: time of the performance of the ode (Arcesilas IV)
> T2: time of the act of foundation (Battus)
> T3: time of the unrealized program (Danaans)
> T4: time of the prophecy (Medea)
> T5: time of the manipulation (Euphemus)

This complex process of temporalization is evidently determined by the necessity of placing the narrated time and the time of the narrative in relation to that of the enunciation of the poem of praise. The ode praises the virtues of one of the most brilliant kings in the Battiad dynasty. Succeeding his father Battus IV, who was responsible for Cyrene's prosperity, Arcesilas IV developed his court in the fashion of a Sicilian tyrant, after the probable repression of an oligarchic attempt.

2.2. *Ariadne's Thread in a Labyrinthine Narration*

From the point of view of semionarrative syntax, a comparison here seems appropriate with the analogous narrative found in the fourth book of the *Argonautica* of Apollonius of Rhodes, written three centuries later. The narration there has both temporal development and linear causality: the meeting of the Argonauts with Triton-Poseidon represents nothing more than a stage in the sequence of trials imposed on the voyaging heroes, corresponding to one of the numerous divine interventions aiding their return to Iolcus. In the course of the narration of the entire expedition, this meeting with the divinity will come to assume the role of a phase of *manipulation* of the particular story of the foundation of Thera, recounted in the final stages of the Argonauts' voyage. During their brief stay on Anaphe, the island of Apollo, the heroes are actually very near Santorini. But in Apollonius, this narrative within a narrative retains an entirely subordinate position in relation to the development of the principal story.

To fulfill his commitment to praise the Cyrenaean victor, Pindar has completely reversed this subordinate relationship. In *Pythian* 4, the narrative of the expedition of the Argonauts (70–246) is included within that of the foundation of Cyrene, with all its temporal disjunctions (4–63 and 249–62), in terms of both narrative logic and the plan of the structure of the ode. Even if, echoing this poem, Apollonius of Rhodes indirectly transfers the Pindaric praise of Arcesilas IV to Ptolemy III, the *Argonautica* eschews all explicit reference to Cyrene; subordinated to a narrative of the expedition of the Argonauts, the narrative of foundation becomes that of Thera alone, an internal echo of the episode of Anaphe.[20] The performative context of the narrative of Cyrene's foundation becomes an essentially literary one.

This is a phase of *manipulation* of a secondary narrative program, we might say; it is engaged in the text of Apollonius by a situation of lack. Without *mêtis* (1539), the Argonauts are in effect incapable of finding the "passes" (*póroi*, 1538) by which they might leave Lake Triton. From that place comes the offering of Apollo's tripod to the "native" gods (*eggénetai*, 1549); from that place the countergift by Triton of a clod of earth. As ruler over this "littoral," Triton is quickly revealed to be not only the avatar of Eurypylus, born in Libya (*eggegaós*, 1561), but, most importantly, the incarnation of Poseidon. Raised by a sacrifice meant for aquatic divinities (1601–19), the god appears in a form both equine and marine in order to lead the Argonauts' ship toward the high seas. In search of knowledge, the Greek heroes thus acquire at the same time the power that allows them to complete an additional step on their route to return from the "fringes" of the land of Libya (*peírata*, 1567). Certainly, the values characterizing this "fringe" region, nurturer of savage beasts (1561), where terrestrial and aquatic routes intermingle (1566–70), have already been presented in *Pythian* 4.[21] But the prophetic words of Triton, who clearly announces the future stages of the Argonauts' performance — Crete, the Peloponnese — never once include the landing of the clod of earth at Thera. Moreover, Apollo and Poseidon, whose interventions the Pindaric version of the foundation of Cyrene takes great care to distinguish from one another, are present here together! The syntactic linearity of the narrative of Apollonius has in this case the corollary of a sort of semantic leveling. It seeks above all to reintegrate the line of the principal narrative. In the context of a distinct enunciation, the semionarrative syntax is transformed!

Even while referring, in a later phase of his narration, to the consequences of the Libyan episode on the tribulations of the Argonauts, Apollonius does not mention the unrealized narrative program evoked by Pindar's Medea. We return, then, to the text of *Pythian* 4. To the program uttered as an unreal condition, Medea strongly opposes what will be substituted for it in reality, in spite of the latter's at first negative appearance (from the temporal point of view, T2 takes the place of T3). Euphemus in fact loses control of the clod when its guardians allow it to fall into the sea instead of bringing it to the mouth of Hades. This disjunction between the *Subject* and its *Predicate* (see §4.2 of chapter I), however, does not in any way prevent the divine gift from undergoing a transformation of state. In coming to land on the island of Thera, where Medea and the Argonauts are presently to be found (*en tâide násoi*, 42), it is destined to become the "indestructible seed" of Libya. But the intervention of an anthropomorphic actor is indispensable for the realization (*performance*) and the *sanction* of this transformation to occur.

In that way, the negative narrative program, activated by the landing of the clod of earth and substituted for the unrealized program, does not delay in gaining an inflection with a positive meaning. This narrative reorientation is clearly marked on the temporal level. True, the miraculous clod arrives at Thera "before its time" (*prìn hóras*, 43: T4 in place of T3); but now (*nûn*, 50), at the moment of enunciation of Medea's prediction, an anthropomorphic actor will take in his hands the destiny of the divine gift and reorient it. Through interposed analepsis and prolepsis, the prophetic words of Medea (in T4) give us the (to this point still lacking) narrative link, inscribing T2 as the sequel to

T5. We see that on the occasion of their stay on Lemnos, which Pindar situates, contrary to later tradition, at the end of the Argonauts' expedition, Euphemus and his companions will unite with the women of the island.[22] And by a projection of seventeen generations from the moment of the enunciation of the words of Medea, we understand that the *génos* born from this union will come to emigrate to Thera, "to this island" (line 52 reprises line 43); it will give birth there to the future master (*despótas*, 53) of Libya. The *performance* issuing from the *manipulation* of Battus by Apollo (5) and what results from the *manipulation* by Poseidon (37) finally converge and overlap. At the same time, through the intermediary of the voice of Medea (T4), the time of Battus (T2) comes to coincide with that of Euphemus (T5).

This rectification of the course of the narrative program has as a corollary not only the indicated temporal distancing, but more importantly a discrepancy in the line of descent of the founding hero of Cyrene. Battus is not the direct and legitimate descendant of Euphemus, since his ancestor was born of an extramarital union between the king of Taenarum and a foreign woman. A substitution in the *Sender* of the heroic action is added to this displacement in lineage, by means of the narrative reorientation already mentioned: no longer Poseidon but Apollo will guide Battus, according to the oracular speech, toward the "regions of the Nile" where Zeus, son of Cronos, reigns (55–56).

Spoken at Thera, the prediction of Medea is situated spatially as well as chronologically at the center of the narrative it unfolds, and it also coincides with the spatial and temporal pivot point (T4) of the narrative's reorientation. The phase of Poseidon's *manipulation* of the hero Euphemus and Euphemus' failed *performance* are actually situated beyond the place and time of the prediction (T5). The clod of Libyan earth is lost, only to reappear at Thera, the very place of Medea's prophetic enunciation. From this point, through a projection into the future, the illegitimate race born from the coupling of Euphemus and the Lemnian woman is guided from Lemnos to Thera in order to take charge of the abandoned root. From here comes the second phase of *manipulation*: Apollo tells Battus, the descendant of Euphemus, the oracle that will allow his seed to regain Libya and bear fruit there (T2). At the final positive realization of this *performance*, only the phase of *sanction* is lacking for this modified narrative program to find its conclusion.

The prophetess Medea is no longer in a position to offer the *sanction* of the narrative action, but she is nonetheless the object of the narration enunciated through the poem itself. Pindar, taking up again the projective narrative of the sorceress, twice prolongs the ode and gives it its conclusion in the time of enunciation, T1.

First, in a direct address to Battus, the son of Polymnestus, the narrator-speaker connects the time of the narrative of colonization (T2) with that of the enunciation (T1). He insists on the phase of *manipulation* of the Theran hero's colonial enterprise by showing that Apollo's oracular command is repeated three times. Offered as a response to a question on an entirely different subject (the stammering affecting the future founder), the oracle is said to be "spontaneous" (*autómatos*, 60); it makes Battus a predestined king (*peproménon*, 61). As for the *sanction* of the colonial action of Battus, it is still not explicit in these verses. The narrator-speaker, however, makes it indirectly coincide with the prosperity of the king Arcesilas, which is augmented by the god of Delphi. The king lives "now" (*nûn*, 64),[23] in the present of the recitation of the poem (T1). He is the descendant of Battus in the eighth generation.

Interrupted by the longest narrative attested in a Pindaric poem, devoted to the adventures of the Argonauts, the address to Arcesilas is taken up again toward the end of the poem, at line 250. This return to the time of enunciation (T1) after the intervening epic narrative comes at the precise moment when the development of the Argonauts' story merges with the events leading up to the foundation of Cyrene: the detour through Ocean (and thus through Libya, coincident with T5) and the stay among the Lemnians, whom we finally learn have killed their husbands (252). The union of the Greek heroes with these homicidal women takes place upon the outcome of a foot race that reflects not only a prematrimonial trial, but also the Pythian race in which Arcesilas IV is victorious! In addition, the legendary race takes place in spite of the temporary character of the Argonauts' stay on Lemnos.[24] The union is in the end a fortunate one because it will produce the privileged "race" of Euphemus, destined to rediscover the land of Libya where the king of Taenarum had received the miraculous clod. The colonial itinerary is thus traced: from Lemnos to Lacedaemon, whence they adopt Spartan culture, from there to Calliste-Thera, which they will colonize (*apoikeîn*), and finally, by the will of Apollo, to Libya, where they will administer (*dianémein*) with prudent intelligence (*mêtin*, 262) "the divine city of Cyrene" (*ástu theîon Kuránas*, 261).[25]

In moving from Santorini to Libya and Cyrene, the act of colonization becomes an act of government. This is to say that in the phase of *sanction* of the narration, the king Arcesilas implicitly takes the place of the founder Battus, and thus the time of the foundation narrative (T2) coincides with that of enunciation (T1). Apollo has taken the place of Poseidon, and the narrative ends by recovering its own logic. While in the most distant time (T5) Euphemus, under the control of Poseidon, intervenes in the composition of the actual land of Libya, in the most recent, Battus establishes a Greek city protected by Apollo on land manipulated by the Greeks.

2.3. Enunciative and Semantic Echoes

The complexity of semantic development in *Pythian* 4 is matched by that of its syntactic articulation. The interlacing of recurrent figures, articulated in isotopies and ensuring the ode's coherence, is so dense that a commentary on the entire poem would require a monograph all its own. But the different semantic strata built into the narrative tissue of *Pythian* 4 intimately depend on the enunciative voices that carry them. Thus a recent book entirely devoted to this captivating poem focuses particularly on the skillful polyphony of the utterance of the poem, which interlaces the voice of the narrator-speaker addressing *hic et nunc* its receiver Arcesilas, the prophetic words of Medea spoken in direct discourse, and the oracles of Apollo relayed through the voice of the Pythia and cited indirectly. We could add also the individual voices of the Argonauts, the protagonists of the narrative to whom Pindar voluntarily cedes the floor, such as Mopsus, the seer of Zeus. These are all prophetic voices in a context in which the clod of Libyan earth itself becomes an oracular portent (*órnis*, 19).[26] The poem's narrative is indeed a polyphonic one!

So far, we have not emphasized the hierarchical relationships that organize the first three voices mentioned within the legend of Cyrene. These take shape at first through the intermediary of the temporal organization of the narration: the prophecy of Medea is situated in the *pote*, the chronologically most distant "once" (10; T4), inspired (*apépneuse*, 11) perhaps by Aphrodite (cf. 216–19); seventeen generations later (T2), we find the oracles of the Pythia inspired by the Delphic god; finally, in the "today" (*sámeron*, 1) of the performance of the poem, eight generations later (T1), it is the narrator who speaks, brought to the side of Arcesilas by the Muse.[27] We could add to the number of these oracular voices that of the clod itself as *órnis* at the most removed time (T5). The spatial organization of the places of enunciation of these different voices is most significant here. We have already noticed the central position the narrative ensures for Thera, the location of Medea's prediction. We can add Delphi, the explicit place of origin of Apollo's oracles. And the voice of the poet from Thebes, through the intermediary of the Muse, definitively places Delphi and then Thera in relation to Cyrene.

The spatial order of the varying voices' places of enunciation in the poem concludes by inverting the temporal organization of these same voices. The earliest is also the least centered, while the most recent is able to sketch, after Thebes, an initial course between Thera, Delphi, and the land of Libya. To the temporal mark "today," which opens the poem, corresponds the spatial mark that concludes it, creating a ring structure: *Thébai*; Thebes, the source of "ambrosial songs" (299), that is to say the point of origin of divinely inspired songs. But this return to the present and to Thebes not only brings us back to the place of enunciation and the voice of the narrator. It is expressed in a direct address to Arcesilas (298) and reveals itself to be inspired by the divinity. The metaphorical spring representing this place is in fact only a transposition onto Greek soil of the spring of Apollo (294) that forms the geographical center of Cyrene.[28] Beside one, as beside the other, Damophilus has benefited from hospitality (294 and 299). As championed by the narrator, his wish to live again in Cyrene draws together and finally identifies the two places of enunciation of the poem: inspired at Thebes beside the "ambrosial spring," the ode is performed at Cyrene beside the fountain of Apollo.

From the modes of enunciation of the narrative and the homologies organizing its space, from time and the common reference to divine inspiration, we should now move to the substance of the utterances intersected by these voices. Before bringing out the spatial image the narrative constructs though the complexity of it structure, we can attempt to define the isotopies that organize its content. We know that in Classical Greece, as in other societies, the reproductive moment of matrimonial union is readily compared to cultivation. The metaphorical relation is quite frequently between the fertilization of a field worked by the plow and then sown, and the essential goal of the Greek institution of marriage, the production of beautiful children, themselves envisaged, in a vegetal image, as offspring or young shoots. Agricultural activity, in particular cereal cultivation, in opposition to pastoral activity, for example, also serves as a metaphorical expression of the achievement of civilization; agriculture and the production of cereals are thus situated at the foundation of Greek representation of social life in the city, whereas political activity is the realm of offspring born of legal marriages between citizens.[29]

It is precisely upon these three levels — agricultural production, foundation of a family, and development of civic life — that Pindar, in playing on their reciprocal metaphorical connections, articulates the semantic values of the narrative of the foundation of Cyrene. These values are organized according to a vegetal isotopy and a human isotopy, which is itself doubled. But a third isotopy, on a mineral level, is added to the two others at the beginning of the narrative. The clod that Euphemus receives from the hands of Eurypylus-Poseidon as a gift of hospitality is, at its origin, only a handful of earth (*gaîa*, 21). But at the moment it is presented to Euphemus, it becomes a piece of "plowed earth" (*ároura*, 34), only to be transformed into a "divine clod" (*bôlax daimonía*, 37) when the hero places his foot on the soil of Libya to receive it.

Moreover, the Argonauts' meeting with the human incarnation of

Poseidon occurs after their long journey through a region of land (*gaîa*, 21) that is completely deserted. Having reached Thera, the clod becomes the "indestructible seed" (*spérma áphthiton*, 43) of Libya. The prediction of Medea then gives two complementary images of the return of the clod to its original land: it is conceived as an act of transplantation (*phuteúesthai*, 15) by Libya, the granddaughter of Zeus, and as the transplantation of a root (*rhíza*, 15), pulled from the "land battered by floods" (*halíplaktos*, 14), representing Thera. This root is destined to be the stock of numerous cities on soil already prepared, in earth consecrated to Zeus Ammon: the term *thémethla* used in line 16 implies by its etymology the act of foundation expressed in the verb *títhenai*. The gardener responsible for this transplant, however, will no longer be Libya, but Battus, the future master of these plains covered by rain clouds (*kelainéphea pédia*, 52), fertile territory (*pîon*, 56) under the control of the son of Cronos. As with the play on time, the metaphor spun from the fecundation of the earth contributes to the conjunction of the two narrative acts, the two narrative *performances* distinguished by their respective phases of *manipulation* at the beginning of the poem: the failed act of the hero Euphemus and the founding act of Battus. At the start of the ode, Libya was already seen as a "productive" (*karpophóros*, 6) land. In this context the hill that probably formed the acropolis of Cyrene can be defined as a breast (*mastós*, 8). We should note that this *mastós* corresponds to the *omphalós* of Delphi, the center of a "wooded mother" (74), that is, a fertile land. Nearby this navel of the earth the prediction is offered that will be at the vegetal (*phúteuthen*, 69) origin of the honors due to the Minyan Argonauts, but also, through the intermediary of Euphemus, to the ancestors of the founders of Cyrene.[30] Having served as a way station for the fecund clod, the metropolis Thera can henceforth figure in the proper sense of *matrópolis* (20), of a "mother city." Engaged by a city figured as a mother, the fertilization of the soil is thus productive of other nurturing cities.

But, because of its wholly feminine aspect, this manipulation of the earth is unable to accomplish fully the act of founding a city. The *génos* of Battus supplied by the play of narrative displacement discussed above fills the role of the lacking masculine element. This *génos*, conceived in the bed of foreign women (*allodapaí*, 50), is the object, at the end of the poem, of significant reinterpretation: it is a "predestined seed" (*spérma moirídion*; *spérma* is the result of a correction by Hermann); it has been planted in "foreign fields" (*árourai allodapaí*, 254). The "race" of Euphemus assumes in turn plantlike growth (*phuteuthén*, 256).[31] Its activity will affect as much the administration of the city of Cyrene (261) as the mastery and the fecundation of the well-watered plains of Libya, made "to fatten" (*ophéllein*, 260) by the benefaction of the gods. Thus the offspring of Euphemus will eventually control both the political activity of the city and the agricultural production of its territory. Significantly, the large number of cities whose foundations are announced by Medea at the start of the poem (14–15, 19–20), just as the extensive colonized territory implying, in the "foundations" of Zeus Ammon, all of Libya (16, 42–43, 56: extension to the Nile), are reduced at the end of the poem to a single city and its *khóra*: Cyrene (161) and the "plain of Libya" (259, in contrast with the "plains" in line 52). This double process of synecdoche makes any attempt at exact territorial identification illusory. This is illustrated clearly by the configuration of the monument to Battus the Cyrenaeans erected at Delphi: the founding hero was represented crowned by Libya and standing on a chariot whose reins were held by Cyrene! The success of this transplant of Thera to the soil of Libya will display its full effect at the very moment of enunciation of the poem of Pindar. Here is realized the blossoming (*thállei*, 65) of a spring flower, Arcesilas IV, the eighth descendant (*méros*, 65) of the founder Battus.[32] Mineral having become vegetal, the key isotopy of the Pindaric narrative is constantly combined with the human isotopy, itself doubled in its matrimonial and political dimensions.

2.4. The Meanderings of a Cosmogonic Journey

The overlapping and interweaving of these three metaphorical levels, none of which is hierarchically superior to another, is not, however, sufficient to express the foundation of a colonial city in its specificity. We still lack a properly cosmogonic dimension, and for this we must return to the mineral isotopy. The spatial journeys followed respectively by the clod — the feminine element — and by the race of Euphemus — the masculine element — are particularly significant in this regard.

The now-famous clod issues from the shore of Lake Triton in Libya. In turn described as a lake, a sea, or even a river, this strange expanse of water is surrounded by dry land even while remaining in communication with the sea; the Argonauts, as has been noted, reach it over land. Existing between sea and land, the lake is further distinguished by its shallows. From the time of Herodotus the lake was known for the cult those who inhabited its shores were reputed to practice in honor of Triton, Poseidon, and, most importantly, Athena. In fact, one of the numerous versions of the birth of Athena situates the event on the shores of Lake Triton. Tritogeneia is in this case "born from the earth" (*gegenés*).[33] That presence of the sea on the mainland recalls not only the mentioned passage of the descendants of Battus, the founder of Cy-

rene, from an island to a fixation on a continental country, as is foreseen in Medea's prophecy about the root of Libya, or the parallel story
of the symbolic earthly voyage of Odysseus when his oar was to be
confused with a fan, as is foreseen in Teireisias' prophetical words on
Odyssey book 12, but also the presence of the sea on the Acropolis
itself through the mark of Poseidon's trident as it is honored in the
Erechtheion next to Athena's olive tree!

But this terrain, auspicious for chthonian births, does not suffice to
assure the fertility of the clod, Poseidon's gift of hospitality. Its first
destination, as we have seen, is one of the extremities of the Greek
continent, the cape of Taenarum in the Peloponnese, with its mouth of
Hades (44) and the sanctuary of Poseidon associated to it.[34] Through
this very opening, situated at the "extremes" of Greece, Heracles had
brought Cerberus up to the light of day. As early as Bacchylides, the
Hades visited by the heroic son of Zeus is described as the home of
Persephone, and Euripides reformulates a version of the legend in which
Heracles was initiated into the cult of the Eleusinian Mysteries to allow
his descent into the Underworld. In addition, in the sacred wood dedicated to the chthonian Demeter, next to Hermione, the hero buried the
captured canine monster.[35]

To throw the clod of Libyan earth into the mouth of Hades on Cape
Taenarum is thus to cause it to reach the kingdom of Persephone by an
act of consecration characteristic of communication with the world of
the dead. Indeed, to throw into Hades a bit of Libya is perhaps to
anticipate the act of legitimate Athenian wives who threw piglets into
pits during the Thesmophoria. The piglets' bodies are not meant to remain inactive in the bowels of the earth. Recuperated in the period of
cultivation and sowing, and mixed with seeds, these putrid remains represent the promise of an abundant harvest. We know the exemplary act
thought to legitimate this strange ritual is nothing other than the story
of Core's travels between Hades and the surface of the cultivated earth
or Olympus. But the clod of Libyan earth will undergo no final rebirth
through the process of agricultural growth, such as defines the tale of
Core and Demeter. Through the negligence of the king of Taenarum,
there will be no fall to Hades, and thus no Calligeneia, no "Beautiful
Birth." In the frame of the Athenian Thesmophoria, in fact, this rite is
specifically associated with the growth of agricultural produce and the
generation (*spóra*) of men; as Epictetus teaches, the seed (*spérma*) must
be buried for a time in the earth before bearing fruit.[36]

Because of the neglect of Euphemus and his guards, however, the clod
of Libyan earth vanishes into the sea instead of being swallowed in the
depths of the earth. An island, then, receives it, a portion of land anchored in the marine expanse. The intervention of Thera is marked as

much by its intermediary geographical position between Libya and the Peloponnese as by its hybrid status as an island, shared with it by many Greek insular lands.

Delos, for example, "battered by waves" like Thera, is itinerant up to the moment when the hospitality it accords Leto and Apollo finally fixes its location. Asteria becomes Delos in the same way that Calliste becomes Thera at the moment of its colonization by the descendants of Euphemus (258). At Delos, the civilizing intervention of Apollo is all the more indispensable because in the Greek representation the islands are at first the product of a cosmogonic act by Poseidon. In order to form them, the god threw savage mountains into the sea, where they took geological root. Thus, before the birth of Apollo, Delos offered terrain more fit for seabirds than for horses; the Delos the *Homeric Hymn to Apollo* describes is devoid of herds and vegetation, a rocky land threatening to disappear beneath the waves.[37] Rhodes plunges its roots directly into the depths, and emerged through the action of Poseidon *Genéthlios*, the "Generator," in order to satisfy Helius, forgotten by Zeus in his distribution of *tímai*. In contrast to Delos, Rhodes is a land that nourishes men and is favorable for flocks. In addition, as Pindar adds in *Olympian* 7, it had the benefit of the shower of gold that Zeus caused to fall on the occasion of the birth of Athena, who, for her part, hastened to accord to the Rhodians excellence in every artistic technique. Like Delos, however, Rhodes will only know the achievement of urban civilization through the injunction and under the protection of Apollo, upon its colonization by Tlepolemus.[38]

*

Surely for some time the word "autochthony" has been in the reader's mind. Yet this is a strange autochthony, since certain of these islands as mineral entities undergo themselves, in a metaphorical way, an "autochthonous" birth, from which the founding heroes from continental *khôrai* usually benefit. What is more, their birth is from the ocean's depths and not from the depths of the earth. As far as the heroes are concerned, at Sparta for example, the first king of the land, the founder of the aboriginal dynasty, was said to have been born from the earth and consequently to rule over the soil of his own mother: not only *gegenés*, but *autókhthon*.[39] The double legend of Athenian autochthony is also well known. The first king of Attica, Cecrops, is not only born from the earth, as numerous primordial beings are, but emerges from the soil of the city over which he then extends his sovereignty. Like Triton, he is a *diphués* being, part man, part serpent. Following the example of other hero-colonists, his intervention over the land he rules is signified by a change of name, as Acte becomes Cecropia, before taking the name Attica. But more importantly, the autochthonous birth of Cecrops coincides with the moment when the gods reapportion the Greek cities among themselves, as *tímai* granted by the sovereign Zeus; each god or goddess will receive in his or her turn a portion. Thence stems the celebrated quarrel between Athena and Poseidon for possession of Attica. Thanks to the olive tree, Athena is able to extend her power over the country, while Poseidon, asserting the same control, accomplishes the inverse of the act of founding islands. At the striking of the god's trident, the sea surges up in the center of Athens, over the very rock of the Acropolis.[40] Like primordial Libya, the Attica of early times knows the admixture of earth and water.

The second legendary narrative of Athenian autochthony reverses the terms of the metaphor of vegetal implant. No longer does the idea of a germ and root transposed in the geological domain represent the creation of a territory and anticipate, by this image, the birth of a *génos*. Instead, the seed of a god is literally implanted into the already existent earth in order to engender there the first king of a long dynasty, Erichthonius-Erechtheus. It is an inversion, but also an impoverishment: at Athens, the process of human generation assumes a vegetal figure, certainly, but it abandons geological and cosmogonic expression. The reason for these modifications in the functioning of the symbolic process are twofold. First, from the perspective of the historical reality underlying the invention of symbolic narrative, Attica, according to the evidence, was never the object of an act of colonial foundation and was never represented as being so. Second, we must consider the medium of the narrative. The rationalized mythographic account that transmits the Athenian legend to us, perhaps by the pen of Apollodorus, does not lend itself to the constant play of metaphorical cross-references peculiar to Pindaric epinician.[41]

Thebes presents a mythical and metaphorical situation analogous to that representing the birth of Attica, but without man as an intermediary. The autochthony to which the Cadmeans lay claim is based on the cultivation and seeding of the soil of the motherland, from which are born the *Spartoí*, the "sown men." Aeschylus, in *Seven against Thebes*, recaptures this metaphor of the generation of a *génos* by illustrating the incestuous act of Oedipus, the parricide who inseminated the sacred furrow of his own mother, inserting there a bloody "root" (*rhíza*). With the dramatic poet, we notice again the three levels — mineral, vegetal, and human — of the metaphoric expression of the birth of a ruling family, albeit here an accursed one.[42]

There are thus numerous narratives for the autochthony of continental cities that place the roots of their royal line and their inhabitants in the soil of the motherland. But there exist also legends of "marine" autochthony, elaborated through the definition of a mineral isotopy, that seek to give terrestrial roots to islands afloat on the expanse of the sea. As soon as they find anchorage, these islands can accommodate emigrants from the continent, capable of founding civilization. While Santorini occupies an intermediate geographical position between the Greek continent and Libya, and while its foundation by Theras most likely confers upon it the "hybrid" and metaphorical autochthony of Delos or Rhodes, Libya itself assumes a position more marginal still, exemplifying a third type of representation of autochthony. Centered on Lake Triton and placed under the control of Poseidon, Libya is, in truth, neither land nor sea. In order to acquire "autochthonous" status, it would be most fitting for its roots to sprout from the outside, in the depths of the continent, near Cape Taenarum. But, in another confusion of distinct categories, the land of Libya runs aground on the island of Thera, and it is only in this intermediary territory that it acquires the generative force of a germ and sprout. At this moment, the human actors decisively intervene.

2.5. From Actors to Struggles with Deviance

There can be no realization of autochthony without anthropomorphic actors. True, even before its arrival on Thera, the clump of Libyan earth was already manipulated by Euphemus, but the absence of care by the son of Poseidon caused the clod to fall short of its initial destination. Should we be surprised when Apollonius of Rhodes, followed by a commentator on Pindar, informs us that Euphemus is particularly capable of intermingling the categories of sea and land, through his ability to walk on the ocean? Conversely, does not the legendary king reach Lake Triton by land, but on a boat? This ability to transgress the limits of the semantic categories of cosmology is inscribed, perhaps, in the very genealogy of the king of Taenarum: his mother, Europa, is the daughter of Tityus, a Giant born from Earth. Note that the Trojan king Erichthonius (!), with his intermediary position between Dardanus (a son of Zeus), the founder of an early city in the Troad, and Tros, the founder of the city of Troy proper, possessed horses capable of running both on the "nourishing glebe" and on the "back of the sea."[43] These particular qualities are clearly capable of making Euphemus the king of a harbor city situated on the shores of a continent, but not the founder of an essentially continental colony.

Under the control of Battus, the illegitimate descendant of Euphemus, the Libyan clod could not have fallen into better hands. We should

examine briefly the ancestry of this founding hero. Not only does the
union that produces him take place on an island, but, more importantly
still, his Lemnian ancestor — the wife of the king of Taenarum during his
stay upon the island of Lemnos — murdered her legitimate husband.[44]
Before establishing themselves on Thera, however, the descendants of
Euphemus and the murderous woman sexually "mix" with the Lacedaemonians (257).[45] The emigration of these islanders will have for its
own frame the colonial enterprise undertaken by the Lacedaemonian
Theras, the eponymous hero of the island. In order to understand how
the descendants of Euphemus and the founding hero Theras converge at
Sparta, we must look to Herodotus. We shall limit ourselves at the moment to filling out the Pindaric allusions by specifying that Theras, of
Cadmean origin and thus a Theban, comes from a continental city, but
lives in Lacedaemon as a foreigner. He is, in fact, the maternal uncle of
Eurysthenes and Procles; he thus belongs to a collateral line of the Heraclids, the heroes who take over the original autochthonous dynasty in
Sparta and found the two dynasties that exercise political power over
the city.

Like the descendants of Euphemus, Theras is a marginal figure in the
legitimate politics of Lacedaemon. But on the island of Calliste, which
his arrival transforms into Thera, the hero recovers his own people.
During his search for Europa, Cadmus, in fact, had left one of his par-
ents on the island and founded a sanctuary consecrated to Athena and
Poseidon. From this, explain the scholiasts, stems Pindar's qualifier for
the island, "holy" (hierá, 6). Hierocles adds (much later) that the cult of
Apollo took root there afterward, on the occasion of the installation of
colonists from Lacedaemon.[46] The colonial enterprise launched at Calliste-Thera thus finds itself in the hands of two lines with ties in part
continental and of royal ancestry, but both strangers to the génos hold-
ing political power in the metropolis. These different aspects are re-
flected in the genealogy of Battus, the oecist (properly speaking) of Cyrene, and we shall see that the narrative of the foundation of Tarentum
inserts its protagonists into a similar ancestry. But in founding a colony
with a continental character, Battus enjoys an additional quality: he
maintains a privileged relationship with Apollo, on which Pindar does
not fail to insist (5–9, 50–56, 59–69, 259–61). We thus should note
that the function traditionally attributed to Pythian 4 — to affirm the
legitimacy of the dynasty of the Battiads and in particular of Arcesilas
IV — is realized in an indirect way.[47] This legitimation was probably all
the more necessary since Arcesilas IV had just faced a stásis aimed at
overthrowing the royal power. The Sender, in this respect, plays a central role.

2.6. Apollonius of Rhodes: Narrative Rectifications

Before discussing the qualities invested in the *Senders* of the action, we should compare the fate the anthropomorphic actors reserve for the clod of Libyan earth in the narrative of Apollonius of Rhodes. The comparison will reveal some telling divergences.

Inserted into a simple exchange of gifts of hospitality at the moment when the Argonauts attempt to extricate themselves from the marshes of Lake Triton, the clod of earth given to Euphemus by Triton-Eurypylus-Poseidon does not seem to hold the promise of any narrative future. It does not reappear until the end of the final book of the *Argonautica*, in Euphemus' dream on the island of salvation that Phoebus Apollo makes appear (*Anáphe* from *anaphaíno*, 1730), a luminous apparition meant to save the Greek sailors lost in the sepulchral night. As has been shown, the clod is thus engaged in a narrative program that remains secondary to the principal action. This secondary program ends, after all, with emigration to Thera, erasing the Libyan extension of this colonial enterprise. Once presented with Anaphe, virtually the end of the Argonauts' itinerary, the concern of the erudite poet is to give an *aition* for the creation of Thera, the neighboring island. At this point in Apollonius' learned narrative the foundation of Cyrene no longer has any pertinence. Nonetheless, though it is distant from the logic of the narrative of Cyrene's foundation as represented by Pindar on the level of semionarrative syntax and dependent upon quite different circumstances of enunciation, this Hellenistic narrative is still largely reliant upon the Classical representation of the process of colonization, particularly in the four interpretations it receives, nested within the narrative itself.

We begin with the dream of Euphemus, which substitutes a form of remembrance for the disregard of the clump of Libyan earth in the Pindaric version. Divine (*daimoníe*, 1734), as in *Pythian* 4, the clod is nurtured by Euphemus himself. The king of Taenarum is thus placed in the role of the nourishing mother; he then becomes its lover when the clod is transformed into a beautiful young girl. Through inversion of sexual roles and incest, all familial identities find themselves confused. But on a second level of interpretation, undertaken by the young girl who speaks herself, it is revealed to Euphemus that she is actually the daughter of Triton and Libya. She, in fact, is destined to nourish the offspring of Euphemus after having been herself entrusted to the Nereids.[48] The distinction between the familial roles that devolve on each of the sexes is thus reestablished by the negation of the incestuous relationship and the assumption by a woman of the nurturing function. Moreover, the young girl will have a mediatory position between the marine domain and the surface of the earth. She will follow the same course as the island of Anaphe, which came to light from the depths of sea by the will of Apollo. Entrusted for her upbringing to the marine daughters of Nereus, she will receive the descendants of Euphemus in the light of the sun.

The oneiric memory of Euphemus is coupled, on a third level, with the waking memory of Jason. Thus the oracle of Apollo given to the leader of the Argonauts at the beginning of the expedition comes to confer a third meaning on the dream and its interpretation. The oracular words transport us beyond the anthropomorphic surface of the narrative, while still remaining figurative. Euphemus must throw the clod into the waves so that, with the aid of the gods, it will become the island of Thera, future dwelling place of the descendants of the king of Taenarum. This handful of mud is, in reality, nothing other than a piece of *terra firma* (*épeiros*, 1753) representing Libya, a gift from Poseidon. For the prediction of Apollo, little remains at this point other than gaining its realization, in a narrative reality forming a fourth interpretative level and in which the mineral, anthropomorphic, and divine actors act in concert. Euphemus throws the clod into the depths of the sea and Calliste surges up. Sacred (*hieré*, 1758), the island becomes nurturer to the children of the Taenarian Argonaut, whose migratory course we now learn: Lemnos, from which the heroes are chased by the Tyrrhenians; then Sparta, where they are accorded the rights of the city; finally to Calliste, led by the Theban Theras, who gives his name to the island risen from the waves. Of Battus, we hear not a word.[49]

*

The hierarchical inclusion of four enunciative and semantic levels, by which the Alexandrian poet breaks down the narrative of the clod of Libyan earth, seems to supply the contemporary interpreter with unexpected hermeneutic confirmation. It will suffice to privilege in this explication one of the levels constructed by the narrative, since the psychoanalyst, the narratologist, the theologian, and the historian will all find in it something of profit. We shall be limited here to a brief comparison with the parallel narrative of Pindar, avoiding reduction to a single level of what can be explanatory of the others.

From the syntactic point of view, the narrative of Apollonius, with its etiological aims, does not present the diversion of the program found in the Pindaric narration. Memory has replaced forgetting in representing Thera as created by Euphemus, manipulated by Poseidon and brought to light by Apollo. Instead of existing already at the time of the king's arrival, the island is born from the clod and then changes its name when the descendants of Euphemus leave Sparta to colonize it, led by the descendant of Polynices. The triple coincidence in the generation of Thera — the explicit course of the clod, the itinerary of the descendants of Euphemus, and the itinerary of Theras — corresponds to the joint interventions of the two divinities. On the other hand, the Pindaric narrative seeks to distinguish these. In its syntax, the narrative of Apollonius follows the narrated time (*temps raconté*), as does the narration of Herodotus, as we shall soon see. From the figurative point of view, as well, the different enunciative levels of the narrative all seek to deny and to invert the deviations that reveal, on the first level, the dream of Euphemus. Finally, in its general development, the narrative undergoes a type of symbolic rationalization, since Thera, as a morsel of earth removed from the Poseidonian continent and given root in the open sea, follows the model of the demiurgic foundation of islands.

On the other hand, within the same semantic domain, Apollonius does not completely efface certain of the figurative values of the Pindaric narrative that in other cases he modifies by keeping to his etiological objective. The clod keeps its power, and keeps also its metaphorical capacity as the nurturer of the *génos* of Euphemus. In addition, it is the point of transition between the marine domain and the terrestrial surface that we have noted is characteristic of the cosmogonical aspect of myths of insular foundations. Also significant from this point of view is the collaboration between the demiurgic activity of Poseidon and Apollo's founding intervention, although Apollonius' narrative has a tendency to superimpose them. In its semantic dimension, the Hellenistic narrative can still be considered a narrative of (insular) "autochthony," or rather a narrative of the "autochthonous" birth of an island, but its different levels of metaphorical expression are made explicit and integrated into the narration itself through the enunciative play of interpretations. In so doing, it gains narrative plausibility. Through this hermeneutical play the temporal and political relationships between the legendary narrative and the occasion of the poem vanish!

2.7. The Triad of Founding Gods

As *Senders* of human actions, the gods in the Pindaric version of the colonization of Cyrene play the determining role. The phase of foundation, during which the very soil of the colony is manipulated, is placed entirely under the control of a "terrestrial" (to avoid the overused "chthonic") Poseidon whose activity is an indispensable part of creating and stabilizing the foundations of any city. Even at Thera, the cult mentioned above is offered to Poseidon *Gaiéokhos*, "who holds the earth" (or "who leads Gaia"). The sons of the earth god are then made the first kings of those cities just established on firm ground.[50] But on the islands and in the colonies, the primordial act of demiurgic foundation accomplished under the auspices of Poseidon remains without effect unless it is followed by the immigration of men originating on the continent, under the control of Apollo. Even Delphi adheres to this model. Chthonic Gaia and Poseidon furnish the oracles before Apollo takes over his prophetic function from these two primordial deities. The avowed goal of this divine succession is civilization itself (*hemerótes*).[51]

In speaking of Poseidon the founder and Apollo the colonizer, we have yet to consider the third *Sender* of Greek civilizing activity on the Libyan continent as it is narrated by Pindar: every phase of this activity is favored, however discreetly, by Zeus. The father of the Olympian gods is present, we recall, to mark the gift of Libyan earth from one son of Poseidon to another with an auspicious clap of thunder (*aísion*, 23). After its detour to Thera, this terrestrial root will germinate in the soil that already forms the foundation of the cult of Zeus Ammon (16), and Battus receives the oracle of Apollo enlisting him in the act of colonization under the watch of the eagles of Zeus, protectors of the *omphalós* of Delphi (4).[52] Why Zeus? He alone is capable of guaranteeing the fertility of the Libyan land, of creating out of it the "rich sanctuary" consecrated to him (56).

The association of Libya with Zeus is not evident solely in the cult of Ammon. It can be seen also both in the ancestry of Libya, the granddaughter of Cronos by Epaphus (14), ancestor of the Danaans, and in the particular climate attributed to the region of Cyrene, where black clouds accumulate to fertilize the soil (56).[53] Thus the presence of Zeus in Libya is necessary as much because he is responsible for organizing the terrestrial surface as because he is the keeper of the fecundating water found "on high." The god from above thus combines his own activity with that of the god of the depths in order to create in the intervening space, the terrestrial surface, a world that nurtures men.[54] But under the control of Poseidon and Zeus, the African continent still exists only as the land of Libya. It is only with the foundation of Cyrene under the auspices of Apollo that this land will be marked by the seal of (Greek) civilization. To simplify to an extreme, we can represent the collaboration of the three divinities in the colonizing act as a repartition of isotopies traversing the narrative: to Poseidon, the mineral; to Zeus, the vegetal; to Apollo, the human! Or, in an even more schematic spatial repartition: to the first the depths, to the second the heights, and to the third, the surface!

2.8. Metaphorical Resonances of the Ode

The theme of generation/germination taking up in turn figures organized in mineral, vegetal, and human isotopies; the attachment of a motherland to a masculine political legitimacy; the complementarity of Poseidon, Zeus, and Apollo, and so on: these different lines of semantic development ensure the coherence and richness of the Pindaric narrative of the foundation of Cyrene. Solidified by the assimilation of different enunciative voices that carry the narrative, this play of semantic resonances and reciprocal metaphors recurs in the two other narrative portions of *Pythian* 4, devoted to the expedition of the Argonauts and to the fate of Damophilus, a Cyrenaean aristocrat and contemporary of Arcesilas IV.

We may simply recall here, relying for more detail on the recent study already mentioned, that the Pindaric version of the expedition of the Argonauts presents the capture of the Golden Fleece as the "root" (*phúteuthen*, 69) of the glory of the Minyans who accompany Euphemus, the ancestor of Battus. The arrival of Jason at Iolcus is predicted by an oracle given beside the *omphalós* at Delphi, at the center of Earth the mother (74). Under the protection of Apollo, the hero arrives to claim the power accorded to his great-grandfather Aeolus (107); he thus returns to the land of his fathers (97–98, 117–18), the control of which was usurped by Pelias, a son of Poseidon and a descendant of Zeus, as is Jason (138, 167). The capture of the Fleece is itself placed under the protection of Zeus in an episode that is, figuratively, an inversion of the gift of Libyan earth to Euphemus. Jason stands at the stern of the ship, once the anchor is raised, when he receives the favorable sign from the father of the gods (191–202). Entrance into the Euxine Sea places the Argonauts in the domain of Poseidon (204). On its savage shores Jason manages to accomplish a fabulous deed of plowing, after having placed the raging oxen of Aeetes under the yoke and gained the hand of his daughter Medea (218–41). Finally, the dragon guarding the Golden Fleece submits, under Jason's blows, to the same fate as the Python at Delphi under Apollo's sword.[55] As for the heroes' return to Greece, it has been anticipated by the narrative of the adventure of Euphemus, with which it coincides in part. Pindar thus breaks Jason's circular course into two segments, whose order of succession he inverts. But reestablished in its circularity, this itinerary repeats, with the aid of adjacent figures, that of the miraculous clod. As an "autochthon," it becomes in Libya the foundation of a city, after a long detour through Thera.

Again, the narrator-speaker wishes an analogous course based on the same circular schema for Damophilus, the Cyrenaean exile at Thebes, but with the second portion of the schema projected into the future in relation to the time of enunciation. After having frequented the palace of Battus (280) and although he has learned to hate *húbris* (284), this just exile lives far from "the land of his fathers" (290). He is compared to Atlas, the son of a Titan and an Oceanid; other texts inform us that this monstrous being is banished to the fringes of the earth in order to ensure, from the depths of the ocean, the cosmological separation of earth and sky. In order to liberate the Cyrenaean from this assimilation with the quasidemiurgic role of the Titan and thus to reestablish the order desired by Zeus, the poet demands that Arcesilas, who enjoys the protection of Apollo Paean, intervene as a physician would (270). Damophilus, in effect, desires to regain his "house," that is to say, his proximity to Apollo's spring, in order to taste the pleasures of the symposium and poetry among citizens living in harmony (*hesukhía*, 296).[56]

In short, it is again a matter of the same circular and yet transformational passage from a potential state of civilization to a state of civility, attained through an intermediate stage in which the protagonist is at odds with primordial forces that form, once they are overcome, the foundation for the birth of culture.[57] The terrestrial germ of Libya becomes a Greek city after settling deep in the sea's waves; Jason, a king in power, will reign in Iolcus after having imposed the plow, yoke, and marriage on the savage forces — geological, theriomorphic, and anthropomorphic — of a marginal territory; Damophilus will return to the activities of civilization encouraged by Apollo and those of the political community of men united at the "banquet" after having atoned for his presumption by submitting to the primordial punishment of Atlas. But, in a reversal clearly exclusive to Pindar, the Titanesque exile of Damophilus at Thebes is transformed in extremis into an initiation into poetry nearby an inspiring and welcoming spring (299, compared with 21–25). Subtly, the poet inserts into the domain of civilization the location of his own enunciation, all the while resuming the poetic itinerary that opens the poem, leading from Delphi to Cyrene by way of Thebes. The ode thus concludes as it began, at a symposium conceived as a place of literary inspiration. But this most skillful movement of recuperation is bound by the constraints the occasion imposes on Pindar's narrative: celebration of the king Arcesilas IV on the occasion of the Panhellenic victory of his chariot at Delphi.

From the point of view of narrative composition, Apollonius of

Rhodes practices his craft in a similar way to what we shall see in the work of Callimachus. He seeks chronological coordination of the narrative within its versions and respects some of its figures, but does so in guiding them toward a unique and reoriented theme; generative "autochthony" becomes cosmogony. Moreover, from the perspective of the legend of the Argonauts, his narrative of foundation—which concludes, as we have seen, with the creation of Thera—originates with the gift of the marvelous clod and not with Apollo's rape of Cyrene. But if we consider again the quadruple semantic interpretation centered upon the clod itself, we note that mineral, vegetal, and human figures are all to be found there; they are organized into isotopies perhaps less interwoven than in Pindar, but still distributed over the four distinct interpretative levels, themselves focalized on the theme of generation. The coincidence of these four levels with the realization of the narrative defines the theme of generation, in the sense of a veritable cosmogonic act. Thrown into the sea, the marvelous clod changes into an island that nurtures the descendants of the Argonauts. Rationalized, in a way, by this simple operation, the Hellenistic legend of foundation paradoxically reveals the representation that underlies it.

In Pindar, cosmogonic acts motivate the different versions of the legend of Cyrene's founding. This is cosmogony in the Greek sense of the term, since it establishes civic order and transforms a location in its geology, flora, and fauna. This order is differentiated from what forms the basis of cities in continental Greece because, under the control of Apollo, it establishes a pastoral civilization that prolonged an otherwise largely obsolete monarchic model up to the middle of the fifth century. These symbolic manifestations are necessarily dependent on the historical situation in which they arise and on representations particular to social circumstances marked in time and space.

3. *Pythian* 9: A Pastoral Civilization

The Cyrenaean legend recounted in *Pythian* 4 took as a figure the manipulation of the land of Libya. This activity, through the intermediary of vegetal growth slowly becoming humanized, was eventually taken over by the quasi-historical figure of Battus and centered on the city of Cyrene. *Pythian* 9 leaves to the side metaphorical echoes of these three interwoven isotopies centered on the theme of (autochthonous) generation in order to fix the listener's attention immediately on the colonial city. Returning once again to metaphorical expression, the narrative of foundation is constructed around a theme that develops according to an entirely different isotopy, the theme of the matrimonial union of Cyrene herself, the eponymous nymph of the city.

3.1. A Biography between Hunting and Husbandry

It is much easier to reconstruct the plot of this story from Pindar's fragmented narrative than it was for the preceding ode. In the mountainous confines of Thessaly, the young Cyrene guards the flocks of her father and defends them from the attacks of wild animals. During the course of her athletic struggle with a powerful lion, Apollo is smitten by the young girl, creating a situation of *lack* provoked by the desire for amorous fulfillment. In typically Pindaric fashion, the advice sought by the god from the Centaur Chiron concerning the realization of his desire affords an anticipation of the outcome of the intrigue and also furnishes it with its phase of *manipulation*. Paradoxically, the sage Chiron, in revealing the oracular god's future to him, appears as the *Sender* of Apollo. To the query by the god about the origin of the young girl, the Centaur responds by predicting the transfer of his love affair to Libya. By conforming in this way to the model of an oracular response suggesting a colonial expedition, Chiron becomes a substitute for the Delphic god.[58] The union of the nymph and the god, probably the latter's first experience in love, will thus have Libya as its frame. In order to accomplish the transformation necessary in any narration, this *performance* realized in the form of a conjunction must be accompanied by a spatial disjunction. In this particular case, the amorous intrigue is transformed, through spatial displacement, into a legend of foundation! *Sanction* is promised: the birth of a son destined to exhibit, through his own immortality, divine qualities.

The prophetic advice of Chiron, with its reflexive aspect, is surely an artifice meant to break the linearity of the narrative. Even so, exercising the *competence* his divinity confers upon him, Apollo immediately realizes in *performance* the content of the Centaur's oracular prophecy. He is united in love with the girl Cyrene. A second *sanction* is reserved for her, in addition to the promised son: the control of a city distinguished by its beauty and its achievements in the games. This forms the pretext for the narrator to return to the occasion of the poem, the brilliant victory in the Pythian games of Telesicrates of Cyrene.[59] *Epinicie oblige!*

*

It is often remarked that the matrimonial union, doubled by the young couple's transfer to Libya, constitutes the heart of Pindar's narrative. We could now add that the narrative of the biography of Cyrene occurs on the semantic plane according to a matrimonial isotopy. The figures assumed by this simple narrative transformation, however, have been little analyzed. Critics have generally considered it a normal event, and have been insensitive to the change of status the wedding implies for Cyrene herself.

Cyrene is a virgin huntress (*parthénos agrotéra*, 7). But in contrast to an Atalanta, for example, her rejection of women's work and conviviality with her companions (18) is not the corollary of a refusal to marry. Cyrene combats wild beasts because she is the shepherdess of her father's flocks (21–25).[60] Like the young Theseus combating the monsters that infest the way from Troizen to Athens, she fights a lion with her bare hands (26–28); in the fashion of that adolescent hero, she is armed with javelins and a sword (20).[61] Precisely these masculine qualities of strength and courage (30–35) attract Apollo, himself represented as an adolescent with long hair (5). Moreover, the young girl's genealogy places her close to the founding gods of the Greek cosmos. Her father Hypseus, the king of the Lapiths, is in fact born from the union of the river Peneus, a son of Ocean, with the naiad Creusa, a daughter of Gaia. Their union is sheltered by the vales of Pindus, the great mountain chain separating Thessaly from the west.[62]

Transported to Libya on the divine chariot of the Delian god, Cyrene, along with Apollo, enjoys the hospitality of Aphrodite. She becomes the sovereign (*déspoina*, 7) of this continental territory, but equally the mistress of a veritable city along with its territory (*arkhépolis*, 54), as the context of that particular expression shows. Even in adulthood, the nymph retains the masculine role of protector; an athlete as an adolescent, as an adult she assumes the function of a sovereign. But the marriage of Cyrene and Apollo does not simply mark the ascendance of the young woman to a politically masculine role. It also assumes its traditional role for the girl as a point of transition. Through the marriage, the nymph acquires the very quality that in Greece characterizes the state of a married woman, maternity. As we have seen, Cyrene gives birth, on Libyan soil, to a son who will be raised and immortalized by the Seasons, as well as by his great-grandmother Gaia. There is nothing surprising in such a destiny for a son who will grow up to assume the old task of his mother, guarding flocks (64), but he will also assume roles, by means of interposed epiclesis, identifying him with Apollo and Zeus: *Agreús* "the hunter," *Nómios* "the shepherd," *Aristaîos* "the excellent" or "the benefactor" (65).[63] Hunting and husbandry merge into the perfect order, established by Zeus. As for Cyrene, her status has undergone a twofold transformation through marriage. The young girl has become a mother, and the athlete huntress has gained political sovereignty.

The contrast between the two poles of spatial displacement that accompany Cyrene's simultaneous transformation into an adult woman and an adult man repeats this transformation. Thus it is at the eastern extremes of Thessaly, in the Pelion range battered by winds (5), that Apollo catches sight of the young Cyrene, who inhabits the "thickets of shadowy mountains" (33–34).[64] From these deep valleys (51), Apollo wishes to take the huntress into the "extraordinary garden" Zeus maintains in Libya (53). Aphrodite seems to rule there, just as she does in the *Symposium* of Plato, in the garden of Zeus that accommodates the loves of Poverty and Necessity; we should not forget, in addition, that in the *Argonautica*, the same garden shelters the play of Eros and Ganymede.[65]

Transported from Thessaly to Libya, the young girl who refused domestic labor is then united with Apollo in a palace of gold (56 and 69).[66] Cyrene, now a sovereign, has at her disposal a portion of the land (*khthonòs aîsa*, 56) of "vast prairies," whose production would be considered remarkable even today. This land represents — by an image already used in *Pythian* 4 — the "flowering root" (8) of Libya, the third continent, according to the Greek conception of the inhabited world; this image may refer to the foundation by Cyrene itself of other Greek cities in Libya. We find here a spatialized type of synecdoche, familiar from *Pythian* 4. While the residence promised to the young nymph corresponds at first to the whole of a continent referred to by the name Libya, it is subsequently reduced to this garden of Zeus, which, beyond the poetic image, coincides with the territory delimited by the presence of sanctuaries consecrated to Zeus Ammon. But this designation of the Cyrenaica undergoes a final metamorphosis when the dimensions of the territory attributed to Cyrene are restricted to a "portion of land," an expression that recovers the *khóra* of the colony to be founded.[67] But there is no *khóra* without an urban center. This center will be the city bearing the name of the wife of Apollo, built on a hill, where Cyrene will assemble "an island people" (54–55).[68] The rule of the Thessalian woman over this fertile territory thus does not preclude in any way its future colonization by the Therans.

3.2. Matrimonial Variations on Civilization

The symbolic narrative of the union of Apollo and Cyrene thus stages a transformation that assumes different figures of the theme of matrimonial union. *Pythian* 9 reproduces the process that formed the narrative in *Pythian* 4, through a reprise of the same theme, but with its own particular figurative variations.

The legitimate marriage, with the conquest of the fiancée that introduces it (*manipulation* and *competence*), and the procreation that is its consequence (*sanction*) together form an isotopy consisting of marriage as a transformation of state, as passage from an old status to a new one, as an "initiatory" rite. It is thus an isotopy that, far from being reduced to a reiterated semantic unit, finds its articulation in the development of the narrative on the syntactic plane.[69] The marriage of Alexidemus with the daughter of the Libyan king of Irasa, who takes as his model the marriage of Danaus' forty-eight daughters; the potential wedding of Telesicrates, the *receiver* of the ode, with one of the young girls of Cyrene; also, generally overlooked by interpreters, the joint union of Alcmene with Zeus and Amphitryon, which produces Heracles, the hero par excellence, introduced by the invocation of Iolaus, his nephew — these are all narrative and figurative variations.[70] They are all unions that have, in their narrative development, well-marked antecedents and consequences.

Antaios is the king of Irasa, the father of the young Libyan girl offered in marriage. If there were not in legend two cities named Irasa, one to the east and one to the west of Cyrene, this Antaios could be the son of Poseidon and Ge; according to Pindar in *Isthmian* 4, he is a giant with whom Heracles will fight to prevent him from offering his guests in sacrifice to his divine father.[71] These monstrous traits, which associate this second Antaios with a Polyphemus or a Cercyon, would probably prevent him from organizing races, those most Greek of competitions, to choose among the candidates for his daughter's hand. However that may be, the fastest competitor, the Cyrenaean Alexidemus, will be wed (*gámos*, 112 and 114) to the exceptionally beautiful young girl. The *xénos* then leads his fiancée through an assembled mass of nomadic cavaliers (123). Even if certain ancient commentators on Pindar rightly hesitated to identify the Antaios of *Pythian* 9 with the adversary of Heracles in *Isthmian* 4,[72] it nonetheless remains that the union of the Libyan daughter with the noble Cyrenaean symbolizes, in patriarchal terms, the integration of the indigenous population with the first group of Greek colonists.

According to Herodotus, Irasa is the most beautiful region of Libya, a place the indigenous peoples managed to conceal from the first Greek colonists. The site was the location of the celebrated battle recounted by Herodotus in the course of which the Cyrenaeans, led by Battus II Eudaimon, managed to defeat a coalition of indigenous revolters and Egyptians led by the Pharaoh Apries one hundred years before the performance of *Pythian* 9. In later tradition the daughter of Antaios bears the name Barce, the name of the city founded under Arcesilas II by dissident aristocrats, aided, apparently, in their political activity by the indigenous population. Are these discreet Pindaric allusions to the political conditions at the moment of the poem's enunciation in the fifth century?[73] Be that as it may, the legend is reformulated in the poems of Pindar to evoke, through particular figurative means, the Greeks' struggles to impose themselves on the native population. It is an excellent example of the constant functioning of the process of symbolic creation and re-creation, stimulated by the succession of historical events, in this particular case especially by the Greek occupation of North Africa.

In addition, the choice of Alexidemus is not a random one. According to the scholiast's commentary on this passage, he is an ancestor of Telesicrates (105), the Pythian victor celebrated by the narrator. We learn that year after year, in the course of the celebrations of the games at Cyrene or on his return from the Panhellenic games, this great athlete gains the admiration of young women (*parthenikaí*, 99), who dream of making this brilliant victor their husband or son, thus becoming women capable of ensuring the fame of their city (74). Does this situation, in representing the young girls infatuated with an athlete crowned by success, invert the relationship between the lover Apollo and Cyrene, the admired female athlete, as one critic has suggested?[74] This would perhaps be to forget that the contest of the suitors (in which Alexidemus, the ancestor of Telesicrates, participates) fulfills a mediatory role and acts as a narrative pivot. By granting access to the hand of Antaios' daughter, this legendary contest closely associates agonal victory with conjugal success. It thus tends to draw the victory gained by Telesicrates at Delphi closer to the ritual wedding that the celebration of the athlete at Cyrene evokes.

This reconciliation is given more depth by two complementary narratives. On the one hand, a mention of the exploit of the Theban Iolaus and his connection to Heracles, while returning us to the place of composition of the poem, allows the evocation of Alcmene's exemplary union with Amphitryon and Zeus (79–88). On the other, the matrimonial contest organized for Alexidemus the Cyrenaean is modeled on the race Danaus imposed upon those wishing to marry his forty-eight daughters (111–25). The future marriage of Telesicrates, blessed by his Delphic victory, as well as the agonal marriage of Alexidemus, thus follows the heroic model.

*

Through these interwoven narratives, mortal man progressively becomes the *Subject* of the central action: a feminized Apollo subjected to the advice of Chiron kidnaps the nymph Cyrene from Thessaly and makes her the queen of Libya; Alexidemus takes the daughter of the Libyan Antaios from Irasa to Cyrene, thus integrating indigenous royalty and Greek power; as for Telesicrates, he does not delay in marrying Cyrene — this is in any case what the imbrication of the three narratives suggests — one of the young Cyrenaeans whose admiration and desire he has aroused.[75] Husband or son? This is one way to summarize in a single formula the twofold narrative consequence of the conquest of a fiancée explicit in the two preceding narratives: as a husband, Telesicrates will be the Apollo or the Alexidemus of the Cyrenaean woman dear to his heart; but, inasmuch as his own *génos* is the product of the marriage of his ancestor Alexidemus and the beautiful indigenous daughter of Antaios, Telesicrates will be capable, for his part, of engendering a descendant worthy of himself. The three narratives are virtually bound in a single "canonical schema": *manipulation* and *competence* in the exemplary loves of Apollo and Alexidemus, *performance* in the marriage of Telesicrates, and *sanction* with the probable birth of a son! What varies, on the other hand, are the secondary antecedents and consequences particular to each of these unions: transfer to Libya of a Greek woman who combats wild beasts and who will come to rule over a colonial city under the control of a Greek god; transfer to Cyrene of an indigenous woman, member of a nomadic people, who becomes the spouse of a Greek colonist and citizen of an established locality; union at Cyrene of a Cyrenaean woman and a Cyrenaean man who has just gained a victory at games celebrated in honor of the god who initiated the whole series of events.

In these interlocking actions, each of which has a corresponding echo, each *performance* becomes the phase of *manipulation* for what follows. And each of these transformational matrimonial unions is the point of a modification that extends the progressive masculinization and Hellenization of Libya. The narrative development of *Pythian 9* thus must be read not only horizontally, but vertically. The matrimonial isotopy, deployed in at least three intertwined narratives, has constant metaphorical echoes on the plane of colonization. The three matrimonial unions — Apollo, Alexidemus, and Telesicrates — are nothing other than foundational acts meant to anchor a Greek city in foreign territory. Moreover, toward the end of the poem, the very victory of Telesicrates, subtly assimilated to a matrimonial union, is interpreted as an act of colonization. In lines 68–75, in fact, the union (*mígen*) of Cyrene and Apollo in the "*thálamos* of Libya," the city so famous for its performance in the games, directly introduces the celebration of Telesicrates. By his victory, the athlete "has united" (*sunémeixe*) with a brilliant fortune. And who is to say whether the anaphora of *nin* (73; cf. 6) refers to the city of Cyrene (*pólin*) or to its foundress, the eponymous nymph! Besides, the glory that Telesicrates brings to Cyrene from Delphi, by a course analogous to that followed by Cyrene herself, has the charms of love (*dóxan himertán*).[76] The play of the Pindaric metaphor thus transfers the matrimonial isotopy to a colonial one by integrating it with agonal victory.

Supported by a spatial transfer, these different marriages consequently introduce their respective protagonists to a new status. The passage from the figurative isotopy to the theme of the ode is assumed to be from nature to culture (as the most recent interpreters, clearly influenced by Lévi-Strauss, have affirmed). Matters, however, are more complex, and we should mistrust the binary logic too often applied by anthropologists without nuance.

It is hardly a controversial point that Pelion, where Apollo falls in love with Cyrene, corresponds to the Greek representation of savagery. But in this hostile environment, Cyrene defends an island of what the Greeks considered a first stage of civilization, pastoral activity. Here, "wild animals" (21) are opposed to "paternal cattle" (23). Without taking into account the production of fruit (7, 58), also evoked in *Pythian* 4 (6), pasturage is exactly the activity to which the "vast prairies" (55) of Libya are most suited, most particularly the region of Cyrene, which is called "rich in flocks" (*polúmelos*, 6). We shall see that in the reported narratives of Herodotus, reference to husbandry is constant in his description of the green Cyrenaica situated in the midst of a deserted and wild Libya. The suitability of this soil for pasturage is recalled in the oracles given to Battus encouraging him to colonize this moist region. Cyrene itself benefits from rains falling from the sky and from water rising from the ground at the spring of Apollo, ensuring the extraordinary fertility and productivity of the *Kurenaíe khóre*, the land of Cyrene.[77]

The installation of the Greek Cyrene in Libya has as a consequence the creation of the most beautiful of cities (69), surrounded by a *khóra*, a productive land, essentially consecrated to pasturage, not agriculture. The foundation of Troy, as described in the *Iliad*, follows a similar model. General control of operations is in the hands of Zeus, though Poseidon builds the city's walls, and Apollo, as a good pioneer, opens the folds of Ida to grazing.[78] When Cyrene enjoys the complementary state of civilization, by way of the marriage of Alexidemus with the daughter of the indigenous king, it is the activity of the natives — nomadic cavaliers (123) — that is integrated by the Greeks into the colonized domain. Here they undergo an essential transformation: the vagabond equitation of the natives is modified, through the impetus of Hellenic technical knowledge, into the art of driving the chariot, a skill destined to make the city famous (4).[79] As far as the future marriage of Telesicrates is concerned, it will establish on Cyrenaean soil one who will be distinguished as a hoplite at the greatest games of continental Greece.

3.3. Callimachus: Hellenistic Variants

The establishment of this first stage of Greek civilization in Libya is also one of the narrative functions of the version of Cyrene's colonization as rewritten by Callimachus in his *Hymn to Apollo*. If we turn our attention to this poem's semantic aspects, we see that the narrative portion of the poem is developed in four episodes. These four narrative programs are articulated in succession according to the same isotopies, ensuring the coherence of their progression on the semantic level. After the various domains of Apollo have been defined (archery, song, divination, medicine), the narration begins; each of its episodes is under the control of an epiclesis of the god and, according to the etiological design characteristic of the erudite poet, each constitutes a type of explication.

First, Apollo is *Nómios*, the "shepherd," caring for (*étrephe*, 48) cattle, goats, and sheep. From the narrative point of view, his solicitude is also a reference to the episode in which he guards the mares of Admetus. In a fit of homophilic desire, the young god is impassioned for the beautiful adolescent who rules over the banks of the Amphrissus in Thessaly.[80] The sojourn of the shepherd god on the shores of this river defines a first space consecrated to the activity of animal husbandry.

Apollo *Phoîbos*, the "brilliant," leads us from the north of Greece to Delos, where he exercises his talents as the founder of cities. It is first at Delos, in fact, that he "wove" the foundations (*themeília*, 57, 58, 64), bases (*edéthlia*, 62) of a cult building, the Ceraton, "plaited" with the horns of wild goats hunted by the god's sister Artemis on Mount Cynthus. This foundational construction also incorporates the supplementary aspect of Apolline *tékhne* as craft of the architect (42).[81] The "weaving" of the Altar of Horns, with its foundations and encircling walls, seems to represent figuratively a passage from the state of savagery that reigned on Delos before the arrival of the god to the state of civilization embodied in the construction of the altar itself. From here, the center of the Aegean Sea, the narrative itinerary of the *Hymn to Apollo* makes a brief return to the continent, at Sparta, but then moves again across the sea, now under the conduct of Apollo *Karneîos*, to the new continent of Libya. The course is direct: from Lacedaemon to Cyrene via Thera (72–74); all three cities are represented as foundations (*édethlon*, 72; *apóktisis*, 75). The narrative of Callimachus thus follows in its broad outline the version Pindar presents in *Pythian 5* and what is also found in the *lógos*, the story told by Herodotus. As in the latter, in the Alexandrian poem the narrated time (*temps raconté*) and the spoken time (*temps énoncé*) match the rhythm of narration and the development of the time of enunciation (*temps de l'énonciation*).

But the Hellenistic poet reserves a few surprises for the reader upon arrival in Libya. After the description of the construction (*deîme*, 77; likewise the construction of the Ceraton, 62) of a temple to Apollo by the founder Battus and of the celebration there of the Carneia, the festival dedicated to Apollo Carneius, the hymnic narration begins a gentle and subtle return to "historical" times. It is not at Cyrene itself, but at the indigenous site of Aziris (or Azilis) "with thick vales" that the colonists, along with the Libyan women, engage for the first time in the dances of the Carneia.[82] In fact, they have not yet reached the geographical center of the future city of Cyrene, near the Cyre spring sacred to Apollo. On the other hand, without the slightest respect for spatial plausibility, it is at Cyrene, this very site, that Apollo admires the dances of the Dorians mixed with indigenous women. Accompanied by his young wife, the god has naturally chosen the horn (91) that represents the Mount of the Myrtles, the still unsullied site of the future Cyrene, as his vantage point.[83] This spatial displacement is also accompanied by temporal slippage. In fact, the mention of the eponymous nymph of the future colony, in the narrative evocation of Apollo's rape of the young girl, brings us from the legend of the colonization by Battus to the divine version told by Pindar in *Pythian* 9. Through the first and paradigmatic celebration of the Carneia on Libyan soil, the times of colonization, both "historic" and heroized (Battus), come to coincide with the divine foundation of the city (Apollo and Cyrene).

In parallel to this twofold narrative displacement (in space and time), the *Hymn* of Callimachus also transfers the heroic struggle between Cyrene and the lion from Thessaly to Libya. Hypseus' daughter is no longer guarding her father's flocks, but instead those of Eurypylus, the native king. This change has not failed to preoccupy Callimachus' readers. Stretching back at least to the *History of Cyrene* of Acesandrus, a work in the local historiographic tradition, the transfer was interpreted simply as situating the exploit of the city's eponymous nymph in a purely Cyrenaean milieu.[84] But, moving beyond a narrative point of view, this transfer also has as a consequence the transfer of the triumph of the first stage of civilization to Libyan soil, represented by the victory of the Thessalian huntress and shepherdess over a savage beast. Indeed, Acesandrus recounts that Eurypylus had set his own kingdom as the prize for whoever managed to kill the savage lion ravaging his flocks. Thus by her athletic exploit, Cyrene not only succeeds in establishing agriculture in a foreign region threatened by savagery, but also causes the sovereignty of the place to fall into Greek hands. In Callimachus' narrative, the allusion to this seizure of indigenous power by a Greek woman finds an echo in the first celebration of the Carneia, where the Greek colonists take Libyan women as partners.

This is not all, however. Since it does not conclude at Cyrene, the narrative of the *Hymn* still requires its *sanction*. This is found at Delphi, in the fourth episode of this series of foundations (97–104). Having already been Nomios, Phoibos, and Carneios, Apollo now becomes the god Paean. The poetic and etiological explanation given for this new epithet recounts how the archer god managed to kill the savage monster which infested this mountainous site.[85] In gratitude, as at Azilis, the people of Delphi sing the praise of Paean the liberator and purifier, in echo of his very name; the words themselves constitute the refrain of the *Hymn*.

The Callimachean narrative thus sketches in succession four different spaces: a pastoral space framed by mountains in Thessaly; one appropriate for building an altar on the fallow island of Delos; one measured by the construction of a city and accompanying temple and by the installation of royal power in a land menaced by wild beasts in Libya; and one purified of its flaws by the god of Delphi himself. Not content to return us to the African continent, nor to guide us from an Aetolian territory to an Ionian island, then to a land colonized by Dorians, before returning us to a Panhellenic site, the episodic narrative of Callimachus finally leads us — as we have already seen — to the very establishment of Greek civilization, by means of two isotopies. The first, which is spatial, has already been described. Centered on the theme of construction, it successively marks out traits that little by little transform a region inhabited by nomadic shepherds into a territory controlled by a city, with local cults and ties to a Panhellenic sanctuary. The other isotopy is social, centered on the theme of intimate relationships. Engaged by the god's homophilic love for the young Thessalian Admetus, it is afterward built into the fraternal relationship of brother and sister at Delos, then in the protection accorded by the god to the oecist Cyrene and in the privileged relationship that the god, as Paean, maintains through cult and song with the people of Delphi.[86] Even here, there is progress toward established civilization as the Greeks imagine it.

By means of narratives that are linearly organized instead of woven together, through novel manipulations of narrative and chronological time, and by recourse to figures connected through different intrigues and actions, the narrative of Callimachus — and probably that of Acesandrus — serves to confirm the underlying theme of the narratives in *Pythian* 9: the establishment of civilization in the form of a Greek city on foreign land. Before considering, as will be done below, the poetic program in which the Callimachean version of Cyrene's foundation is inserted, the perspective adopted in the hymn by the Hellenistic poet must be understood in the context of the transfer of Greek culture from Athens to Alexandria precisely during the third century B.C.

3.4. The Mediators of Civilizing Activity

It is possible to understand the role played by the mediators Chiron, Aristaios, and Heracles in *Pythian* 9 in the context of this transition from a savage state to the (pre-)civilized activity of pastoralism. One recent analysis has shown that Chiron teaches the very arts, hunting and fighting, in which Cyrene excels. Equally a prophet, pedagogue, healer, and horseman, the Centaur is similar to the god he is called upon to advise. His double nature — human and equine — defines him from the start as a mediator. He assumes an intermediary position not between "nature" and "culture," however, but between the savagery of the mountainous forest in which he lives (30) and the pastoral domain Cyrene and Apollo protect.[87]

Precisely these two poles designate the epithets attributed to Aristaios, the Hunter and the Shepherd (65). This son of Cyrene and Apollo is also endowed with these qualities in the *Argonautica* of Apollonius of Rhodes. Instead of being inserted in this version of the Argonauts' passage to Libya, the brief exploit of Aristaios represents in the Alexandrian poem an *aítion* explaining the origins of the Etesian winds — proof of the flexibility of the narrative function of Greek "myths"! This narrative detour, however, does not prevent the Hellenistic version of the legend from retaining its main semantic values. Born in Libya, Aristaios is brought to Thessaly to be entrusted there to Chiron for his education. As an adult, he becomes the double of Apollo, practicing the arts of healing, divination, and husbandry. He guards flocks on the Phthian plain, situated between mountain and river. He is then called to Ceos, where, assuming another function of his father, he saves the island from the curse of drought. By offering a sacrifice to the burning Sirius and to Zeus *Ikmaîos*, the "moist," Aristaios' means of intervention evoke both the moisture necessary for the exercise of his pastoral function and the god who is master of such things. In recognition, Zeus sends the Etesian winds to Ceos from that time on to refresh the land.[88] We should remember that the soil of the plain of Cyrene also owes its fertility to the benevolence of Zeus; the god favors its climate by accumulating black clouds above the land.

Heracles, Panhellenic in notoriety, is skillfully introduced through an evocation of his local homologue Iolaus. Mention of this hero related to Heracles recalls Thebes, the location of the poem's composition and perhaps also of another victory of Telesicrates. As other epinician odes by Pindar, *Pythian* 9 offers, from the point of view of its relation with its situation of performance, a meaningful tension between the place of composition and the place of performance of the poem. This same tension is also to be found in the melic *I*, divided between the poet-author and the choral group.[89] Like Telesicrates and his ancestor Alexidemus, Iolaus and Heracles are athletes. Moreover, in the course of his athletic struggles, Heracles, the son of the Theban Alcmene, liberates Greece from its monsters and allows development of true civilization.[90] His combat with the Nemean lion particularly connects this great hero of Greece with the nymph Cyrene, while his qualities as an exemplary son (84–85) evoke Aristaios. The transformation of the young girl into a masculine and heroic figure is achieved through this assimilation.

To be sure, the different myths in play in *Pythian* 9 aim principally to enrich the praise of the Cyrenaean Telesicrates' brilliant victory. The physical strength of the athlete finds its culmination, by a pun on his own name, in his victory at the games, just as a marriage is fulfilled in the birth of a legitimate son.[91] The legend of the foundation of Cyrene profits from Pindar's "serialization" of different legends by means of this metaphorical assimilation of agonal victory and matrimonial union. It is effected through figures articulated according to the matrimonial isotopy, in order to express an essential transition. This transition, a more abstract thematic passage from savagery to husbandry, informs the Classical representation of the birth of a flourishing colony and its singular civilization, developed through contact with three of the essential sources of Greek culture: Thessaly, dear to Apollo; Delphi, dear to Telesicrates; and Thebes, dear to Pindar, enunciator of the poem.

4. *Pythian* 5: Calling All Heroes!

In singing for a second time the praises of the victory won at Delphi by the chariot of Arcesilas IV, *Pythian* 5 does not use metaphorical entanglements of different isotopies, as does the fourth, nor superposition of narrative transformations on homologous figurative content, as in the ninth. The development of the ode presents a gallery of portraits, on a course moving forward and backward in time, and is involved in a constant spatial alternation between different sites in continental Greece and Cyrene itself. This double series of temporal movements and spatial displacements constitutes the narrative action of the poem. As for the actors, their sequence of appearance follows the communal enjoyment of an *ólbos* (14, 55, 102) granted by the gods, a prosperity that always maintains Cyrene as its frame.

4.1. Actors and the Heroic Age

First, the victor celebrated on the day of the enunciation of the poem is Arcesilas, the rightful sovereign of numerous cities by the authority accorded to him by the gods (12–20). Next, there is the narrator, who has entrusted his song to a chorus of men under the authority of Apollo (20–22), thus establishing a spatial link between Thebes and Cyrene. Next again is Carrhotus, the brother-in-law of Arcesilas, the charioteer and architect of the victory, who has consecrated his chariot to the Delphic god (23–54), connecting that site again with Cyrene in Libya. Carrhotus' return to the "plain of Libya," the city of his fathers (*patroía pólis*, 53), while recalling the city and its *khóra*, also arouses the memory of the *ólbos* of Battus, founder of the city on Apollo's order (55–62), whose colonial activity solidifies the relationship between Delphi and Cyrene. Apollo favored as well the settlement of the Heraclids, founders of enduring continental Greek cities in the Argolid, Messenia, and Laconia (69–72); their course sketches a new relationship between Thessaly and the Peloponnese.[92]

Having reached back to the most distant point of legendary history, in the *palaiá*, the narrator quickly retraces the chronological line forward by developing the isotopy of the favorable welcome reserved for all the protagonists who suffer spatial displacement. To evoke the Heraclids' work in refounding city-states is thus to recall the itinerary followed by the *génos* of the Aegids. The evocation of this clan's legendary origins marks an opportune supplementary connection between the place of the poem's composition (Thebes) and the place of its enunciation/performance (Cyrene). Pindar enumerates the stages of the migration, by the will of the gods and destiny (*moîra*, 76), of those who are both his ancestors (*emoì patéres*, 76) and the fathers of the colonists of Cyrene: they move from Thebes, to Sparta, Thera, and then Cyrene, the "well-built" city (*agaktiména*, 72–78). The beginning of the migration of the future Aegids is paralleled by the arrival of the Trojans, sons of Antenor, in Libya; driven away by the destruction of their city and accompanied by Helen (82–85), they now establish a connection between Troy and Cyrene.

The spatial coincidence at Cyrene of these two *géne* has a consequence, serving to efface the chronological distance separating the arrival of the Trojans in Libya from the expedition of the founder Battus. In this respect, the repetition of the isotopy of hospitality allows the possibility of a double return to the present, reinforcing the impression of the simultaneity of these two events that are in fact quite separate in time. Actually evocation of the Theban Aegids' emigration, willed by the gods (*híkonto* in the aorist, 75), brings about the mention, for the first time, of the present celebration at Cyrene (*sebízomen*, 80; celebration assumed by the narrator-speaker): the Apollonian festival of the Carneia, handed down in the past (*anadexámenoi*, 78) from these heroes who emigrated from Sparta. Evocation of the Carneia induces in turn mention of a more ancient migration, that of the Trojan strangers (*xé-*

noi, 82), descendants of Antenor (*mélon* in the aorist, 83). The Cyrenaeans now recall and honor this "horse-loving" race, in the time of the poem's enunciation (*dékontai* in the present, 86), probably on the very occasion of the Carneia.[93] This double passage from past to present thus assumes the figure of a transition from narrative to ritual, all coming to pass as if it were in the end the Theran colonists, descendants of the Aegids, who had received the Antenorids in Cyrene!

The movement back in time continues with a reprise of the isotopy of hospitality, now figured by the honors following from it. Thus Battus himself, after his founding work, is honored by the people as a hero (89–101). The same is true for the kings of Cyrene, successors of Battus, who have become "sacred" (*hieroí*, 97), by the burial reserved for them at the gates of their palace, contrary to the common habit of extramural burial. Under the earth, they in fact perceive the ritual praise addressed to their authority, which is itself aroused by the agonal achievement of their descendant. The succession of Battus' descendants leads us naturally to Arcesilas IV, who is associated with the same songs of praise (102–17). The actual king of Cyrene thus benefits, along with his forefathers, not only from the *ólbos*, but also from a "communal and justified recognition." Ritualized, the grateful reception reserved for Battus, his descendants, and finally Arcesilas IV is transformed, as we return to the present, into honors addressed to a divinity. Thus *Pythian* 5 is dedicated to the *génos* of Battus in its entirety. The poem ends with the wish for an Olympic victory by the sovereign act of Zeus, thus projecting the historical time, once returned to the present of the narrative, into the future (118–23).

*

The legendary version of Cyrene's colonization presented in *Pythian* 5 complements the one developed in the fourth. For the purpose of praise, *Pythian* 4 made use of a narrative of the origins of a territory's foundational act as acted out by its human manipulators and its divine protectors. *Pythian* 5, celebrating the same victory, is centered upon the ascendance of a *génos* in conformity with a temporal movement and spatial course that organize the entire narrative of the poem. Certainly, in *Pythian* 4, the integration of the itinerary followed by the magical clod with the narrative of the Argonauts gave precise indications of the familial origins of Battus, and consequently also that of Arcesilas IV, the receiver of the ode. The course followed by the ancestors of Battus, from Sparta to Cyrene via Thera, indeed already found expression there. But in *Pythian* 5, this itinerary does not have the same point of origin. It is now Thebes, not Lemnos. Thanks to the mixed composition of their group, in this ode, the Aegids, founders of Thera and descendants of the Theban family of Oedipus, take the place occupied in *Pythian* 4 by the illegitimate descendants of the union of Euphemus and one of the murderous women of Lemnos.

Led by Theras, as we noted in discussing *Pythian* 4, the Aegid line represents the collateral branch of the double family of Heraclid origin that holds the royal power in Sparta. A matrilineal legitimacy is thus substituted, from the Spartan point of view, for the line's illegitimate origins. Theras, the founder of Thera, is only a Heraclid through his mother Argeia; through his father Autesion, he is the descendant of Polynices, the king of Thebes of Cadmeian ancestry.[94] Connecting, by stretching back in time, the *génos* of Arcesilas and Battus with the Theban and Labdacid origin of the other group of colonizers of Thera establishes a privileged relationship between the narrative and the place of origin of its author, and inserts this family into the age of heroes, in the manner of Hesiod, for example, in the *Works and Days*.

In fact, it is in the context of this insertion of the ascendance of the Cyrenaean sovereigns into the heroic age that we must understand not only the intervention of the Aegids but also the much-discussed mention of the Antenorids. In the Hesiodic "myth" of the ages of men, the family of heroes includes those who struggled to divide the flocks of Oedipus at Thebes and the warriors who died under the walls of Troy for the beauty of Helen. The Thebaid and the Trojan War correspond exactly, moreover, to the content of the heroic poems that formed the celebrated *Epic Cycle*.[95] It is no surprise, then, to find a legend concerning the Labdacid ancestors of the Cyrenaeans striving to attach the Libyan colony to the past of the Trojan War. By a clever play in space and time, Pindar manages to make coincide two perfectly distinct colonizing interventions, that of the Aegids, Lacedaemonians stemming from the family of Oedipus, and that of the Antenorids, Trojan descendants of the hospitable husband of Theano. This combination is accompanied, through the intervention of the Spartans, by movement from the Euphemian ancestors of Battus toward the colonists of Labdacid origin.

Does this mean that, prior to the arrival of the Theran descendants of the *génos* of Theras, led by Battus, Cyrene had been the object of Trojan colonization? That Greeks had already occupied the site of Cyrene in Mycenaean times? We can easily imagine that historians have succeeded in separating out what Pindar intended to confuse in order to reestablish the linearity of the legendary chronology, thus transforming it into history: first, in the thirteenth or twelfth century, the Trojans or another "Predorian" people, then, in the seventh, Battus and his Spartiate companions.[96] But an historicist hypothesis of this sort does not take account of the process of heroization prevalent from the beginning of the Archaic period. Every renascent city, beginning from the end of the eighth century, attempts to attach its present to Greece's legendary past.

By a twofold movement of memorial expression that tends to establish a bond of continuity between the political reality of the Archaic age and that of the heroic age, the traces left by the Mycenaean kingdoms, attested in monuments and epic poetry, become the places of ritual celebration of legendary figures, exalted as heroes. These heroes thus receive the honor of a double *mnêma*: a tomb, object of commemorative cult activity, and epic, song reactivating the memory of their heroic deeds.[97] As concerns Cyrene, the mention of a mount of the Antenorids attests to the existence of a cult of this type, rendered to the Trojan heroes of legend.[98]

4.2. Foundation and the Process of Heroization

In *Pythian 5*, the evocation of the Trojan Antenorids' stay on Cyrene moves directly into praise of Battus. By design, the song of praise leaves the date of his arrival in Libya in the uncertainty of the distant past. Battus is, above all, the founder of the city, its architect; he organizes its space in order to receive there the festivals of Apollo. But the line Battus imposes on the central axis of the city is revealed to be "autotelic." This Apollonian way leads, in fact, directly to the "stern" of the agora (*prumnoîs agorâs épi*), exactly where the tomb of the founder stands! Battus is a hero twice over: because he lived blessed among men (*mákar*, 94), that is to say, as a god; but also because he is now the object of cultic veneration by his people (*héros laosebés*, 95).[99]

The entire semantic articulation of the legend of Cyrene's foundation as presented in *Pythian 4* developed the theme of "autochthonous" generation on foreign soil destined to become Greek. *Pythian 9* was concerned with defining, essentially through the different figures implicated in the matrimonial transformation, the process of civilization of this land, as it slowly gave way to cultivation. *Pythian 5* now concentrates on the different heroic protagonists of the foundation and civilization of the land of Cyrene, in demonstrating the permanence the cult rendered to them confers on their figures.[100] The theme of heroization ensures the ode's semantic coherence.

Viewing the narrative from this angle clarifies the emphasis placed on the Aegid branch of the Theran founders of Cyrene instead of the Lemnian or Euphemian ones. By means of the Aegids, Battus and his colonists not only are discreetly attached to Thebes and the circumstances of the composition of the poem, but are also given a Heraclid ancestry. Indeed, innumerable ruling families in Greece claim Heraclid or Heraclean descent, attaching their authority to the Dorians or even the Achaeans. Apart from the three regions of the Peloponnese that can properly be called Heraclid, the great Corinthian aristocratic family of the Bacchiads

traces its origin to Aletes, a "Dorian" descendant five generations removed from Heracles. In Sicyon, the Dorian and Heraclid dynasty is
merely a substitute for a sovereign, Cacestades, whose ancestor is none
other than Heracles. On the islands, Tlepolemus, the founder of Rhodes
mentioned above, is a son of Heracles; he claimed to have been forced to
leave the continent under Heraclid pressure. The Catalog of Ships confers
a Heraclid ancestry, through the intermediary of Thessalus, on the founders of Cos. Perceptible from the age of the diffusion of Homeric epic in
the eighth century, this process of heroization continues through the
Classical period. Even at the margins of Greece, the king Candaules of
Lydia attached his *génos* to an eastern branch of the numerous descendants of Alcmene's son, and Alexander the First of Macedon, the Phil-
hellene, claimed descent from the Heraclid Temenus of Argos.[101]

In the Cyrenaean tradition evoked by Pindar, Heraclid ancestry is explicitly attached, through the intermediary of Theras and the Aegids, to
the figure of Aigimius and by consequence to the control exercised by the
Dorians over the Peloponnese (72).[102] This in no way excludes a second
lineage seeking to attach the colony to the Achaean and Trojan past of
Greece, especially since the mention of Trojan lineage is not explicitly
founded on a genealogical relationship. Pindar limits himself to inscribing
the arrival of the Antenorids at Cyrene in the context of a *nóstos*, a
"return," without indicating that the Trojans had founded a line in Libya.

Why Trojans rather than Greeks? Colonial Cyrene seems to share this
singular characteristic of the "Homeric" past with other cities situated at
the geographical boundaries of the Greek world. Samothrace claims Dardanus; Sarpedon, who fought on the side of the Trojans, is said to have
founded Miletus; at Salaminian Cyprus, from the fifth century on, the
descendants of Teucrus are confused with the Trojans.[103] Surely the Antenorids found an even warmer reception at Cyrene, because Antenor
distinguished himself from other Trojans by receiving the Greeks with the
honors due to them as guests. Reference to these descendants of Antenor
in *Pythian 5* is thus inscribed in the isotopy of hospitality; in parallel with
the isotopy developed through different figures of the hero on the theme
of heroization, it helps to ensure the semantic coherence of the entire
poem.[104] The heroes from Troy were, moreover, accompanied by Helen,
whose figure leads us back to the Spartan origins of certain of the colonists of the Greek city in Libya.

*

Pindar does not choose the Carneia from all the Cyrenaean festivals at
random to reinforce the genealogical and historical bond between the
city's present and Greece's heroic past. From ancient times, the Carneia

was the festival most characteristic of the Dorian cities. Imported by the Aegids, ancestors of Pindar and of the Greeks of Cyrene (74–76), and instituted in the city by the heroized oecist himself (89–93), the sacrifices of the Carneia were made in honor of the Antenorids (82–88). The rite's trajectory, with the temporal confusion it masks, is doubtless made possible by the duplicity of the legend that explains its institution. The celebration is either a ritual meant to expiate the involuntary murder of the divine Carnus, who accompanied the Heraclids in their conquest of the Peloponnese, or a rite seeking to appease the anger of Apollo, whose cornel-trees (*kráneiai*) were cut down to construct the Trojan horse. In addition, by seeing in Apollo Carneius the very expression of the *archegétes*, metaphorically incarnated in the figure of a ram and a leader of flocks, a recent reader of the Carneia has considered this festival the celebration par excellence of colonial activity and of foundation.[105]

The allusion to the return of the Heraclids and the parallel reference to the war of Troy that together present the double *aítion* of the Carneia aim to efface the chronological distinctions that *Pythian 5* as a whole strives to weaken. Under these conditions, we might ask whether Pindar does not subtly include within the Cyrenaean celebration of the Carneia the sacrifices of hospitality offered to the Antenorids (86) and the festival of the Apollonia promised by Battus (90).[106] In any case, there is every reason to think that, in the cultic reality of Classical Cyrene, the heroic cult rendered to the oecist, closely linked with Apollo in his colonizing and apotropaic (if not oracular) functions, coincided with the celebration of the Carneia, the greatest festival of cities with cultural ties to Sparta.[107]

Furthermore, the narrator of *Pythian 5* engages in subtle enunciative play that supports the likely coincidence of the celebration of the Carneia by the Cyrenaean descendants of the Aegids with the ritual of hospitality offered to the Antenorids. Though expressed as a singular *I* while revealing his bond of kinship with his "fathers" (*emoì patéres*, 76) the Aegids, the narrator-speaker becomes afterward a plural *we* that celebrates the festival in honor of Apollo *Carnéios* (*sebízomen*, 80) at Cyrene. While the *I* seems to refer to Pindar by reason of the Theban origin of the Aegids, on the other hand, the *we*, situated at Cyrene, refers to a choral group gathered to celebrate the Carneia, in particular by singing of the victory of Arcesilas IV, at the present moment. Pindar thus makes profitable use of the undifferentiated forms *I/we* employed in Archaic choral lyric to coincide, within the choral performance of *Pythian 5* at Cyrene, perhaps at the Carneia, with his own position as author of the ode and the position of the chorus invited to sing it.[108] This coincidence is confirmed in the preliminary definition of the narrator's function (*tò d'emón*, 72): to proclaim the glory of the Aegids, reference to whom, in this context, involves not their Theban ascendancy, but their colonial activity from Sparta to Thera. The Pindaric perspective is at once transformed into a Cyrenaean one.

We may press the question further whether the occasion of the performance of *Pythian 5* actually does correspond with the celebration of the Carneia.[109] The movement from a singular narrator to a plural locutor is also seen in the narrator-speaker's direct address to Arcesilas after the evocation of the celebration of his Battiad ancestors. The song performed by the young people (*en aoidâi néon*, 104), which the narrator-speaker advises Arcesilas to address to Apollo, is only an echo of the song (*mélos*) that the king of Cyrene has received as compensation for the occasional expenses of his Pythian victory. This song of praise is itself undertaken by the narrator in person (*legómenon eréo*, 108). This is again the situation that allows the use of the present in the form *sebízomen* (80): the honors paid to the city of Cyrene in the context of a banquet dedicated to Apollo *Carneîos* probably also include the ritual glorification of Arcesilas IV on the occasion of the (choral) singing of *Pythian 5*, if not celebration of the hospitality offered to the Antenorids or the cultic acts consecrated to the founding hero Battus.

Whatever the case may be, the heroization of Battus and his successor kings of Cyrene is achieved through a double reference, to Heraclid ancestry and to the heroes of the Trojan War. This process of heroization, achieved by means of both reference to the heroic past and acts of cult, left its traces in the spatial organization of the city of Cyrene, in the form of the tomb of Battus, vestiges of which have been recovered at the very spot Pindar indicated "at the stern of the agora" (93), and perhaps the hill of the Antenorids.[110] The circular temporal path sketched by the gallery of portraits Pindar puts on display in *Pythian 5* and the spatial reciprocity of relationships established between Cyrene and the Greek continent have as their goal to make Arcesilas IV benefit from the cultic and legendary heroization of the founder of the colony. While awaiting the ability to be represented at the Olympian games and to be compared to Zeus with his sovereign qualities, Arcesilas IV, the victor at the Pythian games and the addressee of *Pythian 5*, appears with the traits of a second Apollo through the intermediary of his ancestor Battus, the founder of Cyrene. In this ode, the superposition of heroic destinies attached to the city of Cyrene has replaced the play of metaphorical echoes among multiple interconnected isotopies. In this way, the poem gains it strong pragmatic dimension and function.

5. Herodotus and the Chronology of History

The same heroic vision is pervasive throughout a foundation narrative in prose almost contemporary with Pindar's *Pythian 5*. After having narrated Darius' difficulties in his expedition against the Scythians in the north, as a symmetrical counterpart Herodotus turns to the south to examine the events that determined history there in the same period. The expedition of the Persian governor of Egypt, sent against Barce at the request of the mother of Arcesilas IV, allows Herodotus once again to employ the twofold perspective, "historical" and ethnographic, of his *Histories*.

5.1. Convergent Genealogical Lines

An exhaustive history of the installation of the Greeks in a land they believed to be a third continent precedes a long description of the peoples of Libya. We find here all the stages dispersed in the fractured narratives of Pindar ordered in a linear chronological succession. The narrative of the foundation of Cyrene is now situated in the perspective of the history of Sparta. Herodotus employs this technique of synchronization in his material even if it leaves occasional inconsistencies in his narrative.[111] We recall that in the legend, two genealogical lines converge at Sparta to form the mixed contingent sent to colonize Thera. These two lineages — Minyans on the one hand, Aegids on the other — are clearly distinguished in the Herodotean history of the antecedents of the Greek expedition to Cyrene.[112] This first part of Herodotus' narrative is all the more compatible with our modern conception of history because it is cleansed of all divine intervention. Motivation of the narrative action is to be found among men, more particularly among men moved by political considerations.

First, there are the grandchildren of the Argonauts and the women of Lemnos, driven from the island by the Pelasgians (situation of *lack*). The exiles seek refuge at Sparta where they lay claim to their Minyan roots (phases of *manipulation* and *competence*) in order to demand from the Lacedaemonians the rights of the city, allowing their cohabitation with the citizens, access to political functions, assignment of land lots, and repartition into the tribes. The Spartans' acceptance (*performance*), in the name of the active role taken by the Dioscuri in the expedition of the Argonauts, is sanctioned by an exchange of women. The descendants of the Minyans marry the citizens' daughters while the Lemnian women are given in marriage to Spartans.[113] But the Minyans do not rest there. Dissatisfied with merely obtaining citizens' rights, they make demands for the royalty, normally reserved for the two dynasties descended from the Heraclids. Their inordinate demands land them in prison (rupture of the contract and of the narrative equilibrium), but a *performance* reversing the terms of the matrimonial exchange saves them from incarceration: after a scene of nocturnal travesty, the wives

of the Minyans, daughters of the most prominent Spartan citizens, take
their husbands' places in prison, and the Minyans regain their marginal
position on the savage spurs of Taygetus (new situation of *lack*).

These events coincide chronologically with the (voluntary) marginal-
ization of another clan, whose members, though possessing the rights of
the city, are not authorized to assume royal power. The Theban descent
of this family nonetheless brings it closer to the two ruling families of
Sparta. As has been shown, their representative, Theras, the descendant
of Polynices in the fifth generation, is the maternal uncle of the two
Heraclid ancestors of the Spartan royal families.[114] After having ensured
the kingship, Theras chooses exile on Calliste-Thera, reasonable enough
since the island, as Pindar also recounts, was colonized by Cadmus, the
founder of Thebes, eight generations before. For Theras, as for the Minyans of Lemnos who take refuge in the Taygetus, the exile on Calliste is
a return to his own without setting foot in the land of his ancestors.
This common destiny allows a portion of the Minyans to follow Theras
and the Spartan citizens he chooses in converging on the neighboring
island, which then takes the name of its second founder. Only then can
the son of Theras, remaining in Sparta, found the family of the Aegids,
whose members take the name of his son, Aigeus, Theras' grandson. We
notice that Pindar, through the process of heroization he puts in play in
Pythian 5, did not hesitate to anticipate in some way this familial denomination. At Sparta, the position of this influential family will remain
for the most part marginal, marked by the malediction that comes to
weigh on its various representatives.[115]

5.2. Two Foundational Plots

Compelled to begin from the destinies of these two lineages, the history
of Thera in the Herodotean narrative is, from this point on, confused
with the preliminaries of the legend of the foundation of Cyrene.[116]
Nonetheless, the narrative of the actual colonization is separated from
that of the preliminaries of the Theran expedition to Libya by a strong
enunciative intervention. In fact, up to the occupation of Thera-Santorini by the Minyan and Lacedaemonian ancestors of the future colonizers of Cyrene, the *lógos* to which Herodotus refers is homogenous:
"The Lacedaemonians tell (*légousi*) the same story as the Therans." But
when he speaks of the colonial enterprise itself, the historian is forced to
make reference to two divergent versions. The narrator of one is identified with the people of Thera, the other with Cyrenaean informers. Beginning with the explanation of the colonists' motives for their depar-

ture, each of the two narratives forms an autonomous whole, open to the semionarrative approach.

We start with the Theran version. It begins with a significant absence. The phase of *manipulation* and of the contract between the *Sender* and the *Subject* of the action is not provoked by a habitual situation of *lack*. Instead, the Pythia at Delphi invites the people of Thera to found a city in Libya on the occasion of a sacrifice and consultation of the oracle on unrelated questions. The elderly king Grinnus, a descendant of the Lacedaemonian Theras, unwittingly designates Battus, of Minyan descent, to respond to this unexpected invitation. The phase of *manipulation* of the foundation narrative is thus marked by an early diversion of the narrative progression.

In reaching a conclusion that coincides with the Cyrenaean narrative, the Theran *lógos*, beginning with this first oracle, assumes the canonical narrative schema three times over, with different realizations in each case. It is thus articulated in three connected sequences.

The first prophecy transmits to the Therans both duty (*devoir*) and knowledge (*savoir*): these are the two modalities implied in the sense of the verb *khráomai* ("to make known by an oracular order") employed here by Herodotus. The prophecy corresponds to the phase of *manipulation* of the Theran version's first narrative sequence. It positions Apollo as *Sender*, through the intermediary of the Pythia, of the Therans, *Subject* of the narrative action. They are represented by their king, who at once delegates his power over the action ordained by the oracle to the future oecist Battus. We have mentioned that this delegation is involuntary. Bereft of precise content, it is moreover combined with only partial knowledge (*savoir*), since the Pythia indicates the general direction of the colony, but not the means necessary to reach it. Equipped with a duty (*devoir*) and partial knowledge (*savoir*), but deprived of capability (*pouvoir*), the *competence* of the hero would not be able to materialize without some will (*vouloir*). Stemming from a *manipulation* insufficient on both cognitive and practical levels, this *competence* cannot lead to a *performance*. What is more, the *sanction*, which is a consequence of the fault of the action, is immediate: for seven years Thera suffers a drought that withers all its trees, save for one. The phase of *sanction* of this first narrative sequence thus ends by presenting an echo of the absence of narrative "lack" noted at the beginning of the narrative.

From here the initial narrative program is reiterated in a double sequence. A new consultation with the first *Sender*, through the intermediary of the Pythia, leads to an analogous response. Next a secondary and subordinate program is engaged, in the course of which the Therans themselves take the position of *Sender*. A fisherman from Crete

supplies them with the knowledge (*savoir*) and capability (*pouvoir*) they
lack. Corobius from Itanus is capable of this, since, blown off course by
unfavorable winds, he came to land on the coast of Libya or, more
exactly, on the nearby island of Plataea. So again chance marks the start
of this second narrative sequence. The *sanction*, projected into the future, of this new (delegated) *Subject*, whose knowledge (*savoir*) and capability (*pouvoir*) are required, is material recompense. Possessing the
necessary competence, the action of the *Sender* of this secondary contract (the Therans) and that of its *Subject* (the Cretan Corobius) finally
coincide. We can recover from here the thread of the principal narrative
program. Some Therans finally leave for Libya, assimilating the *competence* of the Cretan fisherman, who is invited to accompany them. And
so we finally reach Plataea.

The phase of *performance* is also doubled. Corobius is abandoned on
the island by the Therans, who eagerly depart to announce their pleasant discovery to their compatriots (knowledge [*savoir*] and capability
[*pouvoir*] acquired). In a second and subordinate narrative program,
Samian seamen replace the people of Thera by supplying the solitary
fisherman with his promised material support. From here, proleptically,
comes a new secondary *sanction* marked by the gratitude that the
Therans, and in particular the future Cyrenaeans, have for the people of
Samos. After this withdrawal of the *performance* on the cognitive level,
the *competence* of the Therans as *Subject* of the action is finally fully
constituted, realized in the completion of the second narrative sequence.
To the duty (*devoir*) inspired by Apollo, and to the capability (*pouvoir*)
and knowledge (*savoir*) transmitted by Corobius and recovered by the
first colonists, is now added the will (*vouloir*) of the community of the
island's citizens to make the decision to found a colony. They delegate
their capability (*pouvoir*) and knowledge (*savoir*) to a new hero, Battus.
Named leader and king, Battus embarks with two ships and men chosen
by lot (again the role of chance) from each of the seven *khôrai* of the
island, and sets out for Plataea. He thus provides the first realization of
the command of the Delphic god.

*

At the moment the Theran narrative is about to attain its *sanction*, it
becomes confused with the Cyrenaean story, which has reached its second narrative sequence after a different beginning. Following the *lógos*
of Herodotus, we shall trace this second version up to the point of its
coincidence with the Theran version.

The narrator first attracts the reader's attention by noting the divergence of the two narratives he recounts. Since the difference involves the origins attributed to the oecist Battus, it concerns qualities of one of the actors who occupy the actantial position of *Subject* of the narrative. Set at the beginning of the narrative, it is expressed through a subordinated program. In the Cyrenaean version, instead of being the descendant of the Minyans who colonized Thera-Santorini with the Lacedaemonians led by Theras, Battus is the son of a citizen of the island and his concubine, the daughter of the king of a small city in Crete (Oaxus). The young girl was saved from the machinations of her stepmother by a rich Theran merchant. Battus is thus born a bastard, and, as indicated by the meaning attributed to his name (from the verb *battarízein*), he comes into the world with a stutter.

At the beginning of this secondary narrative program, it is precisely his stammering that leads Battus to consult the oracle at Delphi. The Pythia's response transforms what should be the moment of *sanction* of this subordinate narrative into a phase of *manipulation* of the Cyrenaean version of Greek colonial activity in Libya. Playing, according to the narrator, on the double meaning of *báttos* — a stammerer in Greek, but a king in Libyan — the oracle designates the illegitimate Theran with the speech impediment as the *Subject* of a colonial enterprise to Libya. The pertinence, from the perspective of the Cyrenaean version, of this direct designation of Battus as colonizer (*oikistér*) is clear: it focuses the narrative action, from its start, on the figure of the oecist. Thus we have Apollo as *Sender*, through the intermediary of the (perhaps) polysemic prophecy of the Pythia, and Battus, the stuttering king, as *Subject*. But while, as in the Theran version, he imposes a duty (*devoir*), the *Sender* does not confer either the capability (*pouvoir*) (except in the sense implied by the interpretation the narrator gives for the oecist's name) or the knowledge (*savoir*) necessary to develop the *competence* of the *Subject* so designated into a desire (*vouloir*), and consequently into a *performance*. At the conclusion of this first narrative sequence in the Cyrenaean version, again a negative *sanction* results from the absence of action, as a calamity falls upon Battus and the Therans.

From here, as in the Theran narrative, *lack* engages a new narrative sequence. In its phase of *manipulation*, the Pythia is again consulted. This time, she adds to a response similar to that of the first oracle the exact destination of the prescribed enterprise: Cyrene. The transmission of this knowledge (*savoir*) by the *Sender* of the action avoids the detour to Crete (already acknowledged in the secondary narrative on Battus' origin!). The Therans at once decide to send Battus to the Cyrenaica with two penteconters.

This action, in its own way, also shares in the reverse movement seen in the Theran version. Here, it is realized by the return of the islanders designated as colonists, and the repeated injunction of the Therans, now accompanied by the violent threat of stoning, to return and establish the colony in Libya all the same. The *manipulation* of the *Subject* by the divine Apollo takes the form, through the intervention of the people of Thera, of a veritable constraint (*anagkazómenoi*). Battus and his companions thus definitively leave Santorini and found a first colony on the island of Plataea. Before rejoining the Theran narrative at this point of coincidence, we should note that the will (*vouloir*) of the Therans takes over the duty (*devoir*) imposed by the Delphic god. This anticipates the doubling of the action that will be seen to occur within the second narrative sequence. The Cyrenaean version thus marks a sharper separation between Therans and future Cyrenaeans, while erasing the friendship destined to bind the people of Samos with those of Thera and Cyrene.

The Theran and Cyrenaean versions then rejoin in the *sanction* of their respective second narrative sequences. After two years' sojourn on the island of Plataea, the colony remains a failure. The situation of the Theran emigrés is still one of hardship. This signifies that the narrative has not yet realized the primary condition of its existence: a transformation of state.[117]

This new situation of *lack* introduces the third narrative sequence of the two convergent versions. Again, it begins with the consultation at Delphi of the *Sender* of the colonial enterprise. Through the Pythia, Apollo again makes reference to (partial) knowledge (*savoir*) originally transmitted but wrongly interpreted by the people of Thera. The colonists must set foot on the continent of Libya itself, not on an island. Encouraged by this precision concerning the content of their *competence*, without returning to Thera, and merely stopping at Plataea to pick up the lone guarantor they had left there, they establish a colony at Aziris, on the Libyan coast facing the island. After a stay of seven years in this forested spot bathed by a river, the Greeks find a new *Sender* in the Libyans themselves. The natives take over the work of the Delphic god by leading the Theran colonists, while carefully neglecting to show them the most beautiful part of their country, to a place they claim is superior to Aziris. Finally the Greeks reach the future site of Cyrene, near the spring of Apollo. Thus it is an indigenous *Sender* who pronounces the *sanction* of the action finally brought to its conclusion. In this place, the "pierced sky" will ensure for the Greeks the rain the god had deprived the people of Thera of for seven years. The water provided by Apollo's spring and by the perforation of the sky, a guarantee of prosperity, answers to the drought that sanctioned the first narrative sequence of the story. We will return to this second narrative *sanction*.

5.3. The Establishment of Political Time

Fundamentally, the version of the metropolis and the version of the colony answer to the same narrative structure. They are marked by the same triple repetition of the canonical schema, and engaged by an identical *Sender*. The two legends differ, however, in their individual focus. This focus is realized in particular by the specific figures that place the actors on the scene in each narrative, and is thus essentially manifested on the plane of actorialization.

In the Theran version, we have seen that the people of the island replace the god as *Sender* and in part take in their own hands the establishment of their own *competence* as colonists. They go to Crete in search of the knowledge (*savoir*) and, to an extent, the capability (*pouvoir*) they lack. Only at the beginning of the secondary program do they designate Battus as the leader of their colonial expedition. On the other hand, the Cyrenaean narrative first sets the action in motion by means of a chosen founder of the colony. From here, this version follows with the integration of the entire story of the illegitimate origin of the oecist and future king of Cyrene. The Theran narrative is content merely to mention in passing his Minyan descent, passing over his Lacedaemonian roots entirely. While attributing to Battus the same father as the Theran narrative, the Cyrenaean version gives Battus a mother of Cretan descent, as we have seen. In the *lógos* of Herodotus, the Theran version is inscribed within the narrative of the legendary foundation of Thera by the Lacedaemonians and Minyans (4.145–49); the Cyrenaean version, on the other hand, seeks to begin the "history" of the colony at the moment of the intervention of the oecist hero. These divergent emphases, on the Therans in one version, and on the figure of the oecist in the other, clearly distinguish these two narratives from each other. This divergence is underscored by the different interventions of the Therans on the occasion of the first colonizer-explorers' return: a favorable reception in one case, but prohibition from landing and lapidation in the other.

The Theran and Cyrenaean versions are also distinguished, from the point of view of the semionarrative process of spatialization, by the crisscrossed courses defined by each of them:

(a) Thera — Delphi — Thera — Crete — Plataea — Cyrene, for the first;

(b) Crete — Thera — Delphi — Thera — Plataea — Aziris — Cyrene, for the second.

The Cretan stage of the first narrative is integrated into the second through the subordinated history of the oecist's origin. In the Cyrenaean version, the destiny of Phronime, the mother of Battus, is a substitute for the secondary program involving the fisherman Corobius in the Theran narrative. This inversion, doubled by a substitution, also contributes to the two narratives' different focal points in terms of spatialization. The Cyrenaean narrative is in fact focused on a center different from that of the Theran narrative.[118]

In spite of these actorial and spatial differences, the two narrative actions, each engaged by Apollo, both conclude by finally installing the colonists on the banks of a spring consecrated to the Delphic god. They thus establish an essential polarity between Delphi and Cyrene, on simultaneously spatial and religious levels. In doing so, the two versions of the legend are surprisingly close to other narratives of colonization. Though a systematic comparative and contrastive analysis is not possible here, comparison with other narratives of foundations of colonies shows the particular strength of the versions transmitted by Herodotus, while allowing us to pass from the plane of semionarrative syntax to that of semantics.

*

The syntactic analogies connecting these two politicized versions of the foundation of Cyrene with the narrative of the foundation of Tarentum, another Spartan colony, are striking. The latter narrative, also going back to a fifth-century source, attributes the sending of colonists to Tarentum to dissension between the Spartan citizens and the Partheniae.[119] Whether these were the sons of Spartan traitors and thus reduced to the status of helots, or the descendants of illegitimate unions between Spartan women and unmarried men, they constitute a group denied the rights of the city by the Spartans. Their position is closer still to that of the Minyans in the Theran and Cyrenaean narratives of foundation, because their aborted attempt at rebellion takes place outside Sparta, at Amyclae; the conquest of Amyclae was the prerogative not of the Heraclids, but of Timomachus, a Theban belonging to the famous *génos* of the Aegids![120]

Next, in the absence of an intermediate stage equivalent to Thera, the leader of the Partheniae, like Battus, consults the oracle at Delphi. The Pythia advises the Spartan to emigrate to "rich" Tarentum. Like the Theran colonists in Libya, the Partheniae are welcomed to Magna Graecia by the native population. But they also find there the Cretans, who arrived in heroic times, at the time of the arrival of the Antenorids at Cyrene. Unlike the Herodotean narrative of the foundation of Cyrene, however, the Tarentine legend contains the theme of autochthony. The Tarentines find a second oecist in the figure of the native Phalanthus, the founding hero whose negative Parthenine qualities are transformed at Tarentum into the positive features of a true Spartan hero. Taras, on the other hand, the eponymous hero of the city, was believed to be the son of Poseidon and a local nymph.[121] In its different versions, the legend of the foundation of Tarentum thus manages to integrate within its narrative not only the complementarity of the foundational activity of Poseidon and Apollo, but also the theme of autochthony. In the first Pindaric version of the foundation legend of Cyrene, autochthony is figured in the manipulation of the clod by Poseidon and his human representatives, gradually aided by Apollo. Is this to say that the narrative of the foundation of Tarentum leads us figuratively toward what we would consider the realm of "legend," while Herodotus is concerned with "rationalizing" the two versions of the foundation of Cyrene that his *lógos* relates? Can comparison of the two groups of narratives define the division between myth and history?

Certainly in Herodotus there is no marvelous clod engulfed by waves and reappearing transformed into an island, no nymph huntress kidnapped by a traveling god to found a Greek city, no descendants of the heroes of the Trojan War to prepare the ground for colonial enterprise. Herodotus' silence on the subject of the clod received by Euphemus does not stop the historian from acknowledging the Argonauts' forced stay in Libya. But the version he presents within his description of Lake Triton only mentions the exchange of the tripod Jason means to bring to Delphi for the information transmitted by Triton; this gift is presented as a sign of the numerous future Greek foundations in Libya.[122] But as far as the narrative of the foundation of Cyrene is concerned, there appears to be an attempt to construct a new type of discourse, answering to two of the criteria we commonly associate with historical narrative: the construction of a precise chronology and the development of politically active protagonists, who act among peoples or in governments.

In terms of chronology, the Herodotean narrative attempts to fill in the gaps left by those of Pindar. The methods of nascent historiography contribute here; he counts generations along with their corollary genealogies and, when possible, counts years. Synchronized reckoning of generations contributes to the coherence of the narrative. Minyan refugees at Sparta and Lacedaemonians led by Theras can converge on Calliste since the former are descendants of the Argonauts after two generations, the latter from Polynices after four generations, and the island of Thera was colonized by the Cadmeans eight generations earlier. On Thera, the computation of years takes over: seven years of drought after the first oracle, two years at Plataea, seven at Aziris, then to Cyrene where Battus reigns for forty years, thus beginning a new reckoning that follows the number of years of each king's reign over the colony. The system adopted by Herodotus thus conforms to the chronological model used in Attica in the fourth century, first according to the succession of reigns of the (legendary) kings of Athens, calculated in generations, then the list of eponymous archons, computed annually, beginning in 683/682 B.C.[123]

The narrated time (*temps raconté*) thus follows the rhythm of the narration, and thus the spoken time (*temps énoncé*) points the reader to the time of enunciation (*temps de l'énonciation*). This coincidence at least gives the appearance, through chronological measurement, of the construction of historical time, of a historiographical type of temporal configuration. On the other hand, Herodotus gives no indication of the temporal distance separating the arrival of Theras on Santorini and the first oracle given to his descendant, the king Grinnus. Consequently, there is no reference to the chronological data given in Pindar's *Pythian* 4: seventeen generations between Euphemus and Battus, and eight generations between the founder and the moment of the poem's performance, coinciding with the reign of Arcesilas IV. In Herodotus, this lacuna corresponds precisely to the transition from the Spartan narrative to what is, properly speaking, the narrative of the foundation of Cyrene, in its two versions. Historiography that conducts us to the present seems to have reasons not shared by legendary narratives. . .

5.4. The Metaphorical Figures of Political Activity

The protagonists themselves — kings of Sparta, sovereigns of Thera, or leaders of colonial expeditions — act politically among the people they direct, granting the rights to the city or establishing their power over new territories. Based on authority established by genealogy, their activity is a matter of civic order. But there are subtleties, as well. The political isotopy traversing the entire narrative of Herodotus is so strong that the narrator does not hesitate to depart from his normal enunciative prudence when discussing Battus' name. As they tell it (*légousi*), Therans and Cyrenaeans agree in relating the name of the founding hero to a stammer that was apparent from the time the boy took his name. But the narrator-speaker offers a preferable interpretation (*hos egò dokéo*, 4.155.1). Meaning "king" in the indigenous language, the name Battus could only have been adopted at the moment of the future founding hero's arrival in Libya, unless (the narrator prudently adds) it had already been suggested by the Pythia; in giving her answer she would have made known the royal status Delphi foresaw for the Theran pilgrim. Battus, a "stutterer" in Greek, becomes in Libyan a "king." To a question about speech, the Pythia thus responds with a bilingual play on words. In this way, the narrator finally comes to accept a political explanation that concludes by falling under the power of Apollo's knowledge.[124]

We should recall on this point that in *Pythian* 4 the oracle at Delphi transforms Battus' question on his stammering voice into a response that, in three parts, installs him as a "predestined king" (59–63). The Herodotean *lógos*, for its part, does not inscribe the transformation of the stutterer into a sovereign only in his name by placing it under Delphic control. Instead, through the play of translation, the narrative creates a type of indigenous acknowledgment out of this political transformation. Battus' insertion into the land of Libya no longer operates through the figure of the "autochthonous" clod, nor through his marriage to a native woman, but through a linguistic figure with political import. In a similar fashion, Pindar projects on the political isotopy one of the essential figurative transformations through which the colonizing activity of Battus is manifested. In *Pythian 5*, Apollo provides Battus with a voice that, "coming from across the sea" (59), terrifies the lions infesting the site of Cyrene. In this way, the oracle of the Delphic god is realized, while Pindar silences its pejorative allusion to the founder's stammering. What the nymph Cyrene achieved in the post-Pindaric tradition through her athletic struggle, Battus obtains through the effect of his voice, recovered in its full force. Whether by the athletic deed of a woman, as in Callimachus, or by the effects of a masculine voice, as in Pindar, to extirpate the lions that infest the area of Cyrene is, as we have noted, to introduce Greek civilization to Libya. The association of Battus with the struggle against the lions of Libya is similar to the spatial displacement of the nymph Cyrene's hunting (from Thessaly to Cyrene) that serves to civilize the territory of the indigenous king Eurypylus.[125] But on this narrative level, in expressing the theme of passage to civilization, Herodotus prefers to abandon the animal isotopy in order to express the same transformation through the intermediary of a royal figure, developed on the political isotopy. Stammerer and bastard, Battus becomes in Cyrene a strong-voiced sovereign. Through the intervention of the Pythia and the linguistic play, the *lógos* of Herodotus ensures a legitimacy from both the Panhellenic and the indigenous perspectives. The vocal figures with which Herodotus fills his narrative refer us once more to the theme of establishment of Greek civilization through the political figure of sovereignty.

The version of the transformation of Battus' voice given by Pausanias, though of a late date, is still of interest. Describing the statue of the founding hero mounted on a chariot the Cyrenaeans dedicated at Delphi, he recounts the following narrative (*légetai*): having arrived at

the borders of the *khóra* of Cyrene, the stammering hero found himself
face to face with a lion in this still-deserted region; terrified by the sight,
he let out a cry that restored his voice, clear and strong. Surprisingly,
the story, heard by Pausanias at Delphi itself, removes Apollo's influence
over the vocal transformation of the founding hero, instead attributing
it to a natural cause. The same is true, in fact, of the fourth-century
foundation narrative told by Acesandrus, the historian of Cyrene. After
having shifted the combat of the nymph Cyrene with the lion from
Thessaly to Libya, where the nymph thus earns the royal power offered
by Eurypylus, the historian maintains that Battus' trembling voice returned to him of its own accord (*apò tautomátou*). The founder then
becomes a man skilled in speaking as a rhetor is (*anèr rhetorikós*) and a
man distinguished by his capacity for counsel.[126] And when Callimachus, in the *Hymn to Apollo*, installs Battus in Cyrene, as discussed
above, he not only discreetly describes him as *oûlos*, "intact" or "vig-
orous" (an adjective often used for a voice!), but he abandons the
proper name that evokes the stammer, calling him instead *Aristotéles*.
Several centuries later, it only remains for Plutarch to explain that beyond the stammering and the weakness of voice about which Battus
inquired, the god of Delphi recognized, in sending Battus as a founder
to Libya, the qualities of a king: political prowess and a man of spirit![127]

Among the many figures assumed by the theme of transition from
savagery to civilization through the effects of colonization, Herodotus'
narrative forgoes nuptials; it also passes over silently the figurative development of the foundation as a birth from the depths of the earth
through the intermediary of the theme of "autochthonous" generation.
Instead this narrative of the foundation of Cyrene is centered on the
person of the oecist. This contributes to the politicizing of the narrative
by insisting as much on his genealogical ancestry as on the figure of the
transformation of his innate defect. We should note here that both marginal ancestry and physical handicap readily characterize colonial and
political founding figures in other narratives. In addition to the Partheniae, the illegitimate sons of Spartan women and the founders of
Tarentum, we could add the lame Medon, who becomes the first archon-king in Athens after the sedition incited by the death of Codrus. If
we consider establishment of tyrannies instead of the foundation of entirely new centers of power, we could mention the partially illegitimate
and deformed origin of Cypselus of Corinth, or the flat feet attributed
to Pittacus, the *aisumnétes* of Lesbos. But we also should not forget the
recommendation made to the Spartans not to have a lame king, or the
obligation of the deformed Battus III of Cyrene to cede his political
power to the people after the adoption of a new constitution. As concerns illegitimacy, note that legend also makes the founder of Lesbos,
Penthilus, the son of the extramarital union of Orestes and Erigone

(herself a product of the illegitimate love of Clytemnestra and Ae-gisthus).[128] Political power, when conferred on one marked by a physical handicap and by an illegitimate ascent, rests, in general, on ambiguous and unstable authority.

In the Herodotean narrative of the foundation of Cyrene, the political transformation of the handicap is under Delphic control. But before examining the heart of the *lógos* recalled by Herodotus, we should ex-amine another (unfortunately incomplete) foundation narrative, that of Croton. This narrative is also structured in three sequences, describing first the future founder's lack of reaction when faced with a response from Delphi, then his desire to found a colony in a location other than that designated by the Pythia, and finally the definitive establishment of Croton. In this narrative, known only from a late source, the Pythia's response inviting the colonial enterprise has only a very indirect connec-tion to the question posed: the hunchback Myscellus will only gain a legitimate descendant — the object of his inquiry — on the condition that he found a colony "in the beautiful fields of Croton." For the fecundity of the man, the oracle at Delphi substitutes the fertility of the soil, in a metaphoric play already familiar from the version of Cyrene's founda-tion transmitted in *Pythian* 9.[129] Another version of the same Crotonian legend stresses the initial motivating role of Apollo, who places a spon-taneous response in the Pythia's mouth, before any inquiry whatsoever. *Pythian* 4 (60), as well as the famous inscription known as the *Agree-ment of the Founders*, interprets the first oracle given to Battus in ex-actly the same fashion: use of the terms *autómatos* and *automatízein*, respectively, designates in a technical manner the spontaneous nature of the Delphic prophecy, previous to any question on the consultant's part concerning any sort of colonial enterprise.[130] In narrative terms, this places the expedition of colonial foundation entirely in the hands of the Delphic oracle and its god.

This brief comparison with other foundation narratives shows how much the *lógos* of Herodotus, with its two interconnected versions, re-mains dependent upon symbolic narrative manifestations incited by the need to legitimate the colonial enterprises of the Archaic period. We have confirmed the political character of the isotopy that traverses the Herodotean narrative, focused on the theme of the establishment of au-thority (*pouvoir*). We may now address the motivation of the narrative action, and consequently the role played by the Delphic oracle.

5.5. The Role of Divinity: Myth or History?

If we take into account the semionarrative *manipulation*, it is apparent that in Herodotus' *lógos* the Theran and Cyrenaean versions of the

colonial foundation are sharply distinguished from the narrative with
Lacedaemonian precedents. While the divinity is absent from the first
portion of the narrative, it comes to influence, as *Sender*, the entire
development of the colonial enterprise. Battus is led to Libya by Delphic
Apollo, the *arkhegétes* god, the god leader and founder.

It is precisely in the injunctions addressed to the civic actors by
Apollo, through interposed oracles, that the figure of the fertility
of Cyrenaean soil and the pastoral activity it permits can reemerge.
Apollo, and then the native people, lead the Greek colonists to Libya,
which "nourishes flocks" (*melotróphos*, 4.155.3 and 4.157.2), Aziris,
bathed by a river and "with beautiful dales" (*nápai kállistai*, 4.157.3),
and finally to Cyrene, with its spring and its "pierced sky" (4.158.3).[131]
The Greeks will find in Libya, as in their own country, a land watered
by rain clouds, not, as in Egypt, irrigated by the flooding of a river. Herodotus' Egyptians are themselves quite aware of this opposition: the
Greeks must await their water from Zeus. Arrian, the historian and
pupil of Epictetes in the second century A.D., still sees in Cyrene a land
that is "grassy, soft, and rich in water" amid a Libya reduced to a desert, while Strabo praises the qualities of the territory of Cyrene, a land
that favors the raising of horses and produces particularly excellent
fruits. Herodotus himself concludes his long ethnographic journey
through Libya by remarking that, contrary to Europe or Asia, the continent is not blessed with fertile land. The *Kurenaíe khóre*, however, is an
exception, for in its different regions, it allows for three successive har-
vests; the period of the *ópora*, which includes the maturation and har-
vesting of fruits, extends over eight whole months.[132] This abundance,
blessing a country located at the fringes of the world, evokes the Greek
image of the Golden Age.

In contemplating the connection between the figurative level of the
foundation narrative and its syntactic articulation, we can note moreover that in contrast with the fecundity of the earth promised by Delphi, the Greeks often placed a situation of *aphoría*, shortage, at the
origin of colonial enterprises. For example, it was due to a famine that
the people of Chalcis consulted the oracle that advised them to decimate
their citizens and consecrate them to Delphi. From Delphi, these men
chosen by lot reached Magna Graecia and founded the colony of Rhegium. They were led there by an oracle whose sexual allusions required
an interpretation in agricultural terms.[133] From a narrative point of view,
in the legend of the foundation of Rhegium, the shortage (famine) creates the situation of *lack* motivating the consultation at Delphi. On the
other hand, in the Theran version of the foundation of Cyrene, the
seven-year drought that scorches all the trees on the island save one is
presented as the consequence of the Cyrenaeans' deafness to the first

oracle given to Grinnus (4.150.4–5). The Cyrenaean version merely mentions the hardships suffered by the Therans following Battus' refusal to obey the oracle's bidding him to colonize Libya (4.155.4–5). This narrative inversion accentuates the role of Delphi in the transformation of an arid land oppressed by drought into one of well-watered soil, favorable for cultivation.

If the two narratives agree from the point of view of spatialization, in the structure of their reiteration of the colonial activity through a preliminary passage on an island they also inevitably evoke a stopover in the voyages of Odysseus in the *Odyssey*. In fact, the transitory stay on the island of Plataea, "equal in area to the city of Cyrene" in the time of Herodotus (4.156.3 and 4.151.3), recalls Odysseus' stay on the island of the wild goats before his arrival at the land of the Cyclopes. An uncultivated land opposite that of Polyphemus and his fellow Cyclopes, where the companions of Odysseus enjoy the hunt, this island nevertheless potentially has all the qualities of a territory, favorable to the development of civilization, that could lend itself to Greek colonization. With its well-irrigated and soft prairies, its natural ports, and its spring of clear water, the rich soil there could be productive of bountiful crops. In a word, the island of the goats in the *Odyssey*, favored by the fertile moisture of its soil (like Cyrene), is *euktiméne*; it is worthy of being exploited and cultivated.[134] What the oracles promise to the Therans sent to Libya is a type of access, once more, to the Golden Age, in a wondrous country on the borders of the world.

In this way, the figures the narrative sets in play through the human protagonists of the action are articulated according to a political isotopy that penetrates the entire history of Cyrene. Alternately, the activity of the god as *Sender* of men introduces vegetal and animal figures that inscribe the theme of civilization into the narrative. Through the voice of the oracles inspired by the Delphic god, the political narrative recovers the metaphorical dimension of a land's transformation into a productive territory, organized by Greek culture.

*

The two narratives of the foundation of Cyrene recounted by Herodotus thus transfer the greater part of the metaphorical and symbolic speculations of the Pindaric versions onto the political level. What if we then return to the question posed earlier about the *Iliad* and *Odyssey* in an attempt to define the modern category of myth: myth, legend, folktale, or history? The repeated interventions of Apollo as *Sender* lead us to the first of these concepts, the heroic past of the grandparents of Theras toward the second, the anecdote on the Cretan origin of Battus toward the third, and the political situation that motivates the action at the moment of landing in Libya toward the fourth — history, as we currently understand the term. Still, an antiquarian historian of the second century B.C., after having likely read Herodotus, seems to have made his choice without the slightest hesitation. The local historian Menecles of Barce, the author of the *Libukaì Historíai*, knows, in fact, the version that motivates the foundation by means of the oracle on the subject of Battus' voice. But he prefers, instead of this, one that places *stásis*, dissensions dividing the citizens of Thera and causing them to confront one another, at the origin of the colonial expedition to Libya. Involved in one of these factions, Battus appears as an influential citizen. Finally driven from his city with his companions and forced to leave the country, he consults the oracle at Delphi concerning the opportunity to found a colony (*apoikía*). The god confirms the interdiction of the seditious Therans and advises him to abandon a "salted territory" for a "better continent." While, in this damaged text, Libya is designated as *sterrà gé*, "terra firma," it is possible that the oracle here transfers the metamorphosis of Battus' speech, from stammerings to a strong and clear voice, into the opposition of an insular land, surrounded by the ocean, with a continent of unshakable foundations.[135] Be that as it may, the judgment of Menecles of Barce on these two narratives is without appeal. The cause (*aitía*) at the origin of the action of the first is more "mythic" (*muthikotéra*), while the second is more credible, more convincing (*pithanotéra*). The criteria for distinction between these two qualifications coincides with a notion of plausibility of the narrative action's motivation: an oracle pronounced by a god on the one hand, a decision taken by a citizen, simply confirmed by the god, on the other. It is no longer a question of fecundity metaphorically attributed to the land of the future colony by the oracle. As in Thucydides, the versions reported by Herodotus are associated with the creation of *lógoi*, and consequently also with the poetic.

But isn't *stásis* the clear charge of history, as we understand the term? In a celebrated passage of the *Laws*, Plato attempts to define the ideal conditions for the foundation of new cities (*katoíkesis*). This pursuit leads him to classify colonial enterprises brought about by constraint in a specific category, and to enumerate their causes. In most cases, we find lack of resources in a territory to be the origin of movement, but sedition (*stásis*) and destruction caused by war are also possibilities. Concerned later with designating the means for choosing a legislator who would not double as a tyrant, in order to purify the city (*katharmoì póleos*) of undesirables, Plato summarizes: colonization (*apoikía*) will be used as a euphemism for banishment (*apallagé*) of those who cause trouble, who carry a stain.[136] In this context, *stásis* placed at the origin of a colonial enterprise appears to have an eminently religious motivation.

Beginning with the *Iliad*, a crime of blood can be a cause of exile and can be matched with a colonial enterprise. In fact, it is after the murder of his great-uncle that Tlepolemus emigrated to Rhodes, where he probably founded three cities on the island that became, with the aid of Zeus, miraculously wealthy. Perhaps more historically, Archias voluntarily went into exile from Corinth and founded Syracuse in order to free the Corinthians from the drought and plague sent by the gods as punishment for the unavenged death of Actaeon. As for *stásis*, Pausanias (or the narrative that he relates) does not hesitate to situate political dissension at the origin of the Athenian colonization of Ionia: the problem of the royal succession after the death of Codrus, the king of Pylos and then Athens, is understood in terms of sedition (*stasiázein*). As we have seen, the Pythia ends the conflict by conferring the royalty of Attica on the crippled Medon. He becomes the first *árkhon basíleus*, the first archon-king, while Neleus and his brothers are forced to emigrate to Ionia. Moving from the heroic to the Archaic age, we recall that colonization also seems to constitute a solution, with the guarantee of Delphi, for the conflict that arises at Sparta between citizen-soldiers and the illegitimate sons of their spouses, the Partheniae, mentioned above.[137] In the last two narratives, the motivation preferred by Menecles of Barce in the name of plausibility (over that of the Herodotean versions of the foundation of Cyrene) is clearly evident.

5.6. Narrative and Oracular Logic

The Hellenistic historiographer thus does not accord belief to the classic narratives of Herodotus. The correspondence is striking, in fact, between the criteria underlying Menecles' implicit definition of *muthikón* and the qualities that define our own encyclopedic category of myth. For Menecles of Barce, as for a modern reader, the truth-value of a narrative concerning the past seems to dissolve at the moment when a protagonist of a divine nature intervenes. Conversely, the narrative becomes more "convincing" when a situation of *stásis* is substituted for the divine intervention of Apollo as motivation for the narrative intrigue. In addition, a comparative analysis has clearly underscored the fact that the two versions of the foundation of Cyrene in Herodotus present an inversion of semionarrative syntax. This inversion places the Delphic oracle at the origin of these two narratives' movements while at the same time assigning subordinate causality to sterility or shortages, causes often presented in ancient Greece, along with political sedition, to justify a colonial enterprise. The same narrative analysis nevertheless greatly lessens the apparent coincidence between the Hellenistic view and the modern one. From the semantic point of view, the narrative preferred by the Hellenistic historian not only includes, for its part, a determining intervention by the oracle and consequently by the god of Delphi, but in representing the consequences of a state of civic unrest, it has religious implications. At the very moment when an indigenous conception of myth seems to sketch what corresponds to the concept as defined by modern anthropology, the relative incompatibility of the two is again revealed.

This is because, when considering the development of the more "historical" narratives of the foundations of colonies, we do not make the same associations concerning oracles as do the Greeks. Integrated into the narration, the repeated intervention of the Delphic god contributes to the construction of a type of predetermination. The oracle does not simply constitute the motivation of the action, as developed in the narrative; it also indicates, in a prospective manner, its goal. This predetermination of narrative action is not without reference to the function of *moîra*, the "destiny" associated with the legendary activities of the Homeric heroes, or that of *ará*, the malediction uttered by heroes and sanctioned by the gods so prominent in dramatic productions of the great heroic narratives on the Attic stage. The role played by Apollo and his oracle at Delphi in the phases of *manipulation* and *sanction* in the Herodotean narratives of Cyrene's foundation places them within a long narrative tradition in Greece, a tradition independent of the narrative forms it assumes through time, and independent also of the indigenous categories distinguishing these forms.

*

In returning to the paradoxical character of the *lógos* of Herodotus, we might ask, in accordance with our encyclopedic sense of what is "mythic," why the historian feels the need to give this particular twist to the narrative of the foundation of Cyrene. Why this insertion of the oracular logic of the god of Delphi into a political narrative, in direct contrast, we might add, with the symbolic narratives in the verses of Pindar and the "historicizing" version of Menecles of Barce? The paradox is all the more striking because in the fifth century the foundation of Cyrene constituted a relatively recent event and very well might have seemed to Herodotus, famously referred to as the *pater historiae* since antiquity, to constitute a verifiable "historical fact"!

We should note first that, generally speaking, the *lógoi* of Herodotus grant oracles, and in particular the Delphic oracle, an essential role in the conduct of narrative action. Of the 157 oracular responses from Delphi attested in ancient sources, from the Archaic and Classical periods up to the eve of the Peloponnesian War, Herodotus, along with the antiquarian historians such as Diodorus Siculus and Pausanias, supplies the greatest number. Without wishing to deny the real influence of Delphi over political conduct within the Classical cities precisely at the time in which Herodotus is writing his *Histories*, and without wishing to underestimate the role played by Apollo's oracle in particular over the direction of colonial movements, it is hard to deny that the oracles, in the narrative of Herodotus or in those of his successor-collectors of *lógoi*, play an essentially narrative role.[138] Within the frame of the different cults actually rendered to Apollo *arkhegétes* in the fifth century, the oracles tend to reintegrate prose narrative of events and actions that have only human will or material circumstances as motivations into the tradition of high epic poetry. Moreover, without the Delphic *Sender*, the colonial expedition as Herodotus recounts it is doomed to failure. Dorieus, the son of the first wife of Anaxandridas, the king of Sparta, is proof of this. Removed from power by Cleomenes, who, though his elder, was born to the second wife of the king, Dorieus is led to Libya by Theran guides (!) in order to found a colony. But without having solicited the support of Apollo at Delphi, the Spartans are repelled by the native people, and after a stay of two years (!), they are forced to return to the Peloponnese.[139]

The narrative hypothesis advanced here is supported by the observation that the moment of the foundation of Cyrene appears to coincide with the very beginning of Delphic expansion. Delphic "propaganda" in this period was still not capable of exerting its full effect, and the influence of the oracle in terms of its extradiscursive reference would be difficult to measure in the narrative. The situation, however, is quite different in the time of Herodotus. Often influential in the political maneuverings of the Greek cities, intervention by the Delphic oracle is within the "horizon of expectation" of the auditors of Herodotus' narrative, through its commentary on the development of what becomes "history." We find, on this point, a significant correlation with Thucydides. The explicit desire to produce a nonpoetic work, devoted to the concept of permanence instead of seductive recitation for a passing auditor, might well find an echo in the scarcity in his work of references to the intervention of the Delphic oracle or the gods in general. The motives for "historical" activity are now to be found in personal undertakings, hopes, and states of mind (*gnomé*), that is to say, in man; this man, while creating facts (*tà gignómena*), must, however, still reckon with *túkhe* (or *sumphorá*), chance, and *anágke*, necessity, occasionally even with the divine (*tà daimónia*).[140] But Herodotus composes a narrative specifically meant for audition. In affirming in the prologue of his *Histories* that he intends to prevent "the renown attached to the remarkable deeds, both on the Greek and on the barbarian sides, from disappearing *(akleâ)*," Herodotus gives his work the same goal as that underlying the Homeric poems. The epic and poetic vision that he assigns to his work is manifested particularly in narrative actions still largely manipulated by the gods.[141] Doubtless it is in this sense that his *historía* can appear to his colleagues in the third century as *muthikóteron*!

In the movement of the Herodotean narrative, the oracle contributes in its way to actually determining the action. Along with other motivations, such as the constant reestablishment of justice, it orients the narrative by fixing its goal and limit. We have noted that the narrative moves along as if the oracle had assigned to the subject of the action what is the equivalent of *moîra* or *aîsa* for Homeric heroes; in the case of Croesus, it explicitly does so, revealing his *peproméne moîra* (1.91.1). The ambiguity of the oracular response can then soften the effects of rigid predetermination by according the *Subject* of the action a margin of freedom, based upon his or her interpretative acumen. In giving meaning to narrative action, the oracles have a cognitive function vis-à-vis the audience of the Herodotean narratives, and it is fair to ask whether their form, often verse, does not tend to compensate, from a narrative point of view, for the inherent deficiencies of prose as a medium for history with an epic view. The one who finally leads and animates the narrative is the narrator-speaker himself, that is, Herodotus, who takes on the oracular voice in order to set his own narrative on its course.

5.7. A Double Memorial

But, as is frequently the case, the *lógos* of Herodotus on the foundation of Cyrene is not merely a reported narrative. It refers to what both the Therans and the Cyrenaeans say *(légousi*, 4.154.1) on the matter. Without necessarily overlooking the possibility of a chresmological poem in oracular form retelling a preexisting epic narrative,[142] it is evident that in the fifth century both Thera and Cyrene had at their disposal local histories that retraced their respective origins in epic or elegiac verse and diction. These narratives of foundation *(Ktíseis)* are probably to be understood in the Classical period as part of the movement to rewrite legendary history as discussed above.

At Cyrene, we can recover material traces of this in the decree on the claim of Thera's citizens to their rights in Cyrene, which quotes the text of the original *Agreement of the Founders* mentioned above. Whatever can be made of the authenticity of this text, which comes to us in an inscription dating to the end of the fourth century, Battus is here at once designated by Apollo as the founder and as king of Cyrene (*arkhagéta-[n t]e kaì basilêa*). In a striking abridgment, the text of the agreement attributes the spontaneous order to colonize (*automátixen*) directly to the god, skipping entirely the intermediary of the oracle. As for the text of the decree itself, it gives to the god of the colonial enterprise the title of Archegetes, inviting an identification of Apollo the *Sender* with Battus the *Subject* of the colonization. The identification is all the more natural because, in designating the capacity to engender a new *pólis*, the quality of *arkhegétes* seems essentially to be attached to the cult of a founding hero.[143]

Moreover, the circular tumulus mentioned earlier, a material and cultural (not textual) token of the ascendancy of the god of Delphi, stands on an elevated part of the Cyrenaean agora. It is the tomb of the leading founder, at the "stern of the agora" according to Pindar's expression. Cyrenaean avatar of Apollo, the founder was there the object of a heroic cult that we have seen existed in probable relation to the celebration of the Carneia. Integrated within this cultural frame, Battus could assume the cathartic and apotropaic functions of the Delphic god, if not also his oracular role. In any case, the ancient commentator on Pindar's *Pythian 5* does not hesitate to describe Battus at once as *herós* and as *arkhegétes*, at the very moment when he demonstrates the veneration Battus enjoyed at Cyrene. And a famous Cyrenaean inscription attributes a purificatory role to Battus the founder as well as to Apollo that contrasts with the errors that mark the preliminaries leading to the legendary colonial expedition.[144]

If we reread the Cyrenaean version of the foundation narrative transmitted by Herodotus in light of the abbreviated version found in the *Agreement of the Founders*, we see the illegitimate stammerer transformed at the end of his long colonial trajectory into a hero who has learned to use *mêtis*, the technical intelligence freely attached by the Greeks to physical defects and genealogical deviation. The impure Theran citizen, rebuffed with stones as one destined to become a *pharmakós* in his attempt to return to Thera, becomes at Cyrene the representative of Apolline *kátharsis*. Only after wanderings and detours on Crete and the island of Plataea does the awkwardness of the colonist become the very medium for opening the "track" over the sea that is the prefiguration of the cobblestone path that, according to the words of Pindar in *Pythian* 5 (87–93), "cuts the plain" to lead straight to the agora and the tomb of the founding hero. It is a royal path, made for processions in the celebrations of Apollo "who protects mortals," a path traced no longer on an island, but on the mainland. Thanks to Apollo, this ambiguous figure, once evocative of a tyrant, is transformed into a captain who, after having led the colonial expedition through a marine expanse with the aid of a marginal fisherman, manages the ship of the city from the stern of an agora to which he himself traced the road of access. Aristarchus is not mistaken when he asserts that Apollo had given Battus talents that were destined to civilize (*hemerósein*) the region. Liberated from his physical handicap and perhaps from the impurity associated with tyranny (thus following in a certain sense the destiny of Orestes), the oecist has become a civilizing hero, endowed with a cathartic gift, the *Sender* of the royal power of his successors. After the reforms of Demonax, this power will be reduced essentially to religious functions. As the charge of the archon-king of Athens, they will endure still in the time of Herodotus.[145]

Assimilated to those of a divinity, the heroic foundational deeds of the artisan-demiurge of Cyrene can only be transmitted to posterity in the form of an epic narrative. To the *mnêma* of the agora corresponds the memorial of the poems (in prose?) to which the *lógos* of Herodotus refers and on which the indirect narrative of the *Agreement of the Founders* undoubtedly depends.[146] The process of symbolic discourse production that has been described is dependent as much on a certain type of "making history" as on the heroic and divine character of the protagonist of the narrative in question. It is determined by the internal rules of the Herodotean *lógos*, in relation to the conditions of its enunciation, and by the pragmatic and cultural function of the Cyrenaean narrative that inspires it, which found its raison d'être in the ritual honors paid to a founding hero. The Herodotean narrative gains its plausibility as much through its correspondence with certain mental categories and representations of its audience as through reference to heroic cult actually rendered to the oecist. Through this double reference it can, in our eyes, constitute a "myth." If we adhere strictly to the narrative category as defined by modern anthropology, it is only a myth inasmuch as the symbolic narrative refers to its situation of enunciation. Of course, one cannot sing of the foundation of a colony in the same way as one writes of the Peloponnesian war. With his explicit intention of the prediction of future events (1.22.4), a historian such as Thucydides thus inserts himself into his narrative as a substitute for the oracle!

6. Callimachus and Apollonius: A Return to Poetry

As far as concerns the pleasure of a narrative, Greek culture undoubtedly did not accept the idea of a line of evolutionary development from *mûthos* to *lógos* conceived as modes of thought. Transformation into a political narrative coinciding roughly with our conception of historiography is by no means irreversible. After Herodotus and in spite of the local chronicles such as that of Menecles of Barce, we find in the Hellenistic period a return to poetic forms and thus to the type of narratives Thucydides classified under the rubric *muthôdes*. The versions of the foundation of Cyrene transmitted by the poems of Callimachus and Apollonius of Rhodes must also be placed within much greater wholes, each with their specific enunciative vision: literary hymn to Apollo in the first case, erudite epic poem describing the voyage of the Argonauts in the second. Inserted into larger narrative systems, these two new versions of the legend of colonization have in common the feature of following a quasi-linear chronological development. But even if, for this reason, it is possible to associate these narratives with expression in a historical mode, this syntactic characteristic does not prevent the reappearance and transformation on the semantic level of isotopies that the Pindaric versions have already made quite familiar.

6.1. Callimachean Enunciative Games

The story of the foundation of Cyrene inserted into the narrative portion of Callimachus' *Hymn to Apollo* is not only inscribed into the narrative sequence that leads the reader from Thessaly and Delos to Delphi by way of Libya. Like the Thessalian, Delian, and Delphic episodes, it is itself also traversed by two isotopies — spatial, centered on the theme of construction, and social, articulated through the theme of intimate relationships — that together ensure the coherence of the narrative as a whole. The figure of the depth and fecundity of the Cyrenaean soil (*bathúgeios*) reappears at the beginning of this narrative development, so that the foundations planned by Apollo are more solidly situated. The manipulation of the land of Cyrene described in *Pythian* 4 by means of the legend of the Libyan clod is thus subordinated here to the foundational and architectural activity of Apollo. The moment of establishment of an autochthony under the authority of Poseidon is passed over in favor of the civilizing activity of the god of Delos and Delphi. Through the intermediary of cult rendered to the founding god, the figure of florescence, most notably expressed by the land's ever-favorable seasons (81–84), is substituted for that of generation.

But as in Pindar, the blooming of the seasons in this humid and verdant locale, attached to the cult of Apollo Carneios, is itself only a metaphor for the potential fecundity of men and women. From here, we move back in time along the course already indicated, following the social isotopy of intimate relations, to the dances of the Dorians with the blond native women in the wooded valleys of Azilis, and from there, to the union of Apollo and Cyrene near the Mount of the Myrtles. This encounter epitomizes clearly the two complementary aspects of the act of foundation: protection guaranteed by Cyrene for the flocks of the indigenous king, and construction by Apollo with the aid of Battus of a city with its own temple and walls (teíkhea, 67; ástu, 73; anáktoron, 77; pólis, 77 and 94). These roles are much more distinct than in Pindar: for the woman, pastoral activity in the khóra, for the men (the god and the colonist hero), the foundation of the pólis.

To return from semantics to the syntactic articulation of the narrative, the figurative continuity created by Callimachus on the semantic level of the acts of foundation of cities allows the poet to include the legendary foundation of Thera by the Theban hero, the "historical" colonization of Cyrene by Battus, and its divine foundation by Apollo accompanied by the eponymous nymph, all within the same perspective. Treated separately by Pindar, these versions are now inscribed in a single narrative. We can, however, find traces of this attempt to coordinate different versions of the legend in the authors of the local histories. Notably Acesandrus, in the work mentioned earlier, places the episode involving Battus' stammering following the combat of the eponymous nymph with the lion.[147] Callimachus, however, prefers the coincidence of different times to this manner of coordinating two distinct versions by inserting them into a single line of chronological succession.

But as I have attempted to show elsewhere, there is more, in particular in those places where the Callimachean narration of the Cyrenaean episode is marked by the strong interventions of the narrator-speaker. At first, the city chosen by Apollo for the founder Battus is presented as "my city" (emèn pólin, 65), that is, as the city of the narrator; this is in relation to "our kings," the kings of Cyrene under whose authority the narrator seems to place himself. But this first picture — within a narrative marked by the use of the third person and the aorist — of a singular relationship between the narrator-speaker and the city of Cyrene is only preparation for a second, still more surprising, enunciative relationship. Apollo, the principal protagonist of the narrative in the third person, at once (69) takes the place of the narratee, by way of a direct address of which he is the object. Facing this narrative actor transformed into an addressee (se, 69), the I of the narrator is strongly asserted (egó and emoí, 71). It is he who introduces by name the epithet under which Phoïbos will be venerated at Cyrene, as at Sparta and Thera. As Apollo Carneius, the "horned" god, he is celebrated at the Carneia in Lacedaemonia, introduced to Thera by the sixth-generation descendant of Oedipus, and installed at Cyrene by Aristoteles the great (72–84). Claimed by the narrator himself in line 71, the epithet Carneius leads to the presentation of the god of Cyrene as the god "of my fathers."[148]

From then on, split between direct addresses to Carneius (72 and 80) and events of foundation narrated in the third person, the narrative focuses on the first celebration of the Carneia on Libyan soil and on the dances of the Dorian warriors with the blond natives. In a reflexive manner, Apollo Carneius and the nymph Cyrene, dedicatees of this part of the poem, can delight from the Mount of the Myrtles in contemplating the development of the choruses of the colonists on their way to the future site of Cyrene (85–95), as traced by the poem itself.

6.2. Narratives in the Service of Poetics

Ancient and modern readers partial to biographical interpretations have not failed to see an echo of Callimachus' Cyrenaean origins in the relationship the narrator establishes in the hymn with Battus, his descendants, and the god of the city. They gain confidence because these same origins seem evident in other poems read from the same biographical angle. The biographizing zeal of readers of the Callimachean *Hymn to Apollo* has been all the more piqued since in the "cultic" portion of the poem the narrator refers twice to "my king" (26 and 27), and associates this king with Apollo. Already the scholiast identified this king as Ptolemy III, though modern interpreters generally prefer Ptolemy II Philadelphus, who is, for his part, associated with the Battiads by way of the allusion in line 68![149]

But before they are extradiscursive, the references to the founder and to Apollo have an essentially textual impact. Through the enunciative play discussed above, they reorient the entire narrative of Cyrene's foundation by focusing it on a third isotopy—a musical one—centered on the theme of choral performance. Engaged at the beginning of the poem by the song of the swan that signals Apollo's epiphany, this isotopy traverses the whole poem, ensuring its coherence. In particular, the connection the narrator-speaker establishes between his narratee Apollo and the group of chorists that celebrate the god for the first time on Libyan soil is simply a narrative echo of the relationship the same narrator forges with his double narratee in the first part of the poem: Apollo and his epiphany, but first a chorus of young people (8) curiously and successively called on to begin singing and dancing and then to silently give attention to the song of the god. Who, in fact, sings Callimachus' *Hymn to Apollo*? The narrator-poet (cf. 11 and 16)? The young chorists in place of the narrator (8, 17, and 25)? Apollo, also invoked in the second person (11)? Moreover, where is the poem performed? At Cyrene? Delos? Alexandria? At the celebration of the Carneia?

In the *Hymn to Apollo*, Callimachus accomplishes the tour de force of setting a melic and choral song in the epic form of a *Homeric Hymn*. It is thus an entirely "mimetic" composition, one that constructs on its own a purely textual, and consequently fictive, situation of enunciation.[150] This intradiscursive auto-reference is borne by a series of enunciative shifts, some typical examples of which have been indicated above. It is all the more pronounced in the *Hymn to Apollo* because the praise of the god in the "ritual" portion of the composition, as in the narrative section, is entirely subordinated to the celebrated metaphorical poetic program that concludes it. This adjustment noticeably influences the narrative of the foundation of Cyrene, at this point focused on the choral celebration of the Carneia and the relationship of the narrator-speaker (and poet!) with a god appreciative of music. If Apollo is praised chiefly as an *aoidós*, as a singer, it is because in the conclusion of the poem he appears as the god of the bow and the lyre in order to defend, through the rejection of Envy and Reproach, the poetics of brief and refined composition as formulated and realized by Callimachus. Only at this moment does the reference constructed in the poem take on an extradiscursive dimension.

The narrative of the foundation of Cyrene, both from the perspective of its plot and on the semantic level, ends with this foundation of a poetic program. While the Dorians, at the moment the narrator leaves them, still were not able to approach the spring of Cyre (98), at least the poet, thanks to Apollo, can drink from the sacred fountain, where precious drops of perfectly pure water well up (111–12).[151] In this poem woven like the Altar of Horns, the development of themes of construction and intimate relationships, a deployment of spatial and social isotopies, finds its purpose through a bard, as does the foundation of a new poetics in the privileged relationship the poet maintains with the god of song. All perfectly outlined, the generosity of the Cyrenaean soil is realized in the poetic fertility from which the *Hymn to Apollo* stems. The poem expresses in the same way the fecundity to which both the dances of the Dorian colonists with the natives at Azilis and the union of the god with the eponymous nymph are dedicated. Here, the effects of the symbolic process and of the metaphorical speculation undoubtedly blur and efface the boundary we could draw between "myth" and literature.

From the perspective of narrative construction, Apollonius of Rhodes engages in a play similar to that of Callimachus: chronological coordination of the narrative in its different versions and respect for a portion of its figures, but at the same time movement to a unique theme that he himself reorients. Generative "autochthony" becomes a cosmogony. Moreover, in terms of the legend of the Argonauts, the narrative of foundation — ending, as we have seen, with the creation of

Thera — has as its beginning the gift of the marvelous clod and not the rape of Cyrene by Apollo. Above all, we should remember the fourfold semantic interpretation centered upon the divine clod itself. We find in it the same mineral, vegetal, and human figures. Organized into isotopies no more interwoven than in Pindar and distributed over the four distinct interpretive levels of Euphemus' dream (see § 2.6), they are all focalized on the theme of generation. The coincidence of the fourth of these levels with the realization of the narrative itself then positions this generative theme as a veritable cosmogonic act. Thrown into the sea, the miraculous clod is transformed into an island that nourishes the descendants of the Argonauts. Rationalized, in a certain sense, through its simplified operation, the Hellenistic legend of foundation paradoxically reveals a representation subjacent in its more ancient versions.

From Pindar on, cosmogonic acts are indeed what motivate the different versions of the legend of Cyrene — cosmogony in the Greek sense of the term, only complete with the establishment of a civic order in a place transformed in its geology, flora, and fauna. This order is distinguished from what lies at the basis of the cities of continental Greece in its establishment, under the control of Apollo, of a pastoral civilization that, even through the fifth century, prolonged a monarchic model largely obsolete elsewhere.

Such symbolic manifestations are necessarily dependent on the historical situation in which they are developed and on representations appropriate to these social circumstances. Expressed by distinctive forms of communication, they are profoundly marked by the contours of the community of belief that fosters them and for which they are intended, through the work of the imagination of a *poiétes*, a true poet in the etymological sense of the word.

Neither Myth nor History

FROM the *Epinicians* of Pindar to the *Hymn to Apollo* of Callimachus, through the *Histories* of Herodotus, the *Agreement of the Founders*, the local history of Menecles of Barce, or the *Argonautica* of Apollonius of Rhodes, the development of the legend of the foundation of Cyrene, in all its different versions, does not outline a passage from myth to history in the sense we commonly attribute to these two notions. There is simply no progressive rationalization defined as a passage from *mûthos* to *lógos*. At most, one might find in the two narratives of Herodotus the sketch of a chronological succession of events that the Pindaric material is precisely involved in effacing. On the one hand, all three divergent versions represented by the poet of Thebes are defined in the end by their connection with the moment of their enunciation, the publication and celebration of victories at the Pythian games. On the other, the two narratives Herodotus spins in parallel, without attempting to reconcile one with the other, do not lose any of their heroizing effect while still responding to the requirements of Herodotean *semaínein*, an indication of the "oracular" sense of history in its narrative configuration.[1] And while Apollonius shapes the story of the miraculous clod in support of that of the expedition of the Argonauts, creating a semiotics in the Alexandrian style, Callimachus resemioticizes the legend in a hymn to Apollo that undergoes a metamorphosis, under the protection of the god of the lyre, into a defense of a poetic program.

In its successive transformations, the foundation narrative is never confronted with a "historical" foundation. It is never compared to events that can be reconstructed and organized in a chronological series on the basis of artifacts and "documents." Its regular reorientation is determined by the function it assumes in the text that presents it and by the pragmatic perspective of this medium, whether the text is composed in verse or prose, whether sung, recited, or read. In particular, the temporal configuration constructed through each of these "poetic" (in the literal sense of the term) versions gains its orientation from the situation of enunciation for which the composition is produced. In this functional connection with the circumstances of its composition and its historically and socially defined communication, a narrative we would consider as a legend reacquires its plausibility, through the variations it undergoes in each retelling. This credibility is thus as much on the semionarrative as on the enunciative level.

1. Strabo's Homer

In the end, is not Homer responsible for this lack of truth-value, this absence of empirical validity of the narratives of foundation? There is room for doubt.

When Strabo makes use of geography to demand whether Homer speaks the truth in describing the imaginary journey of Odysseus, it is in order to make a lively attack on Eratosthenes, the geographer who had dared to consider the poet and his commentators producers of mere rubbish. In this context, the metaphor of language descending from its ceremonial chariot and placing a foot upon the ground is interpreted simply as symbolizing the passage from poetic to prosaic form. On the other hand, Plutarch uses the same image to signify the transition, certified by the development of historical discourse, from poetic *muthôdes* to the truth of prose![2] The geographical approach allows Strabo to envision the problem of the plausibility of Homeric *mûthoi* in terms of their empirical validity. His examination of the truth-value of the Homeric narratives operates by the genetic method already employed by Aristotle in the *Poetics*. According to Strabo, the narratives of the first men are collected not by poets, but by the legislators and civic communities for whom they work; thus these first *mûthoi* are produced in the name of utility (*toû khresímou khárin*). The criterion of civic use at once determines, as for Xenophanes and later for Plato, the choice of *mûthoi* adapted to the city, essentially a matter of responding to the need for knowledge inherent in the nature of man, the "reasoning animal" (*logikós*). As in any genetic sketch, social genealogy, beginning from the primitive state, follows the model of development of the individual. Just as the child takes pleasure in stories, humanity, at a young age, shows itself to be *philómuthos* (adopting the word coined by Aristotle in the introduction to the *Metaphysics*!). True, these narratives do not depict what one sees with one's own eyes (*tà kathestekóta*), but they do have the merit of encouraging knowledge; they constitute a propaedeutic for the understanding of reality (*tà ónta*). At this early stage, reference to reality is thus placed between parentheses. Just as tales of the sorceress Lamia or the Gorgon, seemingly so terrifying, are able to deter children from mischief through the fear they inspire, citizens are encouraged to do good when they listen to the exemplary exploits of a Heracles or a Theseus. They gain understanding by means of the "mythic" (*muthóde*) narratives sung by the poets.

By good evolutionary logic, shouldn't the society that has reached maturity, like the adolescent having attained adulthood, be confronted with the reality evaded by the *mûthoi*? In terms of social evolution, the contradiction proposing a way of understanding reality through the propaedeutic of fable is reduced to a double assertion: not only has the creation of narratives (*muthopoiía*) furthered both the political foundation of human life and the inquiry about reality, but dramatic poetry, like Homeric poetry, remains useful for a population that has no access to the subtleties of philosophy. While at an earlier stage *mûthos* seemed to be defined — as in modern times — through its lack of reference to empirical reality, it recovers now, in terms of an objection formulated specifically to Eratosthenes, a mode of inquiry of the historical type. In this way Strabo can finally present Homer as a practitioner of the truth. He is a poet who most certainly makes use of fictions, but in an educative way, better to convince his public; a poet who, in the end, is pursuing the same goal as the historian who recounts reality (*tà ónta*). Like the wanderings of Odysseus, the Trojan War has taken place (*gegonós*). It corresponds to a historical event. The epic poet thus bases his work on geography and history, composing his narratives (*muthopoiíai*) with a didactic function (*pròs tòn paideutikón*). Once again, what is "mythic" for the Greeks is defined in relation to a poetic form meant to charm and educate a listener, rather than in terms of its (possibly fictitious) content.

More than two centuries after Strabo, Porphyry concludes his allegorical and metaphysical interpretation of the cave of the nymphs that welcomes Odysseus during his wanderings with considerations of the same sort.[3] Homer is the guardian of ancient knowledge (*palaià sophía*). In his moral perfection, he only outlines (*ainízeto*) the images of divine realities by giving them a narrative form (*en mutharíou plásmati*). This outline and form certainly require the allegorizing interpretation of a Porphyry, but their success would not have been assured if they were not founded on elements of truth! And so Homer is indeed a practitioner of the truth.

2. Plato and Fiction

When the poetic form of communication does not determine the definition of *mûthos*, it is its connection to the *palaiá*, events of the distant past, that prevails. Solon had already come to an understanding of the story Plato presents to us in the *Timaeus*. In the course of his discussion with the priests of Neith-Athena at Saïs, the Egyptian counterpart of Athens, the legislator-poet wishes to turn the conversation to the past (tà palaiá). In order to elicit stories (lógoi) from his interlocutors, he tells them (légein) of events that marked the most distant past (tà ark-haiótata) of his own city. Both "mythology" and "genealogy," here nar-ration of legends and genetic narrative merge in describing the birth of Phoroneus, the first man, the tragic destiny of Niobe, and the flood of Deucalion, who escaped the cataclysm with only his wife Pyrrha. The memory of the poet attempts to restore chronological succession and measurement to these narratives of the birth of the human race![4]

Nevertheless, in the eyes of the Egyptian priests, neither stories of primordial cataclysms nor genealogical narratives are very different from tales meant for children (mûthoi paídon). They do not reject them, but instead interpret them in a philosophical manner. Such is the case with the narrative (legómenon, as in Herodotus!) of the fall of Pha-ethon, son of Helios, and his chariot, which caught fire and destroyed the entire earth. This mûthos is not false; instead, its form (skhêma) reveals a recurring physical phenomenon, namely the deviation of the heavenly bodies that traverse the sky and can cause fatal rises in temperature.

From this perspective we can understand the "myth" of Atlantis. It is a story that tells of the Athens of the past (pálai), a story the priests of Saïs were able to conserve in memory through their writings because the Nile allowed them to escape recurring cataclysms. The strong stretches back nine thousand years to the birth of the Athenians from Earth fertilized by the sperm of Hephaestus, presenting under the aegis of Athena an ideal society divided into distinct classes before it is de-stroyed by a disaster that engulfed Atlantis along with the entire Athe-nian army. In modern times the story has been given so much attention that it has indeed become a veritable myth![5] Put simply, a rereading of this narrative, told by the Egyptian priests, recounted by Solon, heard by Critias the elder, and repeated by his grandson of the same name, shows that its adaptation occurs on a social, not physical, level.

Owing to this transposition, and through the discursive mediations and plays on words and notions in which Plato couches the story, we are witness to a veritable interpretative reversal. The theoretical descrip-tion of the ideal city, the sketch of which was presented at the outset of the dialogue, is assigned the form of a mûthos, while the ancestors of the Athenians whom the priest of Saïs describes are considered the true (alethinoí) predecessors of the citizens of the actual city. The "myth" of Atlantis thus allows real substance to be given to a structure that was until now purely theoretical and classified as such, as a mûthos! The realization of this structural outline implies a double movement. Through the intermediary of narrative, not only is the theoretical structure in-scribed in a real past, but, above all, this past is related to the actual city, here and now (through procedures of deixis: *deûro, ténde pólin*). The citizens of the ideal city are thus at once compared to the Athenians in the time of Atlantis and set in relation to contemporary Athens, at the time and place of the dialogue itself. Thanks to the written records of the Egyptians, the "myth" of Atlantis no longer appears to be a fabricated legend (*plastheìs mûthos*), but a true story (*alethinòs lógos*)! It is not a matter of a theoretical construction, but of absolutely verifiable history (*lógos pantápasí ge mèn alethés*). At the beginning of the dialogue Critias reports the history of actual events (*prakhthèn óntos*) in the form of a narrative particularly chosen for the day on which one honors the tutelary goddess Athena. As concerns the gods and the genesis of the world, in any case, as a mortal man, one can only accept a plausible story (*eikòs mûthos*!). Thus it is no surprise that when the story of Atlantis is resumed and developed in the *Critias*, it is presented as a *lógos*, describing the citizens of ancient times (*palaioì polîtai*), but also begins as if it were a poem, with an invocation to Apollo, the Muses, and Mnemosyne.[6] In fact, only the power of memory is capable of reproducing, with the aid of the divinities of poetry, this memorial narrative inscribed in the activity of praise song (*humneîn*).[7]

Perhaps it is appropriate that Socrates supplies us with the final question in this debate, so important for an inquiry into transcultural translation and the dialogue between Greek civilization and Western modernism. How might we understand, on our own terms, a Greek notion of which the principal denomination has been placed in the service of our own attempts to represent and define a concept quite different from the original one? At the moment of facing his death, which the sacred festival for the god Apollo on Delos had temporarily delayed, Socrates remembers a recurring dream in which he had been encouraged to practice the art of the Muses by composing poetry.[8] After having considered, throughout his life, that the highest form of art was the practice of philosophy, Socrates, now nearing the end of his days, intends to respond literally to this invitation to song. He thus makes a return to the popular forms of poetic and musical composition. In honor of the god whose festival is responsible for the delay of his execution, he composes in the Homeric style a hymn to Apollo (a *prooímion*). Then, in order to truly show himself a poet, he abandons *lógoi* to compose *mûthoi*. The stories Socrates chooses for his poems, in lieu of fabricating them himself, are the *mûthoi* of Aesop (which, moreover, before the intervention of the philosopher, Cebes had called *lógoi*!). Without being a genuine *muthologikós*, a true poet and storyteller, one can at least present, in poetic form, the prose narratives of others. In the Athens of the fourth century, *mûthos* is thus still unfailingly attached to poetic activity, if not specifically to honors given to the gods through musical composition.

In consequence, as concerns Cyrene and its foundation, we must envision poetic creations centered on the different moments of the common past the city was celebrating in music.[9] In ancient Greece, as elsewhere, connection with the past can only be symbolic. The making of "myths" from Greek *mûthoi* in intervening times has contributed as much to obscuring their poetic creativity as to effacing their social functions as representations and explorations of the past in relation to the present.

Notes

Preface

1. Keeping myself to the exchanges within the research group on "Cultural transcendence: reconstruction of anthropology and its objects," of which the title "Patomipala" indicates that it includes the anthropologists of Pavie, Turin, Milan, Paris, and Lausanne, I should mention here the profit I have gained from the critical works of F. Affergan, *Critiques anthropologiques* (Paris 1991); S. Borutti, *Per un'etica del discorso antropologico* (Milan 1993) and *Filosofia delle scienze umane. Le categorie dell'Antropologia e della Sociologia* (Milan 1999); U. Fabietti (ed.), *Il sapere dell'antropologia. Pensare, comprendere, descrivere l'Altro* (Milan 1993); M. Kilani, *L'invention de l'autre. Essais sur le discours anthropologique* (Lausanne 1994); and F. Remotti, *Noi, primitivi. Lo specchio dell'antropologia* (Turin 1990). See also the collections published by F. Affergan (ed.), *Construire le savoir anthropologie* (Paris 1999); by S. Borutti and U. Fabietti (eds.), *Fra antropologia e storia* (Milan 1998); and by C. Calame and M. Kilani (eds.), *La fabrication de l'homme dans les cultures et en anthropologie* (Lausanne 1999).

2. "Illusions de la mythologie," *Nouveaux Actes Sémiotiques* 12 (1990).

3. A portion of chapter II of the present book, dedicated to the text of Herodotus, was published in a preliminary form in a volume I edited and entitled *Métamorphoses du mythe en Grèce antique* (Geneva 1988) following a colloquium organized at the University of Lausanne in May 1987 on "The Narrative Forms of Greek Myths." A study on the Pindaric versions of the foundation of Cyrene found publication in a volume edited by L. Edmunds, *Approaches to Greek Myth* (Baltimore and London 1991). I thank the editor of that collective volume and the Johns Hopkins University Press for permission to rewrite and publish that partial text.

4. B. Gentili, P. Angeli Bernardini, E. Cingano, and P. Giannini, *Pindaro. Le Pitiche* (Milan 1995).

Introduction

1. The most recent English edition is *Choruses of Young Women in Ancient Greece. Their Morphology, Religious Role, and Social Functions* (Lanham, Boulder, New York, and Oxford 2001).

2. *Thésée et l'imaginaire athénien. Légende et culte en Grèce antique*, 2nd ed. (Lausanne 1996), 15–68.

3. *The Poetics of Eros in Ancient Greece* (Princeton 1999).

4. See especially A. J. Greimas, *Du sens: Essais sémiotiques* (Paris 1970) and *idem, Tome 2* (Paris 1983). Calame's own discussions of Greimassian semiotics can be found in the introduction to *The Craft of Poetic Speech in Ancient Greece* (Ithaca, N.Y., and London 1995), 3–26, the first chapter of *Thésée* mentioned above, and the first sections of the present volume.

5. I use the term "historical" here in quotation marks to acknowledge that the term, especially when distinguished from the "mythic," creates problems in the interpretation of ancient Greek narratives. The present volume is, of course, dedicated in part to addressing this issue.

6. "Collective importance" and "cultural relevance" are phrases often associated with definitions of the concept of "myth." The more or less canonical definition of the concept, at least among modern critics, seems to be that of W. Burkert, who writes in *Structure and History in Greek Mythology* (Berkeley 1979), 23: "Myth is a traditional tale with secondary, partial reference to something of collective importance." For other recent mainstream definitions and discussion, see especially L. Edmunds (ed.), *Approaches to Greek Myth* (Baltimore and London, 1990), 1–20, and F. Graf, *Greek Mythology. An Introduction* (Baltimore and London, 1993), 1–8.

7. *Kernos* 4 (1991): 179–204.

8. As Calame notes in chapter I, § 1.2, C. G. Heyne (1729–1812) was the first to use the term "mythus" with the sense in which it is employed today. Heyne was most interested in the origins of what he identified as "mythic" thought, and was not, of course, solely responsible for the subsequent development of the term's meaning. His interest in "primitive" cultures does show some affinity, for example, with the work of J. G. Frazer, another important figure in the ontologization of myth.

9. *Infra*, chap. I, § 4.

10. The *locus classicus* is Frazer's introduction to his edition of Apollodorus, Apollodorus. *The Library*, vol. 1 (Cambridge, Mass. 1921), xxvii–xxxi. Cf. *supra* n. 8, and *infra*, chap. I.

11. See *supra* n. 4.

12. A. J. Greimas and J. Courtès, *Sémiotique. Dictionnaire raisonné de la théorie du langage* (Paris 1979) and *idem*, *Tome 2* (Paris 1986).

13. Generally speaking, with gods and heroes populating the category of "myth," humans the category of "legend," and human or subhuman characters that of "folktale." See again the discussion below in chapter I, § 2.1.

14. Perhaps one of the more interesting works to grow out of this "poststructuralist" conception is that of P. Veyne, *Did the Greeks Believe in Their Myths?* (Chicago 1988) (translation of *Les Grecs ont-ils cru à leurs mythes?* [Paris 1983]), in which the belief system of the Greeks is set in stark distinction to our own.

Chapter I

1. Two fundamental works should be noted: Veyne 1983 (Eng. transl. 1989), who questions the ancients' ambivalent attitudes of belief concerning their narrative patrimony, and Detienne 1981 (Eng. transl. 1986), who follows the formation of the concept of myth from its Hellenic origins through its anthropological metamorphoses. These works permit a few allusions to suffice here as introductory remarks. To the two works cited here should be added the more brief, but no less stimulating discussions presented by Vernant 1974, 195–250

(Eng. transl. 1980, 203–60); Graf 1993, 9–56, with the commentary of L. Edmunds, *Bryn Mawr Class. Rev.* 5 (1994): 407–15; and Saïd 1993, 79–110.

2. This assertion begins the article by P. Smith entitled "Mythe — approche ethno-sociologique" in the *Encyclopaedia Universalis*, vol. 12 (Paris 1985), 879. The connection is most likely with the mythological universalism professed by Lévi-Strauss, as presented in the celebrated formula: "Quelle que soit notre ignorance de la langue et de la culture de la population dans laquelle on l'a recueilli, un mythe est perçu comme mythe par tout lecteur dans le monde entier" (1958, 232).

3. Thus it is no mere chance that the attempt at definition cited in n. 2 continues by asserting: "Même dans les cultures qui ne classent pas les mythes à part, c'est ce divorce entre l'adhésion aux récits en question et leur contenu manifestement fictif qui permet à l'ethnologue de les reconnaître immédiatement comme tels, indépendamment des thèmes qu'ils véhiculent"!

4. After being nourished on the *Mythologiae* (*sive explicationum fabularum libri X*) of Natale Conti, published in Venice in 1567 (2nd ed.), Fontenelle — we will return to him — inscribed in the very title of his celebrated essay dedicated to the mythology of the ancients his scorn for this "mass of chimaeras, reveries, and absurdities": "De l'origine des fables," in *Oeuvres diverses de M. de Fontenelle de l'Académie française* (Paris 1724), 567–88, reedited by J.-R. Carré (Paris 1932). In the *Dictionnaire historique et critique*, vol. 2, 2nd ed. (Bâle 1738), 401–3, P. Bayle proposes, following Plato, the rejection of the fictive narratives that are the "fables" of Homer and Hesiod.

5. See O. Gruppe, *Geschichte der klassischen Mythologie und Religionsgeschichte während des Mittelalters im Abendland und während der Neuzeit* (Leipzig 1921), 21–58. On the impact of the great discoveries, see A. Pagden, *The Fall of Natural Man. The American Indian and the Origins of Comparative Ethnology* (Cambridge 1982), especially 119–45 (on Bartolomé de Las Casas).

6. One may consult: *Der Grosse Brockhaus*, vol. 8, 18th ed. (Wiesbaden 1979), 83; *The New Encyclopaedia Britannica*, vol. 12, 15th ed. (Chicago and London 1980), 793; *La Grande Encyclopédie*, vol. 14 (Paris 1975), 8328; *Dizionario Enciclopedico Italiano*, vol. 7 (Rome 1975), 822–23.

7. This definition is presented by W. Burkert in "Literarische Texte und funktionaler Mythos: zu Istar und Atrahasis," in J. Assmann *et al.*, *Funktionen und Leistungen des Mythos. Drei orientalische Beispiele* (Freiburg and Göttingen 1982), 63–82; on this subject, see the prudent remarks of Buxton 1994, 15–17. In response to the question "What is a Greek Myth?" in Bremmer (ed.) 1987, 1–9, the editor of that collection has accepted a definition analogous to that proposed by Burkert, in making myths "traditional tales relevant to society"; he specifies that in Greece in particular, where religion is integrated into society, these legends pertain to gods and heroes. This definition approaches that proposed by Neschke 1993, 119, which is more precisely adapted to Greek culture: "Griechische Mythen sind Darstellungen wichtiger Lebensthemen, insbesondere des Handelns des Menschen, in den Lebensbereichen der kulturellen Gemeinschaft, denen die kollektive Vorstellung dieser Bereiche als transzendente Subjekte in der Rolle von Mitgliedern seines Haushaltes (*oikos*) zugrundeliegt."

8. See Honko 1984, 41–52; Dundes (ed.) 1984, 1, himself returning to encyclopedic knowledge in compiling his collection "devoted to the serious study of
myth," is the author of the following definition: "A myth is a sacred narrative
explaining how the world and man came to be in the present form."

9. G. Vico, *La scienza nuova prima* (Naples 1725), 147–49 of the modern
edition by F. Nicolini (Bari 1931); F. Bacon, *De Sapientia Veterum Liber* (London 1609), *praefatio*.

10. C. G. Heyne proposed to see in myth the "premières origines" of human
knowledge: "Proluduntur nunnulla ad quaestionem de caussis fabularum seu
mythorum veterum physicis," in *Opuscula Academica collecta et animadver-
sionibus locupletata*, vol. 1 (Göttingen 1785), 184–206. See A. E. Horstmann,
"Mythologie und Altertumswissenschaft. Der Mythosbegriff bei Christian Gottlob Heyne," *Archiv für Begriffsgeschichte* 16 (1972): 60–85, and F. Graf, "Die
Entstehung des Mythosbegriffs bei Christian Gottlob Heyne," in F. Graf (ed.),
Mythos in mythenloser Gesellschaft. Das Paradeigma Roms (Stuttgart 1993),
25–43.

11. D. J. ***, "Mythologie," in *Encyclopédie ou dictionnaire raisonné des
arts et métiers*, vol. 10 (Neuchâtel 1765), 924–26. Reflection in this vein can be
followed courtesy of the selected texts presented by B. Feldman and R. D. Rich-
ardson, *The Rise of Modern Mythology. 1680–1860* (Bloomington and London
1972), who unfortunately have the tendency to ascribe the use of the term and
concept of myth to authors who speak of "fable," "religion," or the "divine";
see also the remarks of J. Starobinski, "Le mythe au XVIIIᵉ siècle," *Critique* 33
(1977): 975–97. More pertinently, one can see the historical development carefully traced through the age of enlightenment by Jamme 1991, 17–25 (with an
abundant bibliography), and also in the study of W. Burkert, "Griechische
Mythologie und Geistesgeschichte der Moderne," in *Les études classiques aux
XIXᵉ et XXᵉ siècles: Leur place dans l'histoire des idées* (Vandœuvres and Geneva 1980), 159–99.

12. Among the works of L. Lévy-Bruhl, note in particular *La mentalité primitive* (Paris 1922), 411–25 (reissued in 1976). The citation from E. Cassirer is
taken from *Die Philosophie der symbolischen Formen* (orig. ed., Berlin 1925), in
the translation of R. Manheim (New Haven 1955), 25; see also 95–96, 73–76,
57–59, etc., and also 3. *La phénoménologie de la connaissance* (Paris 1972), 95
(orig. ed., Berlin 1929); for the opposition of myth to "theorico-scientific"
thought, see also *Langage et mythe. A propos du nom des dieux* (Paris 1973), 48–
57 (orig. ed., New Haven 1953). The reflections of K. Hübner in *Die Wahrheit des
Mythos* (Munich 1985), 239–90 are similar; see G. von Graevenitz, *Mythos. Zur
Geschichte einer Denkgewohnheit* (Stuttgart 1987), vii–xxvi. The results of historical development of the subject are traced by Jamme 1991, 94–110; see also the
significant rapprochement begun by Detienne 1981, 192–208 (Eng. transl. 1986,
103–14). If the concept of mythic thought has found its sanction in the work of
Cassirer, we should note that in the *Prolegomena zu einer wissenschaftlichen
Mythologie* (Göttingen 1825), 205–35, K. O. Müller already proposed, in "sub-
stantializing" myth, the strict distinction between "mythischer Stoff" and the
reelaboration of this "mythic material" by poets and writers. Jan N. Bremmer
remarks to me that at the moment I am formulating these critiques in opposition

to the ontologization of myth, other scholars are presenting analogous studies; see the references which he gives in "Mythe en rite in het oude Griekenland. Een overzicht van recente ontwikkelingen," *Nederlands Theologisch Tydschrift* 46 (1992): 265–76 (see in particular n. 19).

13. Cf. Lévi-Strauss 1958, 227–55 for the principles of structural analysis, and *La pensée sauvage* (Paris 1962), 26–33, for discussion of the modes of mythic thought, which are still defined in the sense of analogical functioning on multiple "codes" in *La potière jalouse* (Paris 1985), 227–43; the citation is taken from *Mythologiques II. Du miel aux cendres* (orig. ed., Paris 1966), in the English translation of J. Weightman and D. Weightman (New York 1973), 474. As Dirk Obbink has brought to my attention, it is significant in this regard that, in the paradigmatic analysis of "La Geste d'Asdiwal" (*Anthropologie structurale Deux* [Paris 1973], 175–233), C. Lévi-Strauss defines as versions of the same "myth" the different narratives published by F. Boas as *saga*, *texts*, or *mythology*. For a critique of the notion of primitive or mythic thought and for a questioning of a "great divide," one should read J. Goody, *The Domestication of the Savage Mind* (Cambridge 1977), 1–18 and 146–62; Affergan 1987, 86–103; and the various contributions published in *La pensée métisse. Croyances africaines et rationalité occidentale en question* (Paris and Geneva 1990).

14. These two points of view have been respectively adopted in the quite stimulating contemporary work being done in France on Greek mythology: for the first, see Vernant 1974, 198 and 250 (Eng. transl. 1980, 205–6, 260); also *Les origines de la pensée grecque* (Paris 1962), 127–29, which must be read with the nuanced introduction in the "Préface" to the fifth edition of 1992, and "Raison et déraison chez les Grecs," *Raison présente* 84 (1987): 119–33: the term *mûthos* should only "s'appliquer à une catégorie précise de récits sacrés concernant les dieux et les héros" and thus designates "une réalité mentale inscrite dans la nature humaine." For the other perspective, see the propositions of M. Detienne in the conclusion of "La double écriture de la mythologie entre le *Timée* et le *Critias*," in Calame (ed.) 1988, 17–33, reprinted in *L'Écriture d'Orphée* (Paris 1989), 167–88; see also *Les Jardins d'Adonis. La mythologie des aromates en Grèce*, 2nd ed. (Paris 1989), 259–61 (Eng. transl.: *The Gardens of Adonis. Spices in Greek Mythology* [Princeton 1994], 130–31). Graf 1993, 2–6, combines the two perspectives, in affirming that myth, which transcends the poetic text meant to publicize it, was placed in crisis by the new "critical rationality" pioneered in Greece by philosophers and rhetoricians. For the *mûthos/lógos* perspective, see now G. W. Most, "From Logos to Muthos," in Buxton (ed.) 1999, 25–47.

15. This is the thesis now defended by Dowden 1992, 7–9, and is, in the end, also the sense which Neschke 1983, 125 and 137–38, settles upon, in defining myth as an "Idealtyp." On the *Bibliotheca* attributed to Apollodorus, cf. *infra* § 3.5. When one attempts to pursue the specifics of Greek mythology courtesy of comparative and contrastive analysis, as has recently been done by Konstan 1991, the determining distinctive trait seems to be anthropomorphism. If, however, the actors in the Greek narratives can appear with the traits of animals through the process of metamorphosis, does it not mean that anthropomorphic character is more a matter for theology than for "mythology"?

16. This double definition is taken from the *Grand Dictionnaire Universel du XIXe siècle*, vol. 11 (Paris 1874), 759.

17. Cf. A. M. Ramsay, *Les Voyages de Cyrus avec un Discours sur la Théologie et la Mythologie des Anciens*, 2nd ed. (Deux-Ponts 1792), 35–60 (orig. ed., London 1727), and A. Bannier, *La Mythologie et les Fables Expliquées par l'Histoire*, vol. 1 (Paris 1738), 1–19 (this work in three volumes represents a new redaction of a treatise on the historical explication of fables written in 1711; it is cited in the article of the *Encyclopédie* mentioned *supra* n. 11). The movement from a body of myths to a science of myths (mythology) is carried out in *Nouvelles leçons sur la science du langage*, vol. 2 (Paris 1868), 136–46 (orig. ed., London 1863) of F. M. Müller, through the intermediary of the concepts of "mythological science" and "compared mythology." But we should recall that already in 1825, K. O. Müller titled his work *Prolegomena zu einer wissenschaftlichen Mythologie* (*op. cit.* n. 12), in which he proposed an interpretative approach to narratives understood as "Erzählungen von Handlungen und Schicksalen persönlicher Einzelwesen, welche eine frühere, von der eigentlichen Geschichte Griechenlands ziemlich genau getrennte Zeit betreffen" (59).

18. The works cited of J.L.K. and W. J. Grimm were prepared, in their first editions, in Berlin (Realschulbuch), Berlin (Nicolai), and Göttingen (Dieterich), respectively. J. Frazer presents the definitions summarized here in the introduction to his edition of Apollodorus, *Apollodorus. The Library*, vol. 1 (London and Cambridge, Mass. 1921), xxvii–xxxi.

19. W. Bascom, "The Form of Folklore. Prose Narratives," *Journal of American Folklore* 78 (1965): 3–20, taken up in Dundes (ed.) 1984, 5–29, who has invited Bascom to develop his otherwise not very significative terminology (cf. p. 11). D. Ben-Amos, "Catégories analytiques et genres populaires," *Poétique* 19 (1974): 265–93, has noted the necessity of explicating those classifications that make recourse to several series of contrasting traits.

20. E. Bethe, *Märchen, Sage, Mythus*, 2nd ed. (Leipzig 1922), 6 and 117 (orig. ed., 1904). It is not just chance if, for instance, the two categories of "myth" and "folktale" appear to be blurred in the structural analysis that J. Peradotto, *Man in the Middle Voice. Name and Narration in the Odyssey* (Princeton 1990), 32–58, proposed of some episodes of the Odyssey (in a chapter precisely called: "Polyainos: Myth vs Folktale"!).

21. On this point, see the references given by Graf 1993, 6–7, and by Bremmer 1987, 6–7; but H. Baumann, "Mythos in ethnologischer Sicht. I," *Studium Generale* 12 (1959): 1–17, proposes still other distinctions. Among writers in English, one can find an analogous discussion in Kirk 1970, 31–41.

22. See M. Stanek, *Geschichten der Kopfjäger. Mythos und Kultur der Iatmul auf Papua-Neuguinea* (Cologne 1982), 7–10.

23. Analysis conducted by M. Gaborieau, "Classification des récits chantés. La littérature orale des populations hindoues de l'Himalaya central," *Poétique* 19 (1974): 313–31.

24. The comparison of the narrative genres of Burundi with those of Rwanda is conducted by J. Vansina, *De la tradition orale. Essai de méthode historique* (Tervuren 1961), 138–41. The difficulties of an intercultural system of classification are discussed by Smith 1980, 74–79.

25. B. Malinowski, "Le mythe dans la psychologie primitive," in *Trois essais sur la vie sociale des primitifs* (Paris 1975), 97–154 (orig. ed., New York 1926); W. Bascom, *art. cit.* n. 19, 14–15, exercises a new fierceness toward this careful triadic approach. See particularly the critical remarks of Affergan 1987, 97–103 and 193–206, on the "langue de classement."

26. Aristot. *Poet.* 1450a4f. and 32ff.: *súnthesis* or *sústasis tôn pragmáton*; *Poet.* 1447a9f. and 1449b8f.; see also 1460a11ff. on the role played by the marvelous and irrational in narratives. Cf. Detienne 1981, 236–38 (Engl. transl. 1986, 130–31), Ricoeur 1983, 57–71 (Eng. transl. 1984, 32–42); and V. Cessi, "Praxis e Mythos nella *Poetica* de Aristotele," *Quad. Urb. Cult. Class.* 48 (1985): 45–60. M. Fusillo, "'Mythos' aristotelico e 'récit' narratologico," *Strum. Crit.* n.s. 1 (1986): 381–92, sees in the *mûthos* of the *Poetics* the product of the process of *mimesis*, and as such, it corresponds to the frame, or argument, of the narrative.

27. Aristot. *Pol.* 1341b2ff., 1269b27ff., 1284a22ff.; certainly the same treatise seems to reserve the activity of *muthologeîn* for the elderly (cf. also *Rhet.* 1395a2ff.), but to the ears of the young, *mûthoi* and *lógoi* have the same effects: *Pol.* 1336a30ff.; and if the destiny legend attributes to Sardanapal does not correspond to the truth, it nonetheless remains plausible: *Pol.* 1312a1ff. See also, for the use of *mûthos* without a pejorative sense, 1257b16 (the history of Midas) and 1274a39 (the Corinthian tradition of Philolaos the Bacchiad), and also *EE* 1230a2f., *EN* 1100a8, or *Phys.* 218b24.

28. Aristot. *Met.* 1000a5ff. (cf. 1091b7ff.); 1074b1ff. and 995a3ff.; 982b7ff. The use of *muthologeîn* and *mûthos* to designate an unfounded statement is reserved in Aristotle for the physical and biological works; here, causal explication must be substituted for traditional or theological explication, which is the charge of the "mythic": cf. *HA* 578b24ff., 579b4, 580a14ff., 609b10, 617a5ff., *PA* 641a20ff. in the realm of biology; *Cael.* 284a18ff., *Meteor.* 356b11ff. (essential!), or *MA* 699a27 for the physical world. See T. K. Johansen, "Myth and *logos* in Aristotle," in Buxton (ed.) 1999, 271–91. Finally, note that when Aristotle opposes general demonstrations (*enthumémata*) to examples and stories in the *Problemata* (916b26ff.), to define the second group he uses the terms *lógoi* and *mûthoi* indifferently!

29. Plat. *Prot.* 320c, *Gorg.* 523a, *Tim.* 26e; these passages are still interpreted as representing a strict division between the puerility of myth and the intelligibility of rational discourse, for instance by Vernant 1974, 201–2 (Eng. transl. 1980, 208–10); one can read with profit the nuanced introduction by G.E.R. Lloyd, *Demystifying Mentalities* (Cambridge 1990), 44–49. On this quite complex semantic problem, see also the exhaustive analysis by Brisson 1994, along with the reflections of Detienne 1981, 155–89 (Eng. transl. 1986, 82–102); G. Arrighetti, "Platone fra mito poesia e storia," *Stud. Class. Or.* 41 (1991): 1–22; Graf 1993, 187–93; P. Murray, "What Is a *Mythos* for Plato?" in Buxton (ed.) 1999, 251–62, and Morgan 2000, 132–91. The opposition presented in the *Timaeus* (26e) in particular ought to be reread in light of the discussion presented *infra*, chap. III!

30. It is advisable on this subject to reread in its entirety the long discussion in *Resp.* 376e ff. The role of poets and their *mûthoi* in the future city is also

explained in 392a; see the careful commentary of Cerri 1991, 15–37, with the remarks of Gentili 1992, 92–94, and Detienne 1981, 170–88 (Eng. transl. 1986, 91–102), who complements them with a reading of the *Laws*. Note that in a similar way Hermogenes the Rhetor, *Prog.* 1, at the end of the second century A.D., will identify *mûthos* with the Aesopic fable: even if the tale itself is false, its paedagogical qualities nonetheless become, by imitation of the actions of man, useful instruments for learning about life.

31. Thuc. 1.21.1 and 22.4: cf. *infra* n. 51; Luc. *Conscr. Hist.* 8f. For discussion of dramatic and mimetic history, see especially B. Gentili and G. Cerri, *Storia e biografia nel pensiero antico* (Rome 1983), 5–31. Likewise, for Plutarch, *mûthos* is distinguished by its poetic aspects: cf. *infra* n. 63; see also the remarks of J. Boulogne, "Le mythe pour les anciens Grecs," *Uranie* 1 (1991): 17–30. In a much later time, Heliodorus, the Byzantine commentator on the *Grammatical Art* of Dionysius of Thrace (vol. I.3, p. 449 Hilgard), attaches the *muthôdes* to the poetic form, a form that can communicate elements of truth!

32. Jul. *Or.* 7.205c ff., 219a ff., 216c, and 222c ff. The relationship between the *Republic* of Plato and the discussion of *mûthos* by Julian has been thoroughly studied by R. Guido, "*Múthous pláttein*, un'eco platonico in Jul. *Or.* 73," *Rudiae* 3 (1991): 87–104.

33. Xenoph. fr. 1.19ff. Gentili-Prato, with comments by Cerri 1991, 38–52; see also frr. 15 and 16. Ethical and social criteria also determine the choice of *memuthologeména* reserved for education in the Platonic city: Plat. *Resp.* 377e. For a semantic analysis of Archaic and Classical usage of the term *mûthos*, see my "'Mythe' et 'rite' in Grèce, des catégories indigènes?" *Kernos* 4 (1991): 179–204, and for *mûthos* in Homeric poetry, see R. P. Martin, *The Language of Heroes. Speech and Performance in the Iliad* (Ithaca, N.Y., and London 1989), 14–42; contrast with *lógos*: B. Lincoln, "Competing Discourses. Rethinking the Prehistory of *mythos* and *logos*," *Arethusa* 30 (1997): 341–67, now in 1999, 3–18.

34. Hecat. *FGrHist.* 1 F 1; cf. my discussion in 1986, 81–82 (Eng. transl. 1995, 92–93), L. Edmunds, "Introduction. The Practice of Greek Mythology," in Edmunds (ed.) 1990, 1–20, 4–6, and L. Bertelli, "Des généalogies mythiques à la naissance de l'histoire. Le cas d'Hécatée," in Bouvier and Calame (eds.) 1998, 13–31; on the epistolary meaning of *grápho*, see L. Porciani, *La forma proemiale. Storiografia e pubblico nel mondo antico* (Pisa 1997), 44–76. Research on the concept of the truth in Herodotus through use of the terms *alethés*, *atrekés*, *orthós*, and their derivatives has been conducted with great care by Darbo-Peschanski 1987, 165–84.

35. Hdt. 2.23 and 2.45.1. For the use of *lógos* and its derivatives in Herodotus and on the enunciative stance of the author in relation to the stories of others, see my own reflections in 1986, 73–77 (Eng. transl. 1995, 86–89), and Hartog 1992, viii–xvi and 225–69; see also R. L. Fowler, "Herodotus and His Contemporaries," *Journ. Hell. Stud.* 116 (1996): 62–87. P. Payen, "Logos, muthos, ainos. De l'intrigue chez Hérodote," *Quad. Stor.* 39 (1994): 43–77, analyzes the way Herodotus uses the terms *lógos* or *lógoi* to refer to his own work, while C. Darbo-Peschanski, "Juger sur paroles. Oralité et écriture dans *Les Histoires* d'Hérodote," *L'inactuel* 3 (1994): 161–82 studies the "testimonial" quality of these *lógoi*.

36. This is particularly the case for the legend of Helen: cf. Hdt. 2.120; on the story of Cyrus, cf. 1.95. Concerning the credit given by the historian to his sources depending upon their geographic and ethnic provenance, see Darbo-Peschanski 1987, 91–97.

37. Aristoph. *Vesp.* 1174ff., which should be read with the commentary of Edmunds, *art. cit.* n. 34, 2–8, who nonetheless associates *mûthos* with a category of the *mythical*. Eur. *Phoen.* 469ff.

38. Demosth. *Polycl.* 40 and *Steph.* 149 or *Epist.* 8f.; Isoc. *Paneg.* 158. See my study cited above (n. 33), and "The Rhetoric of *Mythos* and *Logos*. Forms of Figurative Discourse," in Buxton (ed.) 1999, 119–43; see also the pages of Loraux 1993, 159–61 (Eng. transl. 1986, 157–60). Above all, one should note the very exhaustive study S. Saïd will publish, based on the program presented in March 1990 during the graduate seminar of les Diablerets ("Ecritures du mythe et de l'histoire en Grèce et à Rome"), entitled "De l'histoire au mythe. L'exemple des Guerres médiques dans la rhétorique"; see also S. Gotteland, "Généalogies mythiques et politiques chez les orateurs attiques," in D. Auger and S. Saïd (eds.), *Généalogies mythiques* (Paris 1998), 379–93, and *Mythe et rhétorique: les exemples mythtiques dans le discours politique de l'Athéns classique* (Paris 2001).

39. Compare, for example, Paus. 6.3.8 or 2.17.4 with Hdt. 7.152.3; in both cases Pausanias' reservations of belief are expressed vis-à-vis *lógoi*, even while he, in explaining the "myth" of the metamorphosis of Callisto into a bear (8.3.6), is content to declare: *légo tà legómena hupò Hellénon*! Also, at 2.21.5, use of the term *mûthos* to indicate the legend of the Gorgon carries with it no implication of the truth-value of the story. Inquiry into the attitude of Pausanias toward the narratives he recounts has been led by Veyne 1983, 105–12 (Eng. transl. 1988, 95–102), who cites in support of his discussion the most enlightening passages; see also C. Habicht, *Pausanias und seine "Beschreibung Griechenlands"* (Munich 1985), 142–67.

40. Philostr. *Her.* 7.9, cited by Veyne 1983, 81–87 (Eng. transl. 1988, 71–78), who furthermore shows (77) that the master of the purification of Greek mythology in the sense of natural and historical rationalization was Palaiphatos, a student of Aristotle with seemingly multiple identities (cf. *Suda s.v. Palaíphatos*; P 70 Adler), but who was, in all cases, the author of five books of *Apista* ("*Unbelievable Stories*").

41. Paus. 8.8.2ff. This is, in short, the position already adopted by Aristotle in the *Metaphysics* (1074b1ff.) toward the tradition which, in narrative form (*en múthou skhémati*), presents elements of nature in the capacity of divine figures; cf. *supra* n. 28.

42. Sext. Emp. *Adv. math.* 1.263ff. and 252ff.; this distinction perhaps refers back to Crates of Mallos, fr. 18 Mette. See also *Hypoth. pyrr.* 1.147, where the *mutheuómena* about Cronos are accounted "mythic" belief; on the notion of *plásma* in the Second Sophistic, see B. Cassin, *L'effet sophistique* (Paris 1995), 470–84.

43. Procl. *In Plat. Tim.* 20d (vol. 1, p. 75.27 ff. Diehl); cf. *infra* chap. III nn. 5 and 6.

44. Theag. frr. 8 A 1 and 2 Diels-Kranz; cf. G. W. Most, "Die früheste

erhaltene griechische Dichterallegorese," *Rhein. Mus.* 136 (1993): 209–12. The very rich history of allegorical interpretation has been traced by F. Buffière, *Les Mythes d'Homère et la pensée grecque* (Paris 1956); note also the discussion of Saïd 1993, 74–78. On Porphyry in particular, see *infra* chap. III n. 3.

45. Acus. *FGrHist.* 2 F 6 and 23a; Pherec. *FGrHist.* 3 F 2 and 60, who brings his genealogy down to Miltiades I, the close relative of the victor at Marathon. See Thomas 1989, 161–73, along with Graf 1993, 125–31, and C. Jacob, "L'ordre généalogique. Entre le mythe et l'histoire," in Detienne (ed.) 1994, 169–202; see also J. Bremmer, "Myth and Propaganda. Athens and Sparta," *Zeitschr. Pap. Epig.* 117 (1997): 9–18.

46. *Marm. Par. FGrHist.* 239; see the remarks of Saïd 1993, 5–6. On the Greek genealogical and chronological traditions, see the summary of A. A. Mosshammer, *The Chronicle of Eusebius and Greek Chronographic Tradition* (Lewisburg, Pa., and London 1979), 84–127.

47. Diod. Sic. 4.4.1 ff. = Callisth. *FGrHist.* 124 T 24, Theop. *FGrHist.* 115 T 12, and Ephor. *FGrHist.* 70 T 8; see also 16.76.5 = Ephor. *FGrHist.* 70 T 10, along with F 9, where Ephorus shows that he has a natural distrust of those who recount *arkhaîa*. The interesting study of L. Canfora, "L'inizio della storia secondo i Greci," *Quad. Stor.* 33 (1991): 3–19, should also be noted. Concerning the boundaries of historical space in Herodotus, see *infra* n. 51.

48. Diod. Sic. 4.1.1ff.; 2.44.1 and 46.6; 1.2.1ff. and 4.8.1ff.; on this subject see the comments of Veyne 1983, 57–59 (Eng. transl. 1988, 46–48), and the complementary passages cited by H. Funke, "Poesia e storiografia," *Quad. Stor.* 23 (1986): 71–93; see also J. Marincola, *Authority and Tradition in Ancient Historiography* (Cambridge 1997), 119–27, who insists on the aspect of utility assumed by the *mûthoi* according to Diodorus even if they are held at a certain enunciative distance.

49. Dion. Hal. *Ant. Rom.* 1.39.1 and 41.1 with 2.20.1f.: cf. Piérart 1983, 55–60, who gives several examples of the integration of legend and history by Dionysius, F. Hartog (ed.), *Denys d'Halicarnasse. Les origines de Rome* (Paris 1990), 18–21, and E. Gabba, *Dionysius and the History of Archaic Rome* (Berkeley and Los Angeles 1991), 125–29. Historicizing interpretations of "myth" of this type can be found equally in Diodorus of Sicily: see, for example, 5.49.4. See also, around two generations later, the case offered by the orator Dio Chrysostom: S. Saïd, "Dio's Use of Mythology, " in S. Swain (ed.), *Dio Chrysostom. Politics, Letters, and Philosophy* (Oxford 2001), 161–86.

50. Phot. *Bibl.* 442b29ff. and 444a9ff.; cf. H. Verdin, "Agatharchide de Cnide et les fictions des poètes," in H. Verdin *et al.* (ed.), *Purposes of History: Studies in Greek Historiography from the 4th to the 2nd Centuries B.C.* (Louvain 1990), 1–16.

51. Compare the theoretical affirmations of Thucydides in 1.21.1 and 1.22.2ff. with his practical treatment of the "mythic" in 1.4, 1.8.4, 1.9.2, 2.15.1f., 2.29.3f., 6.2.1, etc. On the "time of the gods," a notion implicit in Herodotus 3.122.2 (concerning Minos), see Piérart 1983, 49–51, and Vidal-Naquet 1983, 81–83 (Eng. transl. 1986, 45–47), along with the crucial remarks of Darbo-Peschanski 1987, 25–38. The boundaries of historical space in Herodotus are the object of the excellent discussion of Hunter 1982, 50–115; see also my study "Mémoire collective et temporalités en contact. Somare et Hé-

rodote," *Rev. Hist. Rel.* 215 (1998): 341–67. Veyne 1983, 13, 26, and 63 (Eng. transl. 1988, 1, 13–14, 52–53), notes pertinently that for Thucydides, as for Aristotle or his substitute (*Ath. Pol.* 61.2) and Pausanias (1.3.3), the historicity of a Theseus arouses not the slightest doubt; see now on the subject Dowden 1992, 45–52.

52. As is implied by Detienne 1981, 111 and 120–21 (Eng. transl. 1986, 55–56 and 61–62). In discussing the past of Athens, Thucydides invokes archaeological proofs at 2.15.3ff.; for Mycenae, cf. 1.10.1ff. For Antiochos of Syracuse, a contemporary of Thucydides, the more reliable and obvious of the *arkhaîoi lógoi* deserve to be integrated into his history of Italy: *FGrHist.* 555 F 2.

53. Thuc. 1.2.1, 1.4.1, 1.6.6, 1.20.1 (cf. 1.3.1 and 1.21.1), etc. For the use of *tà arkhaîa,* cf. 1.21.2. There is dispute as to whether *tà palaiá* refers in Thucydides to events up to the Persian Wars or whether it includes equally the period preceding the Peloponnesian War: cf. A. W. Gomme, *A Historical Commentary on Thucydides* (Oxford 1945), 135–36. For the formation of the times of *palaiá* by Thucydides, see Hunter 1982, 17–49, Piérart 1983, 53–54, and the study of R. Weil, "Par quoi commencer?" *Stor. Storiogr.* 7 (1985): 28–37, who notes that contrary to Thucydides, who prefers to use the term *palaión,* Herodotus, more concerned with the problem of origin (*arkhé*), more often uses *arkhaîon.*

54. Thuc. 1.73.2ff., echoing the celebrated programmatic declarations of 1.20.1 and 1.21.1. Note also the use of *arkhaîon* and *palaión* at 2.15.4ff., in reference to the most ancient monuments of Athens and the stories attached to them. In 2.16.1, the combination of *tà arkhaîa* and *tà hústeron* brings us to the Peloponnesian War! The sophist Thrasymachos (fr. 85 B 1 Diels-Kranz) also distinguishes the events that can be heard from very aged persons who had personally witnessed them from those that are transmitted orally through stories about the past (*lógoi hoi palaióteroi*).

55. Hdt. 9.27, cf. 26.1, where the Tegeans add *tò néon* to *tò pálai.* For the respective roles of sight and hearing in Herodotus, see Hartog 1992, 271–302. Demosth. *Andr.* 12f.; see also *Aristocr.* 65f., where the narratives of the judgments of Ares and Orestes at the Areopagus are considered the noble mythic histories of tradition (*kalà paradedoména kaì muthóde*), which, because they pertain to ancient times (*palaiá*), have value as paradigms.

56. Acus. *FGrHist.* 2 T 1; is is only in the third century A.D. that Menander the Rhetor (vol. 3, p. 338.4 Spengel = T 4) notes that some consider these genealogies *mûthoi!* Pherec. *FGrHist.* 3 T 1, F 2, 18a, etc.; Asclep. Tragil. *FGrHist.* 12 T 1 and F 1ff.; Andron *FGrHist.* 10 F 1ff. On the work of Asclepiades, note that the bibliographical information in the *Suda* attributes to the Atthidographer Philochoros of Athens (beginning of the third century) a work entitled *On the Myths of Sophocles* (*FGrHist.* 328 T 1). The titles of the local chronicles of Athens and their relation to "archaeology" are studied by F. Jacoby, *Atthis. The Local Chronicles of Ancient Athens* (Oxford 1949), 79–86 and 111–19; for the beginnings of historiography and its connection to the use of writing, see Thomas 1989, 181–94, and *infra,* chap. II nn. 8 and 9.

57. Phot. *Bibl.* 142b16ff.; there is a useful discussion on the author and composition of the *Bibliotheca* attributed to Apollodorus in the edition of J.-C. Car-

rière and D. Massonie (eds.), *La Bibliothèque d'Apollodore* (Besançon and Paris 1991), 7–23, to be read with the commentary of C. Jacob, "Le savoir des mythographes (note critique)," *Annales H.S.S.* 2 (1994): 419–28.

58. Diod. Sic. 4.7.1 f.; Dion. Hal. *Ant. Rom.* 1.13.2. One should note that while Polybius (4.40.2 f.) clearly distinguishes between poets and mythographers on the one hand, and history, the sole medium in which the hearer (!) should have confidence, on the other, still, on the subject of the Phlegraean fields, he does not hesitate to find plausible the *lógos* told by *muthográphoi*!

59. Strab. 1.2.35 f. (= Theop. *FGrHist*. 115 F 381), cf. 8.3.9 and *infra* chap. III n. 2; *IG* XII.7.273. For the use of *muthológos* in Plato, see *Resp.* 392d and 389a along with *Leg.* 941b, where this status is also associated with the poet: the teller of stories is equally one who fabricates them (exception: *Leg.* 664d), but while avoiding the poetic form; see on this subject the prudent commentary of Brisson 1994, 184–95, who remarks that in its eight occurrences in Plato, the term *muthología* refers to the action of composition and narration of stories, whether in the poetic form or not, when it does not refer to an *anazétesis tôn palaiôn* (*Crit.* 110a; cf. *infra* chap. III n. 6).

60. Con. *FGrHist*. 26 F 1ff. and T 1 = Phot. *Bibl.* 130b25ff.; note on this subject the excellent discussion by Henrichs, "Three Approaches to Greek Mythography," in Bremmer (ed.) 1987, 242–77, and M. K. Brown, *The Narratives of Konon* (Munich and Leipzig 2002), 25–31. On the formation of mythography in general, see E. Pellizer, "La mitografia," in G. Cambiano, L. Canfora, and D. Lanza (eds.), *Lo spazio letterario nella Grecia antica*, vol. 2 (Rome 1993), 283–303.

61. It is no coincidence that Dowden 1992, 8–9 and 18–21, bases his work on the plan of the *Bibliotheca* attributed to Apollodorus in order to give substance to the complete and intertextual system that he calls "Greek Mythology," replete with capital letters . . .

62. Thuc. 1.22.4 (cf. *supra* n. 53); Aristot. *Poet.* 1451a36ff., with the commentary of R. Dupont-Roc and J. Lallot, *Aristote. La Poétique* (Paris 1980), 221–22; Plat. *Hi. Ma.* 285a–e: cf. Detienne 1981, 166–67 (Eng. transl. 1986, 88–89).

63. Plut. *Glor. Ath.* 347e ff., referring to Plat. *Phaed.* 61b, and *Thes.* 1; see C. Ampolo and M. Mandredini, *Plutarco. Le vite de Teseo e de Romolo* (Milan 1988), ix–xvii.

64. The skepticism displayed in these lines with regard to the category of myth, and the limited space granted to them, make an enumeration of the recent trends that characterize approaches to "myth" superfluous. There is a brief summary in Honko 1984, 47–48; for a detailed treatment, see the classic work of J. de Vries, *Forschungsgeschichte der Mythologie* (Freiburg and Munich 1961), or the article by W. Burkert and A. Horstmann, "Mythos, Mythologie," in *Historisches Wörterbuch der Philosophie*, vol. 6 (Basel and Stuttgart 1984), 282–318.

65. The details of this attempt to configure the process of symbolic production can be found in my 1996 work, 29–54. On the notion of production in the Greek sense of poetic *poieîn*, see especially J. Molino, "Interpréter," in Reichler (ed.) 1988, 9–52; on cultural preconstructs, see J. B. Grize, *Logique et langage* (Paris 1990), 27–32.

66. I. Calvino, *Lezioni americane. Sei proposte per il prossimo millenio* (Milan 1988), 86–94. On the role of the symbolic in literary creation, see particularly C. Reichler, "La littérature comme interprétation symbolique," in Reichler (ed.) 1988, 81–113, J. Molino, "Nature et signification de la littérature," *Et. Lettres* 4 (1990): 17–64, and, on the question of reception, the discussion of J.-M. Adam, *Langue et littérature. Analyses pragmatiques et textuelles* (Paris 1991), 12–32.

67. The question of the multiple narrative and literary forms assumed by "myths" is taken up in the collection I edited in 1988: see in particular the introductory remarks entitled "Evanescence du mythe et réalité des formes narratives," 7–17, and Calame 2000, 38–52 ; as concerns tragedy in particular, see C. Segal, "Greek Myth as a Semiotic System and the Problem of Tragedy," *Arethusa* 16 (1983): 173–98. For the definition of "discourse" as "text" + conditions of production and reception, see J.-M. Adam, *Linguistique textuelle. Des genres de discours aux textes* (Paris 1999), 39–41. In including iconography, Buxton 1994, 18–44, rightly stresses the importance of the enunciative circumstances corresponding to different forms of expression of Greek "myths." The idea of the constant adaptation of "myth" to new situations through the intermediary of narration was already formulated by F. Creutzer, *Symbolik und Mythologie der alten Völker, besonders der Griechen*, vol. 4, 2nd ed. (Leipzig and Darmstadt 1823), 103; it is revisited in certain ways by Neschke 1983, 129–31, through the notion of "Darstellung" and developed in his conclusive remarks under the title "Mythe et traitement littéraire du mythe en Grèce ancienne," *Studi Class. e Or.* 37 (1987): 29–60. On the subject of "mythography," see *supra* n. 60.

68. Inscribed in the Archaic use of the term *mûthos* (see *supra* n. 33), the pragmatic, if not performative, value of "mythic speech" has been recognized as much by antiquarians as by anthropologists: note above all the research of P.-Y. Jacopin, notably in "On the Syntactic Structure of Myth, or the Yukuna Invention of Speech," *Cult. Anthrop.* 3 (1988): 131–59, and "Dynamique de la parole sociale en Amérique latine," *Bull. Soc. Suisse Americ.* 57/58 (1993/94): 147–60; for Greece, see especially Konstan 1991, 28–30; G. Nagy, "Mythological Exemplum in Homer," in R. Hexter and D. Selden (eds.), *Innovations in Antiquity* (New York and London 1992), 311–26; and Buxton 1994, 45–52. On the connection of the pragmatic functions of "myths" with what we call literature, see the contribution of A. Deremetz, "Petite histoire des définitions du myths. Le mythe: un concept ou un nom?" in P. Cazier (ed.), *Mythe et création* (Lille 1994), 15–32.

69. The problem of configuration of time, both from a prefigured time and through plot and narration, is the object of the study of Ricoeur 1983, 85–87 (Eng. transl. 1984, 52–54), along with the works cited *infra* chap. II n. 7; see also the comprehensive study by P. Carrard, *Poétique de la Nouvelle Histoire. Le discours historique en France de Braudel à Chartier* (Lausanne 1998).

70. Recently F. Rastier, *Sens et textualité* (Paris 1989), 47–52, has given more substance to the rather disembodied notions of "sender (*émetteur*)" and "receiver (*récepteur*)" in proposing to see in them "places (*places*)" occupied by actors specifically subject to the social and linguistic circumstances of enuncia-

tion; meanwhile J. Fontanille, *Les espaces subjectifs. Introduction à la sémioti-que de l'observateur* (Paris 1989), 13–16, is occupied with highlighting the connection between the two actors of communication by demonstrating the images they construct of themselves through discourse; see also the critique formulated by F. Jacques, "Le schéma jakobsonien de la communication est-il devenu un obstacle épistémologique?" in N. Mouloud and J.-M. Vienne (eds.), *Langages, connaissance et pratique* (Lille 1992), 157–84; see now J.-B. Grize, *Logique naturelle et communications* (Paris 1996), 57–78, and J.-M. Adam, *Linguistique textuelle. Des genres de discours aux textes* (Paris 1999), 101–16. For an enunciative reorganization of structural semiotics, see J.-C. Coquet, *Le discours et son sujet I. Essai de grammaire modale*, 2nd ed. (Paris 1989), 23–67, and for a discussion of the question of reception/interpretation, Adam, *op. cit.* n. 67, 19–32. In the study "Pour une problématique socio-sémiotique de la 'littéralité,'" in L. Milot and F. Roy (eds.), *La littéralité* (Sainte-Foy 1991), 95–119, E. Landowski proposes to "semioticize (*sémiotiser*)" the situation of enunciation by considering it a semiotically constructed reality.

71. For the notion of schematization in the production of discursive objects constructed according to the rules of natural logic, cf. J.-B. Grize, *De la logique à l'argumentation* (Geneva and Paris 1982), 188–95 and 197–200, and *op. cit.* n. 70, 117–41; on the same notion in relation to the problem of reference, see M.-J. Borel, "Le discours descriptif, le savoir et les signes," in J.-M. Adam *et al.*, *Le discours anthropologique. Description, narration, savoir*, 2nd ed. (Lausanne 1995), 21–64.

72. The discursive and semionarrative concepts summarized here are explained in the corresponding entries in A. J. Greimas and J. Courtès, *Sémiotique. Dictionnaire raisonné de la théorie du langage* (Paris 1979) and *idem*, *Tome 2* (Paris 1986), in each case with an equivalent denomination in English; for more detailed definitions of these semionarrative categories, see my books of 1986, 125–32 and 145–47 (Eng. transl.: 1995, 144–51 and 166–69), and of 1996, 55–60; for their application in an analysis of mythic narratives, see Pottier 1994, 49–79. From the point of view of semionarrative semantics, one should remember the propositions advanced by F. Rastier, *Sémantique interprétative* (Paris 1987), 117–19, 172–75, and 177–211, concerning the fruitlessness of attempting to trace a hierarchical distinction between "figurative isotopy" and "thematic isotopy." On the level of semionarrative syntax, we should borrow the notion of causality instituted by the production of plot from J.-M. Adam, *Les textes: types et prototypes. Récit, description, argumentation, explication, dialogue* (Paris 1992), 45–63. For the sake of clarity, I have substituted for the notions of "process (*parcours*)" and "narrative program (*programme narratif*)" that of a narrative program meant as a concrete realization of the (narrative) canonical schema.

73. In addition to the references on this subject given *supra* n. 13, cf. J. Molino, "Anthropologie et métaphore," *Langages* 54 (1979): 103–25.

74. Dion. Hal. *Thuc. 5*, cited and commented upon by Detienne 1981, 146–50 (Eng. transl. 1986, 76–79); see also W. K. Pritchett, *Dionysios of Halicarnassus. On Thucydides* (Berkeley and Los Angeles 1975), 50–57. One can re-read on this subject the proem to the work of Herodotus, with my own com-

mentary of 1986, 71–73 (Eng. transl.: 1995, 78–80), and that of Nagy 1990, 217–28.

Chapter II

1. In spite of their rarity, some objects have caused the thesis of the validity of the earliest date attributed by Eusebius to the founding of Cyrene (he supplies 1336, 761, and 632) to resurface. These dates correspond to renderings in modern chronology of ones given in Olympic time and transmitted in the Latin version of the *Khronikoî Kanónes* (VII, pp. 52.18; 87.16ff. and 96.19 Helm). For an attempt to make the chronology of different versions of the legend coincide with our own reckoning of historical time, see Büsing 1978, 52–66. The hypothesis of the "Mycenaean" colonization of Cyrene has been defended by S. Stucchi, "Aspetti di precolonizzazione a Cirene," in D. Musti (ed.) 1985, 341–47, and "Nuovi aspetti della precolonizzazione della Libya," in D. Musti (ed.), *La transizione dal Miceneo all'Alto Arcaismo. Dal palazzo alla città* (Rome 1991), 583–86; see also L. Bacchielli, "Contatti fra *Libya* e mondo egeo nell'età di bronzo: una conferma," *Rend. Acc. Naz. Lincei* 34 (1979): 163–68. For an argument based on historical linguistics on this topic, see C. Brillante, "Il nome della Libia in un frammento de Ibico," in Gentili (ed.) 1990, 99–122 (with n. 33); see also Giannini 1990, 84–88, and Colomba 1980. The historicist thesis was rejected in its time, on the basis of more important documentation, by Chamoux 1952, 69–91 (in particular 74 n. 1), who was responding to the historical hypotheses of Studniczka 1890, 126–31, and Malten 1911, 112–41.

2. This "arithmetic" time, culturally Christian in its perspective, enters into the larger category of "chronic" time as defined by Benveniste 1974, 67–78. Ricoeur 1985, 154–60 (Eng. transl. 1988, 105–9), takes up this notion in creating a "calendar" time. But neither of these two authors analyzes the material aspect of the time of physical eventuality, or the relationship of "calendar time" with the cyclic time of the festive calendar: cf. *infra* n. 7. For the material *semeîa*, cf. Thuc. 1.10.1.

3. On the occasion of *Pythian* 9, cf. Carey 1981, 65–66 and 93. On that of *Pythian* 5, cf. Lefkowitz 1985, 37, with the complementary remarks of E. Cingano, "Interpretazioni pindariche," *Quad. Urb. Cult. Class.* 65 (1990): 143–62, on the political context of its performance. On the occasion of *Pythian* 4, see Giannini 1979, 35–36; Braswell 1988, 1–6, who privileges poetic intentions in the composition of the ode; and Gentili (*et al.*) 1995, 103–4, who sees in the poem a citharodic song. The date of the thirty-first Pythiad for the fourth and fifth *Pythians* is drawn from *Inscr.* a and b *Pyth.* 4 and *Inscr. Pyth.* 5 (vol. 2, pp. 92, 93, and 171 Drachmann).

4. The circumstances surrounding the publication of the work of Herodotus are evoked by J. Gould, *Herodotus* (London 1989), 4–18. For the historical references probably contained in the *Hymn to Apollo* of Callimachus, see *infra* n. 149, and for the *Agreement of the Founders* (SEG IX.3), *infra* n. 143.

5. The question of the relationship of the *Epinicians* of Pindar to the contexts of their enunciation is discussed by Angeli-Bernardini 1983, 39–79, and Gentili 1989, 153–202 (Eng. transl. 1988, 115–54); for *Pythian* 5 in particular, see

Krummen 1990, 1–27. The studies of Lefkowitz, collected in a volume in 1991, 1–71 and 191–201, have revived controversy over the enunciative reference of the *Epinicians*: chorus or poet? As concerns the enunciator of *Pythian 5*, see the references given *infra* n. 108; Gentili (*et al.*) 1995, 237–38, thinks that *Pythian 9* was sung by Telesicrates himself! Note also on the question W. Rösler, "Persona reale o persona poetica? L'interpretazione dell'io nella lirica greca," *Quad. Urb. Cult. Class.* 48 (1985): 131–44, G. B. d'Alessio, "First-Person Problems in Pindar," *Bull. Inst. Class. Stud.* 39 (1994): 117–39, and G. Nagy, "Genre and Occasion," *Mètis* 9/10 (1994/95): 11–25; for other bibliographical references, see M. R. Lefkowitz, "The First Person in Pindar Reconsidered — Again," *Bull. Inst. Class. Stud.* 40 (1995): 139–50.

6. These different systems for the measurement of time are analyzed in the now classic work of E. J. Bickermann, *Chronology of the Ancient World*, 2nd ed. (London 1980), 62–70; for Athens, see K. Raaflaub, "Athenische Geschichte und mündliche Überlieferung," in von Ungern-Sternberg and Reinau (eds.) 1988, 197–225.

7. For the sake of clarity, I have borrowed the distinction between "narrated time" (*temps raconté*) and "time of narrating" (*temps du raconter*) from Ricoeur 1984, 113–30 (Eng. transl. 1985, 77–88); he himself takes up the traditional distinction between "erzählte Zeit" and "Erzählzeit" in order to develop an unclear opposition between the "uttered time" (*temps de l'énoncé*) and the "time of enunciation" (*temps de l'énonciation*, to which is added "l'expérience fictive du temps") and in order to introduce pertinent nuances in the distinction between "historic time" (*temps d'histoire*) and "narrative time" (*temps de récit*) formulated by G. Genette in *Figures* III (Paris 1972), 122–30 (Eng. transl.: *Narrative Discourse* [Ithaca, N.Y., and London 1980], 117–25). The overlapping of these temporal lines with "calendar" time (cf. *supra* n. 2) in Greek historiography is the object of my study "Temps du récit du rituel dans la poétique grecque. Bacchylide entre mythe, histoire, et culte," in C. Darbo-Peschanski (ed.), *Constructions du temps dans le monde grec ancien* (Paris 2000), 395–412.

8. On this topic, see the reflections of F. Lasserre, "L'historiographie grecque à l'époque archaïque," *Quad. Stor.* 4 (1976): 113–42, and C. Dougherty, "Archaic Greek Foundation Poetry. Questions of Genre and Occasion," *Journ. Hell. Stud.* 114 (1994), 35–46. Surprisingly, Lasserre omits local genealogical history from the list he draws up of the first historiographical forms, although it is well attested from the Archaic period, for example by the *Corinthiaca* of Eumelus of Corinth: cf. Paus. 2.1.1 = *Cor.* fr. 1 and 4 Bernabé; cf. M. L. West, "'Eumelos': A Corinthian Epic Cycle?" *Journ. Hell. Stud.* 122 (2002): 109–132.

9. The relationship between the first forms of historiography and writing has been brought to light by F. Hartog, "Ecritures, généalogies, archives, histoire en Grèce ancienne," in *Mélanges P. Levêque*, vol. 1 (Besançon and Paris 1991), 177–88. Thomas 1989, 173–95, comments on the work of genealogical systematization undertaken by Athenian historiographers; see also Jacob, *art. cit.* chap. 1 n. 45, 176–84. For Hecataeus in particular, see L. Pearson, *Early Ionian Historians* (Oxford 1939), 96–106, along with the references given *supra*, chap. I n. 56.

10. Hdt. 2.116 f.; Paus. 2.18.6; Mimn. frr. 21 and 22 Gentili-Prato; Stes. frr. S 88–147 and 196–205 Page-Davies; Thuc. 1.21.1 f. On the role of "myth" in

melic poetry, see most recently Nagy 1990, 116–23; Gentili 1992, 94–98; and Calame 2000, 95–115.

11. In general, sources postdating the Alexandrian period will not be considered; on these texts, see Malten 1911, 26–41, and Chamoux 1952, 78–79.

12. On the narrative technique of Pindar, considered in terms of temporal interplay, see the study of A. Hurst, "Aspects du temps chez Pindare," in Hurst 1985, 155–97, and the bibliographical references he gives in n. 1.

13. The concepts discussed here are explained *supra* chap. I, § 4.2.

14. Cf. A. Hurst, "Temps du récit chez Pindar (*Pyth.* 4) et chez Bacchylide (11)," *Mus. Helv.* 40 (1983): 146–68, and R. Drew Griffith, "In the Dark Backward. Time in Pindaric Narrative," *Poetics Today* 14 (1993): 607–23; see also E. Robbins, "Jason and Cheiron. The Myth of Pindar's Pythian IV," *Phoenix* 29 (1975): 205–13. A linear reconstruction of the plot of Pindar's poem is presented by Braswell 1988, 23–30 and 78.

15. Hom. *Od.* 11.118 ff. (= 23.268ff.), with the commentary of W. F. Hansen, "Odysseus' Last Journey," *Quad. Urb. Cult. Class.* 24 (1977): 27–48, that of Ch. Segal, *Singers, Heroes and Gods in the* Odyssey (Ithaca, N.Y., and London 1994), 187–94, and that of Dougherty 2001, 172–76. The difficulties of a detailed interpretation posed by this complex passage are discussed by A. Heubeck, *Omero. Odissea*, vol. 3 (Milan 1983), 270–73 (Eng. transl.: *A Commentary on Homer's Odyssey*, vol. 3 [Oxford 1992]), 244–47).

On the modes of intervention of Poseidon in the marine and equestrian domains, see Detienne and Vernant 1974, 176–200 and 221–41 (Eng. transl. 1978, 187–215 and 231–48). The affinity imagined by the Greeks between the two domains was fostered by numerous metaphors: see Braswell 1988, 84–85.

16. While designating the wood of a weapon and consequently of a spear, *dóru* refers, in its primary meaning, to a beam meant for construction; from here comes its triple sense, "framework of a ship" (Hom. *Il.* 15.410 or *Od.* 9.498), "frame of a chariot" (Hes. *Op.* 456; Hom. *Il.* 12.36), and, by synechdoche, "ship" (Aesch. *Pers.* 411 and *Suppl.* 846). For the interpretative problem of the boat's portage posed in line 26, see recently E. Livrea, "L'episodio libico nel quarto libro delle 'Argonautiche' de Apollonio Rodio," *Quad. Arch. Libya* 12 (1987): 175–90.

17. On the bit as a control over the savage forces of the horse, see Detienne and Vernant 1974, 183–91 (Eng. transl. 1978, 195–203), and E. F. Cook, *The Odyssey in Athens. Myths of Cultural Origins* (Ithaca, N.Y., and London 1995), 181–94.

18. Sch. Pind. *Pyth.* 4.61 (vol. 2, p. 105 Drachmann); cf. also the scholia to 4.51 (vol. 2, p. 104 Drachmann), where Eurypylus is presented as the indigenous king of Cyrene (cf. *infra* § 3.3). The characterization of Eurypylus as such goes back in any case to the historiographer Acesandrus of Cyrene, *FGrHist.* 81 F 3, cited by the sch. A. R., 1561c (p. 322 Wendel); cf. also F 4 and Phylarch. *FGrHist.* 81 F 15. On two occasions, the scholiast insists on the familial bond between Eurypylus and Euphemus: cf. also sch. *ad* 4.36a (vol. 2, p. 102 Drachmann). The scholiast to 4.57 (vol. 2, p. 105 Drachmann) repeats the identification that Apollonius of Rhodes (4.1552 and 1561) makes between Triton and Eurypylus: see, in addition, the scholia to the first passage (p. 321 Wendel), which does not hesitate to attribute this identification to Pindar himself!

The scholia to Pindar also cite a fr. of Acesandrus (*FGrHist.* 469 F 1) on this topic. According to this fourth-century historian, Eurypylus was the son of Poseidon and Celaeno, the daughter of Atlas; he was thus the brother of Triton. On this dimorphous being, see *infra* n. 40. Significantly, the Cephisus near which the legend places the birth of Euphemus flows into Lake Copaïs (a Greek homologue, more or less, of Lake Triton) near Orchomenus, the capital of the Minyans (a group to which the Argonauts belong).

19. According to the sch. Pind. *Pyth.* 4.85 (vol. 2, p. 109 Drachmann), the emigration of the Danaans from Sparta, Argos, and Mycenae is provoked by the return of the Heraclids, which has generally been associated with the "Dorian invasion": cf. Giannini 1979, 41 n. 30, and Braswell 1988, 128–30.

The semionarrative analysis shows that we have here an unrealized program of the same legend, not of two different ones; this is affirmed by Burton 1962, 152, along with other critics. Note as well C. Lévi-Strauss, "Mythe et oubli," in *Langue, discours, et société. Pour Emile Benveniste* (Paris 1975), 294–300, who demonstrates (following the lead of J.-P. Vernant) the role played by forgetting, understood as a type of lack of communication, in different narratives of foundation.

20. While the *Argonautica* does in fact include an explicit allusion to the foundation of Cyrene, it is within a very different narrative context (2.498ff.) and through the intermediary of a different legendary version: cf. *infra* § 2.6. Hunter 1993, 152–53, has no doubts as to the allusions to Cyrene and the parallel established between Arcesilas IV and one of the Ptolemies in the Hellenistic version of the foundation of Thera; on the other hand, Corsano 1991, 63–72, drawing his argument from the foundation narrative's stop at Thera instead of at Cyrene, sees a sign of the epic poet's polemic against Callimachus. On the movement of literacy in Alexandrian poetry, see P. Bing, *The Well-Read Muse. Present and Past in Callimachus and the Hellenistic Poets* (Göttingen 1988), 10–48.

21. Concerning this type of sacrifice, see the numerous parallels cited by P. Stengel, *Die Griechischen Kultusaltertümer*, 3rd ed. (Munich 1920), 135–36. Otherwise, the mastery through *mêtis* of the signs that represent the *póroi* over an indistinct expanse is examined by Detienne and Vernant 1974, 147–50 (Eng. transl. 1978, 150–53). On the reading *therotróphos*, which the manuscript offers as a epithet of Libya, cf. *infra* n. 77. Concerning the intermingling of earth and sea, we should note that while the Argonauts erect the tripod on land (*en kthoní*, 1550), Triton makes it disappear into the lake (1590). In discussing the analogies of this meeting with those between Odysseus and Athena in the *Odyssey* (7.14ff. and 13.221ff.), Hunter 1993, 89–90, stresses the role played by Poseidon.

22. Braswell 1988, 347–48, sees political reasons for this displacement of the Lemnian stage of the narrative. The sch. Pind. *Pyth.* 4.455b (vol. 2, p. 160 Drachmann) gives the name Lamache or Malache to the Lemnian woman united with Euphemus. The same commentary, drawing notably on Didymus (fr. II.5.25 Schmidt), distinguishes four different Euphemuses: the founder of the *génos* of the colonists of Cyrene, and consequently also of the Battiads; the descendant of this first Euphemus, and the son of Samos; a third Euphemus who accompanied

Battus in the actual foundation of Cyrene; and a contemporary of Arcesilas IV, whom Pindar indirectly praises in *Pythian 5* according to the sch. *ad* 5.34 (vol. 2, p. 175 Drachmann) = Theotim. *FGrHist.* 470 F 1 (cf. *infra* n. 100). Note that the scholiast designates the first Euphemus as *arkhegós*; this qualification is applied as well to one responsible for the original act of foundation of a *génos*, as to the oecist of a colonial city: see Casevitz 1985, 246–48. The sch. *ad Pyth.* 4.447a (vol. 2, p. 159 Drachmann) notes the inversion the traditional succession of stages of the Argonauts' voyage undergoes in the Pindaric poem.

23. This *nûn* seems to correspond to the *nûn* at line 50, which designates the moment of the birth of the race of Battus and thus of Arcesilas, as well, in the prediction of Medea; in this way, the correspondence between T1 and T2 would be stressed. On the "spontaneous" oracle, see Braswell 1988, 144–46, and *infra* n. 130.

24. According to the sch. *ad* Pind. *Pyth.* 4.450a (vol. 2, p. 160 Drachmann), the occasion was the funeral games celebrated in honor of either the lost husbands or Thoas.

25. *Apoikeîn* designates the establishment of colonists through emigration: see Casevitz 1985, 114–35.

26. Braswell 1988, 88, and Segal 1986, 27, 30–51, 136–45, 171, and 183. A substantial portion of the present study was written with this second work in mind; the views developed there show welcome points of agreement with those presented here. The different enunciative voices of the poem merely recapture that of the poet, who willingly poses as the "prophet of the Muses"; cf. Gianotti 1975, 81–83; see also S. I. Johnston, "The Song of the *Iynx*: Magic and Rhetoric in *Pythian 4*," *Trans. Am. Philol. Assoc.* 125 (1995): 177–206.

27. On the inversion in melic poetry of the traditional roles held by the inspired poet and by the inspiratory Muse, cf. Calame 1986, 47–50 (Eng. transl. 1995, 48–52).

28. The inspiratory spring from which flows water of divine origin and with which the poet quenches his poetic thirst is a recurrent image in Pindar: cf. Gianotti 1975, 110–14, and Braswell 1988, 399. On the spring located at the geographical center of the city of Cyrene, see *infra* nn. 83 and 131.

29. These Greek representations of the foundation of civilization have been analyzed by Detienne 1989, 215–20 (Eng. transl. 1994, 116–19), and Vernant 1974, 148–53 (Eng. transl. 1980, 151–56); on the agricultural metaphors for sex, see also K. Ormand, *Exchange and the maiden. Marriage in Sophoclean tragedy* (Austin 1999).

30. *Rhíza* (15) probably refers to the image of the germination of Cyrene: cf. Braswell 1988, 71–73. On the problem of the geographical localization of this "bosom" of the colonial city, cf. *ibid.*, 81–83. On the other hand, according to the scholia *ad Pyth.* 4.14 (vol. 2, p. 98 Drachmann), Aristarchus, in his commentary on Pindar, connected the image of the *mastós* with the Homeric expression *oûthar aroúres*, "udder of the field," that is, its most fertile part, and interpreting it as "breast of the field," (Hom. *Il.* 9.14 f.; cf. also *HCer.* 450); it is also in this sense of double fertility—vegetal and civic—that the scholia *ad Pyth.* 4.25b and 27 (vol. 2, p. 100 Drachmann) understand the entire passage. In addition, this quality of fertility is probably inscribed in the term *bôla* in the

same sense: in Homeric poetry, the adjectives *eríbolax* and *eríbolos* designate fertile regions (Paeonia: *Il.* 21.154; Phaeacea: *Od.* 5.34; *árourai*: *HCer.* 471, etc.).

31. Segal 1986, 68–71, has demonstrated the bonds that connect the metaphorical cultivation undertaken by the ancestor of Battus and Jason's enterprise to capture the Golden Fleece (224ff.). But in the legend as Pindar treats it, the cultivation of Jason does not bear fruit; it leads implicitly to the reconquest of legitimate power over an existent city (105ff.), and not to the foundation of a new city. Jason is, in a sense, already in possession of a "root." On the metaphoric use of *phuteúomai*, cf. Braswell 1988, 229.

32. Segal 1986, 81–82, is also sensitive to the "urban" isotopy that runs through the entire ode (cf. 7, 19f., 56, 260, and 272), but he overlooks its "rural" counterpart: cf. Paus. 10.15.6. The myth of the foundation of Cyrene does not lead us from the desert to civic life, but from potentially fertile soil to its products: a fertile *khóra* and a well-administered city. The gift of the clod thus represents more than an agreement on the sovereignty over the land in question, as is the case in the legends cited by Braswell 1988, 92–93. Malkin 1994, 163–67, attempts to show that while designating Libya in general, the "foundations" of Zeus Ammon correspond to the geographical reality of the Cyrenaica, with its different sanctuaries of the god apparently established on the frontiers of the land; cf. *infra* n. 67. T. Cole, *Pindar's Feasts or the Music of Power* (Rome 1992), 115–18, is rightly suspicious of too-precise geographical identifications.

33. Hdt. 4.179 and 188; Diod. Sic. 3.70.2, along with the sch. Pind. *Pyth.* 4.36a (vol. 2, p. 102 Drachmann) and sch. A. R. 4.1311 (p. 313 Wendel); see also Diod. Sic. 5.70.4 and 72.3. Athena is born from Zeus' umbilical cord buried near the river Triton of Crete, in a spot afterward called *omphalós* (cf. Call. *Jov.* 42ff.). The location of Lake Triton in the Greek representation of the inhabited world and the aspects of the Golden Age attached to it are studied by Ballabriga 1986, 216–21. S. Jackson, "Apollonius' *Argonautica*: Euphemus, a Clod, and the Tripod," *Ill. Class. Stud.* 12 (1987): 23–30, attempts to retrace the history of this episode in the story of the clod of Cyrene.

34. On the gateway to Hades on Cape Taenarum, cf. Men. fr. 785 Koerte, cited by the sch. Pind. *Pyth.* 4.76d (vol. 2, p. 108 Drachmann), Strab. 8.5.1, sch. Aristoph. *Ach.* 510 (vol. 1.1B, p. 71 Koster) and sch. Lyc. 90 (vol. 2, p. 50 Scheer). On Medea's prophecy and Teireisias' parallel prophetic words to Odysseus, cf. *supra* § 2.1 with n. 15.

35. On Heracles and Cerberus: Bacch. 5.56ff.; Eur. *HF* 23f., 612ff. and 1277ff.; the version is confirmed by Apoll. 2.5.12 and Diod. Sic. 4.25.1 and 26.1; Paus. 2.35.10 and 3.25.5: attempting to sustain his skepticism concerning the cavern that he visits on Cape Taenarum with its supposed path of communication with Hades, Pausanias cites the rationalizing explanation previously proposed by Hecataeus, *FGrHist.* 1 F 27. The hypothesis of a Peisistratid origin of the version that makes Heracles an initiate in the Eleusinian Mysteries is discussed by G. W. Bond, *Euripides. Heracles* (Oxford 1981), 218–19; see also Pind. fr. dub. 346 Maehler. Concerning the cult of Demeter Chthonia at Hermione, cf. Burkert 1977, 308 (Eng. transl. 1985, 200), and Detienne and Vernant 1979, 203–8 (Eng. transl. 1989, 140–44).

36. Clem. *Protr.* 2.17, sch. Luc. p. 275, 23ff. Rabe, with analogous acts given as parallels by Burkert 1977, 365–70 (Eng. transl. 1985, 242–46), and the interpretation proposed by Detienne and Vernant 1979, 191–99 (Eng. transl. 1989, 133–38). Epict. 4.8.36, with the commentary of Detienne 1989, 215–20 (Eng. transl. 1994, 116–19).

37. Call. *Del.* 11ff. and 30ff.; *HAp.* 53ff. and 72ff.; for the cosmogonic activity of Poseidon, see W. H. Mineur, *Callimachus. Hymn to Delos* (Leiden 1984), 77–78. The name change from *Kallíste* to *Théra* is also mentioned by Hdt. 1.147.4, A. R. 4.1763, sch. Pind. *Pyth.* 4.455c (vol. 2, p. 161 Drachmann); we should not forget also Call. fr. 716 Pfeiffer, with the numerous references given in Pfeiffer's critical apparatus.

38. Hom. *Il.* 2.653ff.; Pind. *Ol.* 7.27ff., with the commentary of Angeli-Bernardini 1983, 170–85, and Dougherty 1993, 120–28. The rationalizing version of the founding of Rhodes is in Diod. Sic. 5.56.1ff.; in Apoll. 1.4.5, Rhode, the daughter of Poseidon and Amphitrite, is the sister of Triton; cf. Prinz 1979, 78–97. Note that the island of Syme, inhabited from its origin, is first colonized by men who accompany Triops and are led by a certain Chthonius, son of Poseidon and Syme: see Diod. Sic. 5.53.1.

A semantic analysis of the Archaic use of the of the verb *ktízo* shows that particularly on the islands, the verb designates as much the activity of cultivation of land after it has been cleared as it does the civilizing construction of a civic establishment: see Casevitz 1985, 21–34.

39. Paus. 3.1.1; on other autochthonous heroes and founders of cities, see Brelich 1958, 137–39. In contrast to birth from the depths of the earth, expressed by the term *gegénes*, autochthony implies in addition dwelling on the soil from which one is born: cf. E. Montanari, *Il mito dell'autoctonia* (Rome 1981), 31–37, and V. J. Rosivach, "Authochthony and the Athenians," *Class. Quart.* 81 (1987): 294–306.

40. On Cecrops, see especially Aristoph. *Vesp.* 438 and Philoch. *FGrHist.* 328 F 39, *Marm. Par. FGrHist.* 239 A 1, and Apoll. 3.14.1: cf. U. Kron, *Die zehn attischen Phylenheroen* (Berlin 1976), 84–103. For the dispute between Poseidon and Athena, cf. Hdt. 8.55, Plut. *Them.* 19, Paus. 1.26.5 and 8.10.4, etc.; see R. Parker, "Myths of Early Athens," in Bremmer (ed.) 1987, 187–214, and Cook, *op. cit* n. 17, 129–39.

While the double nature of Cecrops (part man, part serpent) associates him with the earth, that of Triton (part man, part dolphin), associates him, another hybrid being, with the sea — as does his parentage, Poseidon and Amphitrite: cf. Hes. *Theog.* 930 f., A. R. 4.1602ff., sch. A. R. 4.1619 (p. 324 Weidmann) and sch. Lyc. 886 (vol. 2, p. 287 Scheer). Triton is the brother of Rhode, among others: cf. *supra* n. 38. But Lycophron 886 and 892 calls the *dímorphos* god a descendant of Nereus. Libya herself is called *autóchthon* by Hdt. 4.45.3.

41. On Erichthonius, born from the seed of Hephaestus spilled on the soil of Athens without having touched the *parthénos* Athena, see Apoll. 3.14.6, along with Hom. *Il.* 2.546 ff., Eur. *Ion* 266ff. and *Erechth.* fr. 65.55 Austin; other versions of the birth of Erichthonius-Erechtheus are in Parker, *art. cit.* n. 40, 193–98, who shows the impact this birth from a nourishing earth has on the representation of the status of the Athenian citizen; see also on this topic Loraux 1981, 41–72 (Eng. transl. 1984, 42–71); P. Brulé, *La fille d'Athènes* (Besançon

and Paris 1987), 13–79, and Calame 1996, 438–41, and 2000, 133–6. On the visual representations of this birth, see C. Bérard, *Anodoi. Essai sur l'imagerie des passages chthoniens* (Neuchâtel and Rome 1974), 34–38.

We should note that in the *Menexenus* (237dff.), Plato, parodying the *epitaphios* of Pericles in the voice of Aspasia, in a sense inverts the terms of the metaphor by asserting that a pregnant Athenian woman is merely imitating the earth of Attica, which engendered the first men, who were just and respectful to the gods, and produced from the start cereals and oil to nourish them. The myth of autochthony reinterpreted by Plato thus makes vegetal generation the model for human generation!

42. Aesch. *Sept.* 752ff.; on the myth of the autochthonous birth of the Cadmeans, cf. Vian 1963, 158–76. Examining the analogy with autochthony, Malkin 1994, 180, also mentions the legend of Aletes, who creates from an earthen clod a sign of his power over Corinth: cf. Dur. *FGrHist.* 76 F 84.

43. A. R. 1.182ff., who, in his catalog of the Argonauts, attributes the same ancestry to Euphemus as Pindar; see also Paus. 5.17.9, who reports that on the chest of Cypselus at Corinth Euphemus was represented as the victor in the chariot race at the games in honor of Pelias, and Hyg. *Fab.* 14, 15, sch. Pind. *Pyth.* 4.61 (vol. 2, p. 106 Drachmann), and sch. Lyc. 886 (vol. 2, p. 287 Scheer). The Hesiodic tradition makes Euphemus a son of Poseidon and Mecionice, the daughter of Eurotas: Hes. fr. 253 Merkelbach-West, as cited by sch. Pind. *Pyth.* 4.36c (vol. 2, p. 102 Drachmann) and as commented on by the sch. *ad* 4.15b (vol. 2, p. 99 Drachmann). Moreover, Euphemus had married a sister of Heracles: see *ibid.* and sch. *ad* 4.79b (vol. 2, p. 108 Drachmann).

On Tityus, born from Gaia, cf. Hom. *Od.* 11.576. On Trojan Erichthonius and Tros, see Hom. *Il.* 20.219ff. and Diod. Sic. 4.75.1f.; the ability to move over the surface of the sea with a team of horses is also attributed to Poseidon himself (Hom. *Il.* 13.17ff.).

Apart from the conjectures voiced by the scholiasts to explain Euphemus' position at the prow of the ship when the Argonauts come to shore in Libya, we might ask whether this explicit assertion by Pindar (22) is not to be understood in relation to the specific ability of Euphemus to walk on water; cf. sch. Pind. *Pyth.* 4.36c and 61 (vol. 2, pp. 102 and 105 Drachmann), which cite Theotim. *FGrHist.* 470 F 2. The respective functions attributed to the two pilots of Theseus show, in any case, that the *próreus* is the assistant of the *kubernétes*: Philoc. *FGrHist.* 328 F 111.

44. These are the characteristics that Pindar attributes to the Lemnians, even if the union of these women with the Argonauts marks, in other versions of the legend, their return to the institution of marriage under the auspices of the pleasing fragrances of Aphrodite; see on this topic Detienne 1989, 172–84 (Eng. transl. 1994, 90–98).

45. Concerning the polysemy of this expression in Pindar, cf. T. J. Hoey, "Fusion in Pindar," *Harv. Stud. Class. Philol.* 70 (1965): 236–52, and Segal 1986, 64 and 71; for the sense of the verb here, see *infra* § 3.2.

46. Hdt. 4.147, in a text discussed *infra* § 5.1, which should be read with the commentary of Corcella and Medaglia 1993, 337–39; see also n. 94. Note also on this subject the sch. Pind. *Pyth* 4.10b, 10f and 88c (vol. 2, pp. 97, 98 and

110 Drachmann). The first of these scholia cites the fr. mentioned of Hierocles; the second claims to have drawn its information on the sanctuary of Poseidon and Athena from the historian Theocrestus of Cyrene (not Theophrastus): *FGrHist*. 761 F 3. Other analogous insular foundations are discussed by Vian 1963, 60–64.

47. In this way, Battus' role as a founding hero, the quality that distinguishes his character, is made to stand out (cf. *infra* § 4.2); on the political function attributed to *Pythian* 4, see Giannini 1979, 37, 39 and 42–43, and Gentili (*et al.*) 1995, 103–4.

48. In spite of the reservations of some interpreters on this point, the term *népodes* (1745) is particularly suited to designate the descendants of Euphemus. Found in Homer (*Od.* 4.404), where it refers to the baby seals cast out by *Halosúdne*, the "Child of the Sea," the term in Alexandrian poetry readily designates the descendants of a river-god: Call. frr. 66.1 and 533 Pfeiffer (but in fr. 222, the aquatic sense of the term is not actualized; the same is true for Theocr. 17.25). Here the use of the term to designate the descendants of Euphemus can refer as much to the ability of their ancestor, the son of Poseidon, to walk on water (cf. *supra* n. 43) as to their own destiny as island dwellers and mediators between the sea and the land. On representations of the seal as an amphibious and mediatory animal, cf. Detienne and Vernant 1974, 244–52 (Eng. transl. 1978, 260–67); on the etymology of the term *népodes*, cf. P. Chantraine, *Dictionnaire étymologique de la langue grecque*, vol. 3 (Paris 1974), 747.

As M. Steinrück has remarked to me, this manner of placing in the mouth of the principal protagonist the interpretation of her own dream is already found in the explanation of the famous dream of Penelope in Hom. *Od.* 19.535ff. Moreover, Hunter 1993, 153 n. 7, sees in the qualification of the clod as *epimástios* an echo of Pind. *Pyth.* 4.37 and 78 (designation of Cyrene); see also 168 n. 59, along with the study of F. Létoublon, "Rêve d'amour," in J.-C. Marimouton and J.-M. Racault (eds.), *L'insularité. Thématique et représentations* (Paris 1995), 17–26.

49. The scholiasts do not fail to fill in the Alexandrian poet's narrative by mentioning its Cyrenaean conclusion: the sch. A. R. 4.1750/1757 and 1760/1764d (pp. 327–28 Wendel) note the difference between the forgetfulness of which the clod is the object in the Pindaric version and the voluntary act of Euphemus in Apollonius. On the interpretation of dreams in antiquity, see G. Giangrande, "Dreams in Apollonius Rhodius," *Quad. Urb. Cult. Class.* 95 (2000): 107–23.

50. The figure of Poseidon as a divinity of the soil, in particular of its continental depths, as well as a god of marine depths, is noted by Burkert 1977, 217–19 (Eng. transl. 1985, 137–39). On the possible etymology of *gaiéokhos* as "who leads Gaia (as his spouse)" in accordance with *Poseidón* understood as *pósis Dâs*, "Earth's husband," see F. Schachermeyr, *Poseidon und die Entstehung des giechischen Götterglaubens* (Bern 1950), 13–15, with the critical remarks of E. Simon, *Die Götter der Griechen* (Munich 1985), 67–68. On the origin and nature of the cult of Poseidon on Thera, cf. *supra* n. 46.

51. Mus. fr. 2 B 11 Diels-Kranz, cited by Paus. 10.5.6, cf. also 10.24.4 and Ephor. *FGrHist*. 70 F 150 and 31 b; see the commentary of C. Sourvinou-

Inwood, "Myth as History: The Previous Owners of the Delphic Oracle," in Bremmer (ed.) 1987, 215–41, reprinted in *"Reading" Greek Culture. Texts and Images, Rituals and Myths* (Oxford 1991), 217–43; she enumerates the different legendary versions of the succession from Gaia to Apollo in demonstrating the futility of a historicist reading of these narratives; see also the epigraphical attestations in G. Daux, "Le *Poteidanion* de Delphes," *Bull. Corr. Hell.* 92 (1968): 540–49.

52. On the combined intervention of Zeus and Apollo in relation to Metis and Themis in *Pythian* 4, see Giannini 1979, 42 and 49–53.

53. The Libyan cult of Zeus Ammon is already placed in relation to the cult at Dodona by Hdt. 2.54 ff., who attributes a common Egyptian origin to them: see the commentary of A. B. Lloyd, *Herodotus Book II. Commentary 1–98* (Leiden 1976), 251–64, and Braswell 1988, 84. According to the sch. Pind. *Pyth.* 4.28 (vol. 2, p. 100 Drachmann), the entire land of Libya was consecrated to Zeus. In his historical study of 1994, 161–63, Malkin relates the role played by Zeus Ammon in *Pythian* 4 to the different sanctuaries the god appears to have at his disposal on the frontiers of the Cyrenaica.

For the ancestry of the figure Libya, cf. sch. Pind. *Pyth.* 4.25 (vol. 2, p. 100 Drachmann), but also Aesch. *Suppl.* 315ff. and Apoll. 2.4.1f.

54. On the organizing and fertilizing functions of Zeus, see Burkert 1977, 200–203 (Eng. transl. 1985, 125–28), and H. Schwabl, "Zeus," *Realenc. Alt.-Wiss.* Suppl. XIV (Munich 1978), coll. 993–1481 (1046–53); Segal 1986, 171–79, relates these functions to the "patriarchal" role of the god. The tradition also reports, in relation to the fecundity of the soil, a Zeus Chthonius (Hes. *Op.* 465, cf. also 379, 474, and 488).

55. The subtle play of echoes that relates the Pindaric version of the search for the Golden Fleece to the legend of Cyrene's foundation has been brought to light by Segal 1986, 72–85 and 92–93. Segal mainly insists on the transition, through the exchange between sea and land, from instability to civic foundational order. But he is less sensitive to the fact that the principal protagonist of the legend of Cyrene's foundation is neither Euphemus nor Battus, but the miraculous clod itself.

56. This parallelism is noticed by Segal 1986, 84–85 and 160–61; on the cosmogonic echoes of this same episode, cf. *ibid.* 103–5 and 144. Segal also puts forward the hypothesis (91) that Pindar, for his part, follows an itinerary articulated in terms of departure and return. For echoes of reconciliation, festivity, and hospitality in the whole poem, see Hubbard 1985, 96–98. The *mêtis* that Pindar exercises toward Damophilus is discussed by Giannini 1979, 60–62.

For the genealogy of Altas, a hero marked by *húbris*, see Hes. *Theog.* 507ff.; on the cosmogonic role of Atlas in connection with the sea, cf. Hom. *Od.* 1.52ff. and Aesch. *Prom.* 348ff. Note also on this topic the commentary of M. L. West, *Hesiod. Theogony* (Oxford 1966), 311, and that of Ballabriga 1986, 75–91.

57. Some interpret the circularity of this course as a simple return, omitting its transformative aspect; this is the case for Burton 1962, 168; Kirkwood 1982, 163; and also Segal 1986, 89–93. See also N. Felson, "Vicarious Transport. Fictive Deixis in Pindar's *Pythian Four*," *Harv. Stud. Class. Philol.* 99 (1999): 1–31.

58. This paradox has been often noted, most recently by Woodbury 1982, 245–46. Köhnken 1985, 94, also proposes a narrative solution. The Delphic character of the response given by Chiron is also understood by Dougherty 1993, 147–49. In the poetry of Pindar, the figure conferred on Apollo varies according to the addressee of the poem: see Angeli Bernardini 1983, 64–67.

59. The discrepancies in the structure of the Pindaric narrative in contrast to a linear chronological development are thoroughly discussed by Köhnken 1985, 78–79; on the structure of the poem, see Froidefond 1989, 49–51.

60. The two nymphs who guard the cattle of the Sun on a remote island are also the daughters of the owner of the herd (Hom. *Od.* 12.131ff.). On the other hand, in Call. *Dian.* 206ff., Cyrene appears as the companion of Artemis; the nymph is honored by the goddess after an athletic victory as if she were an *erómenos*: see the commentary of F. Bornmann, *Callimachi Hymnus in Dianam* (Florence 1968), 97–98.

In assimilating Cyrene with Atalanta (cf. Woodbury 1982, 251–53 and Giannini 1990, 57–60), commentators have effaced the former's association with the positive activity of hunting, as well as the note of *aidós* that marks her union with Apollo. It is never said that Cyrene *phúgei gámon*, as is the case with Atalanta (Hes. fr. 73 Merkelbach-West, Thgn. 1287ff., Aristoph. *Lys.* 785ff.); other sources and documents attesting to the legend of Atalanta are collected by J. Boardman and G. Arrigoni, "Atalanta," *LIMC* vol. II.1 (Zurich and Munich 1984), 940–50.

61. Cyrene, therefore, should not be assimilated to Artemis Agrotera, as Dougherty 1993, 142–43, has proposed. On the adolescent and ephebic nature of Theseus' armament in his combat with monsters, cf. F. Brommer, *Theseus. Die Taten des griechischen Helden in der antiken Kunst und Literatur* (Darmstadt 1982), 3–34, and my own discussion in 1996, 187–90.

62. Slightly different versions of the genealogical origin of Hypseus appear in Pherec. *FGrHist.* 3 F 57 and Acesandr. *FGrHist.* 469 F 2, cited by the sch. Pind. *Pyth.* 9.27b (vol. 2, p. 233 Drachmann); cf. also sch. *ad* 9.104 and 105 (vol. 2, p. 230 Drachmann).

63. In *Ol.* 6.29ff., Iamus, the son of Apollo and Evadne (herself a daughter of Poseidon), has a destiny analogous to that of Aristaios; he also comes to share one of his own essential functions with his father, namely the oracular art. This analogy is noted by Crotty 1982, 116–17. On the epithets given to Aristaios, cf. *infra* n. 88, and for Greek marriage understood as a rite of passage toward maternity, see most recently my own study *I Greci e l'eros. Simboli, pratiche e luoghi* (Rome and Bari 1992), 87–98 (Eng. transl.: *The Poetics of Eros in Ancient Greece* [Princeton 1999], 116–29).

64. Even if the scholia *ad Pyth.* 9.6a (vol. 2, p. 212 Drachmann) maintain that Pindar draws the legend of Cyrene from the *Ehoiai* of Hesiod, the fr. 215 Merkelbach-West, which the scholiast cites, actually attributes a place of residence to Cyrene more in accordance with the genealogy of her father (cf. *supra* n. 62): the granddaughter of Peneus and Creusa lives in the land of Phthia, near the waters of the Peneus, which descend from Pindus; see nevertheless M. L. West, "The Hesiodic Catalogue: New Light on Apollo's Love-Life," *Zeitschr. Pap. Epigr.* 61 (1985): 1–7. The geographical displacement from Phthia to Pelion effected by Pindar, while locating the story in a place equally marked by

savagery, shows the liberties the poet can take with his supposed source (Diod. Sic. 4.81.1 follows the Pindaric version). This observation ought to contribute to weakening historicist hypotheses seeking to draw on the indications of the scholiast: cf. Malten 1911, 154–63, and Chamoux 1953, 84–88 and 171. On the other hand, A. R. 4.500 takes up again the Hesiodic version of the presence of Cyrene beside the "marshes of the Peneus."

65. Cf. Plat. *Symp.* 203b–c, A. R. 3.114ff., and Soph. fr. 320 Radt, with my own commentary in *op. cit.* n. 63, 124–26 (Eng. transl., 157–60); for the gardens of Aphrodite on Cyprus, see M. Carroll-Spillecke, KEPOS. Der antike griechische Garten (Munich 1989), 23–25. Aphrodite of course exercises the seductive, and then generative, power necessary to accomplish the paradigmatic matrimonial union that takes place in the "garden of Zeus"; Motte 1973, 121–36 and 207–28, collects other references to the gardens of Aphrodite as well as to those of Zeus. Places of fecundity, these gardens are the opposite of the sterile gardens of Adonis: cf. Detienne 1989, 191–201 (Eng. transl. 1994, 101–6). In *Pythian* 5, the Garden of Aphrodite, in which Arcesilas' praise is sung, corresponds to a place of cult within the sanctuary of Apollo (cf. *infra* § 4.2).

66. On the details of Cyrene's conveyance from Thessaly to Libya, the legend has several variations. According to different versions, the nymph is brought to Libya by the swans of Apollo (Pherecydes, *FGrHist.* 3 F 98, Ariaethus of Tegea, *FGrHist.* 316 F 3); she makes a stop in Crete (Agroitas, author of *Libyca*, *FGrHist.* 762 F 1); she emigrates to Libya of her own free will (Mnaseas the Periegete, *FHG* fr. 3, vol. 3, p. 156 Müller); cf. also Phylarchus of Athens, *FGrHist.* 81 F 16. All of these fragments are cited by the sch. A. R. 498/527a (p. 168 Wendel). We should note also that in the myths of topographical foundation that include the carrying off of a nymph by a god, islands and mountains take their denominations from nymphs seduced by Poseidon, such as Mount Rhodope (sch. Theocr. 75d, p. 98 Wendel) or Corcyra (Diod. Sic. 4.72.3), while the loves of Apollo are reserved for continental colonies, such as Sinope on the Euxine Sea (sch. A. R. 2.946c, p. 196 Wendel).

67. The parallelism Pindar establishes between this florescence of the land of Cyre and the blooming of Cyrene is brought to light by Felson-Rubin 1978, 359 and 365. Malkin 1994, 158–67, has attempted to assimilate the "garden of Zeus" on the one hand to the sanctuary of Zeus Ammon mentioned in *Pyth.* 4.15, and on the other, by metonymy, to the Cyrenaica as a whole; for the scholiasts *ad Pyth.* 9.90b, c, and d (vol. 2, p. 228 Drachmann), of which one cites in support of his identification the short fr. 36 Maehler, the "garden of Zeus" simply designates all of Libya; cf. *supra* nn. 32 and 53. The question of whether Libya, and by consequence Africa, constituted a third continent in addition to Europe and Asia was the object of an animated debate in the fifth century, which Herodotus echoes (4.16).

68. For the geographical identification of this hill, see *infra* n. 83.

69. Köhnken 1985 notes that the victorious conquest of the fiancée and subsequent marriage constitute the common denominator of the narratives included in *Pythian* 9. As for procreation, in the poem it takes the form of flowering, as observed by Kirkwood 1982, 216.

70. This last union is overlooked, for example, in the otherwise stimulating narrative analysis of Felson-Rubin 1978, 358–63.

71. Pind. *Isthm.* 4.52ff. with the sch. *ad loc.* (vol. 3, p. 235 Drachmann), which emphasizes the *apanthropía* and *asébeia* of the giant; cf. Angeli Bernardini 1983, 58–62. See also Phryn. *TrGF* 3 F 3a, Diod. Sic. 4.17.4, Apoll. 2.5.11, etc.; other sources are in R. Olmos and L. J. Balmaseda, "Antaios I," *LIMC* I.1 (Zurich and Munich 1981), 800–811.

72. The existence, for chronological reasons, of two Antaioses is supported by the sch. *ad Pyth.* 9.185b, 185d and 217 (vol. 2, pp. 238 and 240 Drachmann): the age of Heracles does not, in fact, correspond with that of the Cyrenaean colonist Alexidemus. A different reading of the Pindaric text, however, allows this doubling of the figure of the giant to be avoided (cf. Chamoux 1952, 281–85, and Robbins 1978, 103 n. 37): the young native woman could be the daughter of the king of Antaios' city; see Gentili (*et al.*) 1995, 616–17. But the preoccupation of this legend — already attested in the seventh century in the work of the epic poet Pisander (fr. 6 Bernabé), before the historical foundation of Cyrene — is probably not the synchronization of historical time!

73. Hdt. 4.158.2, 159.4f. and 160.1; sch. *ad Pyth.* 9.185a (vol. 2, p. 237 Drachmann), citing the fr. of Pisander mentioned in n. 72; the latter gives the name Alceis to the daughter of Antaios. While Herodotus situates Irasa to the east of Cyrene, Pherecydes of Athens, *FGrHist.* 3 F 75, places it to the west, near Lake Triton: cf. Ballabriga 1986, 216–17. In spite of historicizing speculation concerning these different versions, Malkin 1994, 181–87, relates these geographical shiftings to reorientations of the legend related to the progress of colonization in the region. On modern attempts to locate Irasa, cf. Goodchild 1971, 17–18, and Stucchi 1975, 5. For the foundation of Barce, cf. Hdt. 4.160, with the commentary of Chamoux 1952, 136–38. Note that Barce seems to have had an indigenous king by the name of Alazir; Arcesilas IV, having married his daughter, is perhaps repeating the legendary act of Alexidemus (Hdt. 4.164.4).

74. Woodbury 1982, 254–55. Note also the intelligent commentary that he supplies (246–47) on verses 99–100: if these admirers desire to make Telesicrates at once their husband and their son, it is because they project his own generative function onto their conception of a matrimonial union with him. Cf. also Segal 1986, 187–88, and the useful remarks of S. Instone, "Love and Sex in Pindar: Some Practical Thrusts," *Bull. Inst. Class Stud.* 37 (1990): 30–42, who shows that the dialogue between Apollo and Chiron concerning the girl Cyrene contributes to increasing amorous desire for the young athletic victor; see also, in a similar vein, Froidefond 1989, 49–60.

75. Cyrene itself, having become a city, is feminized as a "land of beautiful women" in order finally to receive Telesicrates (74); this movement reminds us that at the beginning of the narrative (9 and 56), it is Aphrodite who receives Apollo. For Carson 1982, 127–28, the return of Telesicrates to Cyrene should be interpreted as a type of *numphagógia*, with power to integrate the community! *Dóxa* would then be the wife of the athlete and Cyrene herself the mother of Doxa.

76. Note on this topic the interpretation of *Pythian* 9 proposed by Dougherty 1993, 137–51, who demonstrates certain relationships between agonal victory, marriage, and foundation that stress the connections Cyrene and Telesicrates both maintain with Apollo at Delphi. See also L. Kurke, *The Traffic in Praise.*

Pindar and the Poetics of Social Economy (Ithaca, N.Y., and London 1991), 127–32, who attempts to interpret these conjugal transfers as exchanges, and, with reference to the Odyssean Pheacians, Dougherty 2001, 130–34.

77. Hdt. 2.32.4; 4.155.3 and 157.2; 4.158.3 and 164.3; 4.199. See also the later evidence, cited *infra* n. 132. In A. R. 4.1561, the reading *therotróphos* should be retained, instead of its rival *melotróphos*, as the qualification of Libya in its primordial state. Note here that Libya was able to support, among other things, the golden goats (not sheep) guarded by a dragon-shepherd described as *ágrios*: Agroitas *FGrHist*. 762 F 3a and b. Moreover, in Lyc. 893, the Libyan people who welcome the Argonauts are presented as a community of shepherds. The miraculous animals that situate this pastoral Libya between uncultivated land and Golden Age are already mentioned by Homer, *Od.* 4.85ff.: the epic poet locates flocks that give abundant milk year-round in this region; see also on this point Hdt. 4.29. Doubtless it is in this context that we must assess the extraordinary qualities attributed to silphium: cf. Aristoph. *Plut.* 925 and sch. Aristoph. *Eq.* 894c (vol. 1.2, p. 211 Koster); all are collected and discussed by Chamoux 1952, 246–63.

78. On the building of Troy: Hom. *Il.* 21.441ff. and also 7.452f.; see S. Scully, *Homer and the Sacred City* (Ithaca, N.Y., and London 1990), 32–33 and 50–53. The complementarity of the construction of a city — with its houses, walls, and temples — and the formation of the *ároura* — the cultivated area that surrounds the city — is well demonstrated in the description of the foundation of Scheria (*Od.* 6.8ff.).

79. On Cyrene's affinity for equitation and the driving of chariots, see also *Pyth.* 4.2 and 5.32ff., 85, 92, and 115, along with Call. fr. 716 Pfeiffer. Even if Pindar does not seem to appeal to it here, we should remember the Greek metaphor expressing conceptions of marriage through the image of the domestication of a horse; see the remarks I have made on this subject in *Les choeurs de jeunes filles en Grèce archaïque*, vol. 1 (Rome 1977), 413–20 (Eng. transl.: *Choruses of Young Women in Ancient Greece* [London, Boulder, and New York 1997], 238–44). The marriage of Alexidemus to a native princess could then be expressed metaphorically through the domestication the passage from nomadic equitation to conveyance by yoked horses represents.

80. P. Voelke, "Ambivalence, médiation, intégration: à propos de l'espace dans le drame satyrique," *Et. Lettres* 2 (1992): 33–58, has admirably demonstrated the liminal character of space reserved for shepherds; for other references on this topic, cf. Calame 1992, 46–49, a study whose results I am summarizing here. For the relationship between Admetus and Apollo, see especially B. Sergent, *L'homosexualité dans la mythologie grecque* (Paris 1984), 124–32 (Eng. transl.: *Homosexuality in Greek Myth* [Boston 1986], 131–37).

81. The origin and location of the Altar of Horns on Delos are explored in the studies mentioned by Williams 1978, 59–60. The term *thémethla*, the first term used by Callimachus to designate the foundations established by Apollo, refers in *Pyth.* 4.16 to those of the sanctuary of Zeus Ammon; it consequently signifies there the foundations of Libyan soil. This same term is even used to designate the foundation by Apollo of the temple of Delphi: *HAp.* 254 and 294, with the commentary of Detienne 1998, 85–104. On the metaphorical usage of

the verb *huphaínein* to denote the construction of an edifice, see Williams 1978, 56–57, along with J. Scheid and J. Svenbro, *Le métier de Zeus. Mythe du tissage et du tissu dans le monde gréco-romain* (Paris 1994), 106–12 (Eng. transl.: *The Craft of Zeus. Myth of Weaving and Fabric* [Cambridge, Mass. and London 1996], 125–32. Weaving here refers to the activity of Apollo as architect: cf. Detienne 1990, 308–9.

82. The probable location of Aziris (spelled Azilis in the Callimachean text) is examined by Goodchild 1971, 19–20; cf. also Corcella and Medaglia 1993, 349. On the warlike appearance assumed by the Thebano-Spartiate colonists celebrating the Carneia, cf. Williams 1978, 5–6; on the military character of the Carneia itself, cf. Burkert 1977, 354–58 (Eng. transl. 1985, 234–36). The implantation of the Carneia in Libya also constitutes the main thread of the version of the Greek migration to the Cyrenaica as it is presented in *Pythian 5*: cf. *infra* § 4.2, with references given in n. 105, along with R. Nicolai, "La fondazione di Cirene e i Karneia Cirenaici nell'Inno ad Apollo di Callimaco," *Mat. & Disc. Anal. Testi Class.* 28 (1992): 153–73, who sees in the Callimachean representation of the first Carneia at Cyrene the act of foundation of the community through the marriage of Greek colonizers with native women. For the meaning of *apóktisis*, see Casevitz 1985, 54–57.

83. The "Mount" of the Myrtles is also mentioned by A. R. 2.505, when he designates the site of Cyrene before its colonization, along with Steph. Byz. *s. v. Múrtoussa* (p. 464 Meineke). On its geographical identification, cf. Chamoux 1952, 268, and Stucchi 1975, 117, who associates Myrtoussa of the legend with the terrace on which the sanctuary of Apollo stands. In this case, the "nipple" of which Pindar speaks in *Pyth.* 4.14 would correspond roughly to the acropolis, as would the "eminence" surrounded by a plain mentioned in *Pyth.* 9.55. The spring Cyre, sacred to Apollo (cf. Pind. *Pyth.* 4.294 and Hdt. 4.158.3) and located at the center of the city, has been identified by Goodchild 1971, 110; cf. also *infra* n. 131.

84. Acesandr. *FGrHist.* 469 F 4, cited by the sch. A. R. 2.498/527a (p. 168 Wendel). Conforming to this version, A. R. 2.509 indicates that in Libya Apollo made an *agrótis*, a huntress, out of Cyrene. On Eurypylus, the indigenous king of Cyrene, see *supra* n. 18. The conflict between this version of the legend and the Pindaric version is the object of attention of Chamoux 1952, 77–83, who also mentions the later sources for this narrative. While Malten 1911, 51–55, wished to see purely local narratives in the versions of Acesandrus and Callimachus, other factors have been proposed to justify this divergence; they are enumerated by P. Radici Colace, "Cirene e Artemide *potnia theron* nell'Inno secondo de Callimaco," *Giorn. It. Filol.* 27 (1975): 45–49, who herself advances a ritualist thesis that is difficult to defend.

85. For a detailed analysis of this episode, with its numerous plays on words, see the commentary of Williams 1978, 82–85, and my own study of 1992, 52–54.

86. See the semantic analysis I have proposed in 1992, 46–49.

87. Robbins 1978, 96–104, in an overtly structuralist reading, confuses this pastoral domain, the second term of the opposition, with the domain of (agricultural) culture; more prudence is to be found on this subject in the commen-

tary by Kirkwood 1982, 223 and 226. For a study of the double nature of Centaurs, cf. Kirk 1970, 152–62.

88. A. R. 2.498ff. with the *sch. ad loc.* (pp. 168–69 Wendel); Aristaios is already defined as a guardian of flocks, in the company of Hermes, by Hesiod, fr. 217 Merkelbach-West (see also fr. 216 and Theog. 977). Call *Aet.* fr. 75.32 ff. Pfeiffer attributes the name Aristaios to Zeus Icmaeus, making it the epithet of the god of the Etesian winds. We should note here that in Hom. *Il.* 13.154 and 14.214, as well as in *HHom.* 23.1, Zeus is described as *áristos*. There is no doubt that this epithet itself has facilitated the assimilation between Aristaios and the god of celestial water. Moreover, Pindar probably uses Aristaios' name in the play of assimilations between different legendary actors in which he engages in *Pythian 9*; the name of the hero is found, in fact, as a designation in the list of suitors for the hand of Antaios' daughter (*aristêes*, 107), among them Alexidemus: cf. Köhnken 1985, 105.

The essentially pastoral function of Aristaios is analyzed by Woodbury 1982, 255–58. Brelich 1958, 171, has noted that the alimentary inventions attributed to Aristaios do not include cereal cultivation: cf. Diod. Sic. 4.81.2 f. and sch. Pind. *Pyth.* 9.112 and 115b (vol. 2, p. 231 Drachmann); other sources are collected by Malten 1911, 77–85. Note also that according to the sch. *ad Pyth.* 4.4 (vol. 2, p. 94 Drachmann), Aristaios himself was honored as oecist by the Cyrenaeans! Cf. S. Ensoli Vittozzi, "L'iconografia e il culto di Aristeo a Cirene," *Lyb. St.* 25 (1994): 61–84.

89. Since the studies of E. L. Bundy, *Studia Pindarica*, vol. 1 (Berkeley 1962), 17–18, and Burton 1962, 48–50, allusions have been noticed in lines 79–103 to other victories won by Telesicrates not only at Thebes but also at Aegina, Megara, and Cyrene, connected to the local festivals mentioned in 97–103: see in particular the studies of J. Péron, "Pindare et la victoire de Télésicratès dans la IXᵉ Pythique (vv. 76–96)," *Rev. Philol.* 50 (1976): 58–78, and L. L. Nash, "The Theban Myth in *Pythian 9*, 79–103," *Quad. Urb. Cult. Class.* 40 (1982): 77–97; the question of the function of these Theban allusions has been raised by Kirkwood 1982, 228–29, and by T. K. Hubbard, "Theban Nationalism and Poetic Apology in Pindar's *Pythian* 9.76–96," *Rhein. Mus.* 134 (1991): 22–38.

90. Amphitryon and Iolaus were both objects of heroic cults at Thebes: cf. Pind. *Ol.* 9.98f., *Isthm.* 5.32f., *Nem.* 4.19ff. and fr. 169.47ff. Maehler; see on this subject A. Schachter, *Cults of Boeotia*, vol. 1 (*Bull. Inst. Class. Stud. Suppl.* 38.1) (London 1981), 30–31, and vol. 2 (38.2) (1986), 64–65, who cites all other evidence for the tomb shared by the two heroes. Heracles, whose brother Iphicles is the father of Iolaus, is doubly attached to the young hero, familialy and amorously: cf. *ibid.*, 15–18. The uncle and the nephew were probably honored in the same festival, the Iolaeia/Heracleia: cf. C. Jourdain-Annequin, "A propos d'un rituel pour Ioalos à Argyrion. Héraclès et l'initiation des jeunes gens," in A. Moreau (ed.), *L'initiation I. Les rites d'adolescence et les mystères* (Montpellier 1992), 121–41. Pindar seems to situate another of Telesicrates' agonal victories on the occasion of this festival: see the references given on this *supra* n. 89, with the discussion on the syntactic articulation of this passage found in Burton 1962, 45–50, and Carey 1981, 90–91. Parallels to this type of eulogy can be found in the study of J. Pòrtulas, *Lectura de Píndar* (Barcelona

1977), 86–96. On the civilizing and foundational nature of the exploits of Heracles, cf. Brelich 1958, 193–96.

91. This metaphorical relationship between victory and marriage is discussed by Köhnken 1985, 108–10, who nevertheless does not perceive that the *télos*, both of the contest and of the marriage, applies equally to Telesicrates (cf. lines 99ff.!). See in a similar vein Crotty 1982, 95; Suárez de la Torre 1984, 203–8 (who gives on 199 n. 3 an abundant bibliography on the subject); and Segal 1986, 187–88. In a very subtle reading, Carson 1982, 123–28, shows that Telesicrates' victory remains without meaning if the athlete is not integrated into the community through the civilizing ritual that marriage represents. On the relationship these two metaphorical levels maintain with colonization, see the references given *supra* n. 76. Other Pindaric assimilations of athlete to fiancé are discussed by C. Brown, "The Bridegroom and the Athlete: The Proem to Pindar's Seventh *Olympian*," in D. E. Gerber, *Greek Poetry and Philosophy. Studies in Honour of Leonard Woodbury* (Chico, Calif., 1984), 37–50.

92. On the intervention of the Heraclids in the Peloponnese, cf. Prinz 1979, 277–313, who considers the rise of Delphic influence to be relatively late (278 n. 82). On the tripartition of the Peloponnese that the Heraclid legend sanctions, see the remarks I have made in "Le récit généalogique spartiate. La représentation mythologique d'une organisation spatiale," *Quad. Stor.* 26 (1987): 43–91. For the structure of the poem, see Hubbard 1985, 124–32, and Froidefond 1989, 90–92.

93. These different temporal movements have not facilitated comprehension of the text of this passage. Lines 85–88 are worthy of special comment from the chronological point of view: "the men rich in the gifts Battus brought on the ships" are able to receive "the people who love horses," that is, the descendants of Antenor the Trojan. Making *dékontai* a historical present only reinforces the contradiction; it is nonetheless the solution offered by Chamoux 1952, 71 and 279 n. 5 (but cf. 389), and by Brunel 1964, 11–21; the latter proposes making *tò éthnos* the subject of the verb *dékontai*, following the various paraphrases of the passage offered by the sch. *ad Pyth.* 5.113 (vol. 2, p. 186 Drachmann); see also Dougherty 1993, 119 n. 31. As Vian 1955 clarifies, the verb in question, explained by *thusíaisin* and the expression *oikhnéontés sphe* (an allusion to the movement of a procession) refers to an act of cult rendered to the heroes. It is pointless to attempt to resolve the temporal contradiction presented in this passage by identifying the heroes received by Battus and his colonists as Libyans, descendants of the natives with whom the Antenorids would be assimilated, as Braccesi 1984, 75–76, proposes. Furthermore, as has been seen, it is not plausible to posit a royal installation of Antenorids at Cyrene before the Theran colonization. Menelaus himself was said to have traveled Libya: see Hdt. 2.119.2 and the allusion to his travels found in Hom. *Od.* 4.85, with the remarks of Malkin 1994, 48–52.

94. The ancestry and political destiny of Theras are described by Hdt. 4.147 ff. in a *lógos* commented upon *infra* (cf. n. 116 and *supra* n. 46); recently Vannicelli 1992 has also insisted on the marginal character of this lineage of the Aegids and on its utilization by Pindar for "personal" ends. For a historicist hypothesis on this subject, cf. M. Corsano, "Mini ed Egidi a Cirene," in Gentili

(ed.) 1990, 123–29. Some have sought to associate the figure of Theras with husbandry protected by Apollo: cf. R. Holland, "Theras," *Ausführl. Lex. der Gr. und Röm. Mythologie*, vol. 5 (Leipzig 1916), 640–52. Also, it should be noted that historians subsequent to Herodotus attempted to remove this Aegid line from the history of the foundation of Cyrene by substituting Samos, a descendant of Euphemus, for Theras, the founder of Thera: cf. *infra* n. 147.

95. Hes. *Op.* 156ff.; on the content of the *Cyclia* as a whole, see in particular the introduction to fr. 1 Bernabé of the *Cypria*: the Theban and Trojan wars are included in the same plan of Zeus. For a reconstruction of the plot of the epic cycle, cf. A. Séveryns, *Le Cycle épique dans l'Ecole d'Aristarque* (Liège and Paris 1928), 163–425, and, for instance, J. Burgess, "The Non-Homeric Cypria," *Trans. Amer. Philol. Assoc.* 126 (1996): 77–99.

96. The ancient historians had already proposed the hypothesis of a precolonization of Cyrene by the descendants of Antenor following the destruction of Troy: so, for example, Lysimachus, *FGrHist.* 328 F 6, a historian of the second century B.C., cited by the sch. *ad Pyth.* 5.110 (vol. 2, p. 186 Drachmann) or by the sch. Lyc. 874 (vol. 2, p. 283 Scheer); see also Timachidas of Rhodes, *FGrHist.* 532 F 17, with the commentary of Chamoux 1952, 72. This hypothesis justified the early date of 1336 proposed for the colonization of the Cyrenaica (cf. *supra* n. 1).

Among modern historians, the hypothesis of a "pre-Dorian" or "Mycenaean" colonization of Cyrene was advanced at the end of the nineteenth century by scholars cited *supra* n. 1, to whom should be added, concerning the Antenorids, A. Gercke, "Die Myrmidonen in Kyrene," *Hermes* 41 (1906): 447–59; this thesis has recently been reformulated in several articles also cited *supra* n. 1. Brillante 1989 offers a useful discussion on this topic. Moreover, attempts have been made to identify the Antenorids with the Tritopatores or the Acamanthes cited in *SEG* IX, 72.21ff.: cf. Leschhorn 1984, 68, and Malkin 1987, 209–12. A very prudent historicist thesis has been presented by Malten 1911, 112–51; Chamoux 1952, 71–91, supplies a refutation of these different hypotheses on "precolonization," while Braccesi 1987 attempts to attribute the insertion of the Antenorids in the legend of Cyrene's foundation to anti-Persian propaganda conducted by Athens in the fifth century; cf. also 1984, 71–74.

97. The introduction in the Archaic period of cults, located on Mycenaean sites, rendered to heroes of the Trojan War has been studied notably by C. Bérard, "L'héroïsation et la formation de la cité," in *Architecture et société. De l'archaïsme à la fin de la République romaine* (Paris and Rome 1983), 43–59; by A.J.M. Wittley, "Early States and Hero Cults: A Re-Appraisal," *Journ. Hell. Stud.* 108 (1988): 173–82; and in an extensive manner by C. M. Antonaccio, *An Archaeology of Ancestors. Tomb Cult and Hero Cult in Early Greece* (Lanham, Boulder, New York, and London 1995). As concerns more specifically the "invention of the mythic founder" and cult consecrated to him, see the study of F. de Polignac, *La naissance de la cité grecque*, 2nd ed. (Paris 1995), 170–76 (Eng. transl.: *Cults, territory and the origins of the Greek city-state* [Chicago 1999]); for Sparta, see the references given *supra* n. 92. The problem posed by the narrative of the foundation of Rome is analogous: constructed, in the legend, by heroes of the Trojan War, Rome has archaeological remains only from

the eighth century; cf. here especially J. M. Bremmer and N. M. Horsfall, *Roman Myth and Mythography* (*Bull. Inst. Class. Stud. Suppl.* 52) (London 1987), 12–24. Other Greek colonies laid claim to a past reaching back to the age of Trojan heroes: cf. Malkin 1987, 153. Herodotus' silence on the passage of the Antenorids to Cyrene is commented upon by Vannicelli 1993, 136–37.

98. The existence of the hill of the Antenorids is indicated by Lysimachus in the fr. cited *supra* n. 96. Chamoux 1949 attempts to locate it; the author repeats there a portion of the arguments developed *loc. cit.* n. 96 in order to refute the historical existence of a pre-Battiad colonization of Cyrene. As concerns cult rendered to Trojan heroes, see the hypotheses presented by Defradas 1952.

99. *Mákar* essentially denotes the pleasant conditions from which the gods, living in privileged regions, benefit: cf. M. L. West, *Hesiod. Works and Days* (Oxford 1978), 193–94. The hero may gain access to it after his existence as a mortal, particularly in the Islands of the Blessed: see Brelich 1958, 352–53, and C. Sourvinou-Inwood, *"Reading" Greek Death. To the End of the Classical Period* (Oxford 1995), 17–56; on oecists, see Braswell 1988, 141–43. The traces that remain in the legend of the process of Battus' heroization are the object of § 5.4, *infra*.

100. If we follow the Cyrenaean historiographer Theotimus, we note that even the charioteer Carrhotus is included in this sequence of founders/civilizers, since, at the demand of Arcesilas IV, he is substituted for a certain Euphemus (cited *supra* n. 22) to take the lead of a colonial expedition to the Hesperides: *FGrHist.* 470 F 1, cited by the sch. *ad Pyth.* 5.34 (vol. 2, p. 175 Drachmann); cf. Chamoux 1952, 173–75.

101. Corinth: Paus. 2.4.3; Sicyon: Paus. 2.6.7. One must not forget that Heraclean or Heraclid descent was used as a means for conferring to certain dynasties either an Achaean or a Dorian origin; cf. especially on this subject D. Musti, "Continuità e discontinuità tra Achei e Dori nelle tradizioni storiche," in Musti (ed.) 1985, 37–71; the question is framed by Prinz 1979, 212–16. Rhodes: Hom. *Il.* 2.653ff., but also Pind. *Ol.* 7.20ff. with sch. *ad loc.* (vol. 1, p. 208 Drachmann) and the commentary of Prinz 1979, 78–97; Cos: Hom. *Il.* 2.677ff., with the commentary of G. S. Kirk, *The Iliad. A Commentary*, vol. 1 (Cambridge 1985), 225 and 228, who shows that the Achaean continuity implied by this genealogical projection of the history of certain cities into the heroic past does not coincide with archaeological evidence. Lydia: Hdt. 1.7; Macedonia: Thuc. 2.99.3 and Diod. Sic. 7.15.3ff.

102. On Aigimius as representing the Dorians, cf. Pind. *Pyth.* 1.62ff. and Strab. 9.4.10. The legend of the alliance of the Heraclids and Dorians for the conquest of the Peloponnese, a pretext for a first "Aegid" emigration from Thebes, is explained by the sch. *ad Pyth.* 5.101b (vol. 2, p. 184 Drachmann), citing Eph. *FGrHist.* 70 F 16; cf also *infra* n. 115.

103. On these different legends, cf. Prinz 1979, 97–111 and 56–78 respectively; also we should not forget the foundation of Rome by the descendants of Aeneas! On the complex relationships between the Homeric *nostoi* and the foundation of colonies in the western part of the Mediterranean, see now I. Malkin, *The Returns of Odysseus. Colonization and Ethnicity* (Berkeley, Los Angeles, and London 1998), 156–257.

104. The favorable and conciliatory attitude of Antenor vis-à-vis Menelaus and Odysseus is described in Hom. *Il.* 3.205ff. and 7.348ff.; cf. also Bacch. 15, Paus. 10.27.3, and the commentary of the sch. *ad Pyth.* 5.110 (vol. 2, p. 186 Drachmann), which cites the fr. of Lysimachus already noted *supra* n. 96. Antenor himself founded Patavium in Venetia: cf. Soph. *TrGF* p. 160f. Radt, Strab. 5.1.4, Liv. 1.1, and Verg. *Aen.* 1.242ff.; other sources are collected by M. I. Davies, "Antenor I," *LIMC* vol. I.1 (Zurich and Munich 1981), 811–15, and Braccesi 1984. The isotopy of hospitality is also actualized in *Pythian* 4: cf. *supra* § 2.1.

105. On the "Dorian" character attributed since antiquity to the Carneia, cf. Thuc. 5.54.2 and Paus. 3.13.4. Celebration of the festival is best attested at Sparta: sources are in S. Wide, *Lakonische Kulte* (Leipzig 1893), 63–87; cf. also Burkert 1977, 354–58 (Eng. transl. 1985, 234–36), with additions supplied by Krummen 1990, 108–14. The double *aítion* of the Carneia is given by Paus. 3.13.3 and 5; see also Alcm. fr. 52 Page-Davies, Theop. *FGrHist.* 115 F 357, Con. *FGrHist.* 26 F 1.26, and sch. Call *Ap.* 71 (vol. 2, p. 48 Pfeiffer); for interpretation of these legends, cf. Malkin 1994, 149–52, who sees in Apollo Carneius the metaphorical incarnation of a "lead ram," and Detienne 1998, 89–91.

106. A similar interpretation is given by Lefkowitz 1985, 45 and 50; see also Krummen 1990, 117–30, and Miller 1997, 261–64. The scholiast, commenting on *Pyth.* 5.121 (vol. 2, p. 181 Drachmann), nevertheless makes the Apollonia a separate celebration. On the subject of the Carneia celebrated at Cyrene, see also Call. *Ap.* 77ff., with the commentary presented *infra* § 6.1.

107. On the Apolline-type cult of which Battus was the object at Cyrene, note the remarks of Chamoux 1952, 285–87 (with an error concerning the location of the tomb of the hero: cf. *infra* n. 110); see also Malkin 1987, 204–12. For his part, Dougherty 1993, 103–12, insists on the assimilation of Battus the founder and Arcesilas IV, the victor at Delphi, through their connections with Apollo.

108. On the flexibility of the use of I/*we* in the poetry of Pindar, see the inconclusive remarks of Lefkowitz 1985, 45–49 (with the studies cited *supra* n. 5), and the more precise observations of G. M. Kirkwood, "*Pythian* 5.72–76, 9.90–92, and the Voice of Pindar," *Ill. Class. Stud.* 6 (1981): 12–23. Krummen 1990, 136–41, refers both the singular in the expression *emoì patéres* and the plural *sebízomen* to the chorus singing the poem. Burton 1962, 146–47, attempts to reduce the contradiction this double enunciative reference presents by imagining that Pindar himself assisted in celebrating Arcesilas IV at Cyrene! Note also that the Theban ancestry of the Aegids is affirmed in *Isthm.* 7.12 ff.: cf. *infra* n. 115.

109. Analogous hypotheses concerning the performative circumstances of the ode have been proposed by Burton 1962, 135–37, Froidefond 1989, 96–100, and Krummen 1990, 114–15 and 148–51. Accepting this hypothesis means admitting that the Garden of Aphrodite, where the performance of the ode takes place (24), is not to be found beside the sanctuary of Apollo (as Chamoux 1952, 267–69, supposes), but instead within it. A small temple of Aphrodite seems indeed to have made up a part of this sanctuary of the tutelary god of the city: cf. Stucchi 1975, 53–54, with n. 3, and C. Parisi Presicce, "Sacrifici e altari nel

santuario di Apollo," in *Da Batto Aristotele a Ibn el-'As* (Rome 1987), 37–40. We should also remember that at Delos the statue of Aphrodite brought to the island by Theseus was raised in the sanctuary of Apollo: cf. P. Bruneau, *Recherches sur les cultes de Délos à l'époque hellénistique et à l'époque impériale* (Paris 1980), 19–21 and 333–34. On gardens consecrated to Aphrodite, cf. Motte 1973, 121–37, and Calame, *op. cit. supra* n. 63, 123–26 (Eng. transl. 1999, 170–74).

110. The identification of the tumulus corresponding to the tomb of Battus is still not completely certain: cf. Goodchild 1971, 94, and Stucchi 1975, 12 and 104 n. 4, and above all the suggestions proposed by L. Bacchielli, "I 'luoghi' della celebrazione politica e religiosa a Cirene nella poesia de Pindaro e Callimaco," in Gentili (ed.) 1990, 5–33 (with diagrams and plates), and "La tomba di Batto su alcune monete di Cirene," in *Scritti di Antichità in memoria di Sandro Stucchi*, vol. 1 (Rome 1996), 15–20; supplementary references can be found in Krummen 1990, 100–108; Büsing 1978, 66–75, attempts to reconstruct the tomb. In the cities of Greece, the heroic tomb is generally located in the agora: cf. Brelich 1958, 129–39. On the hill of the Antenorids, cf. *supra* n. 98.

111. The writing of synchronic history as practiced by Herodotus, along with its faults, has been studied notably by Darbo-Peschanski 1987, 30–32; on the predecessors of Herodotus, see *supra* n. 9. Concerning the problem of Libya as a third continent, see *supra* n. 67.

112. Hdt. 4.145–57 (the ethnographic portion of the discussion of Libya extends from 168 to 199; Vannicelli 1993, 123–25 analyzes the structure of this *Libukoì lógoi*). This Herodotean version of the antecedents of the foundation of Cyrene is taken up and completed by the sch. Pind. *Pyth.* 4.88b (vol. 2, p. 109 Drachmann); see also the sch. *ad Pyth.* 5.99 (vol. 2, p. 184 Drachmann). The coincidence at Sparta of these two lineages at the moment of the decision to found Thera is also described by Pausanias, 7.2.2, who dates this colonial act to a generation after the foundation of Ionia.

113. The Minyans' pretension of considering their return to Sparta a return to the land of their fathers (Hdt. 4.145.4) is marked by a fire lit on the slopes of Taygetus that can be interpreted as representing a sacrifice to Hestia: cf. F. Prontera, "I Minii sul Taigeto (Erodoto IV 145). Genealogia e sinecismo in Sparta arcaica," *Ann. Fac. Lett. Filos. Perugia* 16 (1978/9): 159–66; it should be noted that the interpretation Prontera proposes receives confirmation in A. R. 4.1761, who describes the establishment of the descendants of Euphemus "near the hearth" (*ephéstioi*) of the Spartans; this term is glossed by the word "colonists" (*époikoi*) in the sch. *ad loc.* (p. 327 Wendel).

With the aid of Herodotus, the enigmatic expression *meikhthéntes* used by Pind. *Pyth.* 4.257 in describing the stay of the descendants of Euphemus at Sparta can be understood in its primary meaning of matrimonial union and also in its secondary signification of incorporation into the Spartan civic body.

114. The same genealogy, reaching back to Oedipus, is presented by Call. *Ap.* 74; cf. also the sch. A. R. 1760/4c (p. 327 Wendel).

115. On the Spartiate destiny of the Aegids, cf. Pind. *Isthm.* 7.12ff. along with the sch. *ad loc.* (vol. 3, p. 263 Drachmann), which cites Androt. *FGrHist.* 324 F 60b; see the complex commentary of F. Kiechle, *Lakonien und Sparta*

(Munich and Berlin 1963), 82–95. The reference to Sparta marking the mention of the Aegids in *Pythian* 5 is inscribed in the process of heroization that traverses the ode: cf. Nafissi 1985, 378 and 380, who, however, greatly exaggerates the role played by the Aegids at Cyrene; see also the 1980/1 study by the same author, with the justifiable criticisms of Vannicelli 1992, 64–73.

116. Note that, just as the different legends of the Argonauts, Antenorids, and Aegids have been understood through historicist readings, the narrative of Herodotus itself has recently been used for a reconstruction of the events of the "historical" foundation of Cyrene, attempted by Colomba 1980; see also, in a similar sense, the study of Jähne 1988.

117. Only here does this coincidence in the semionarrative structure of the two narratives fail to interrupt the strictly Cyrenaean version after 4.156.2. The physical force exercised on the colonists by the Therans belongs to the latter; it is a narrative feature corresponding to the order the same colonists receive to found a colony corresponding to Plataea in the Theran version. Giangiulio 1981, 4 n. 7, presents other arguments opposed to the different segmentation of the two versions of the legend proposed by Graham 1960, 97–98. Concerning the structure of the entire Cyrenaean *lógos*, see the wholly sound remarks of F. Jacoby, "Herodotos," *Realenc. Alt.-Wiss. Suppl.*, vol. 2 (Stuttgart 1913), coll. 205–520 (particularly 434–38).

118. Some references on this subject can be found in Chamoux 1952, 71–91, and in Corcella and Medaglia 1993, 345–49. This twofold focus of Herodotus' narrative makes the unity of the legend, as defended from a historicist point of view by Gierth 1971, 98–103, an implausibility.

119. The two versions of the colonization of Tarentum are cited by Strab. 6.3.2 and 3, relying on Antiochus of Syracuse, *FGrHist.* 555 F 13, and Ephorus, *FGrHist.* 70 F 216, respectively. Other sources of the legend can be found in the study of M. Corsano, "Sparte et Tarente. Le mythe de la fondation d'une colonie," *Rev. Hist. Rel.* 196 (1979): 113–40, who presents the best analysis of this legend, with an abundant bibliography.

120. Sch. Pind. *Isthm.* 7.18c (vol. 3, p. 263 Drachmann), which cites Aristot. *Resp. Lac.* fr. 532 Rose; cf. G. L. Huxley, *Early Sparta* (London 1962), 22–23.

121. Dion. Hal. 19.1; Paus. 10.10.4; other texts in the article cited *supra* n. 119.

122. Hdt. 4.178f.; cf. *supra* n. 33. A particularly enigmatic passage of Lycophron (886ff.) presents a probable echo of this narrative: having become a crater brought to Triton by Medea, the gift of the Greeks is presented as a presage of Greek control over Libya. Vannicelli 1993, 128–31, sees more precisely in this transformation of the legend the Spartan desire to appropriate the legend of the foundation of Cyrene through effacement of the role played by the Minyans and their descendants! Be that as it may, detached from its Cyrenaean context, the narrative of Herodotus cannot be considered a Libyan version meant to stand opposed to the Theran version of the foundation of Cyrene as found in *Pythian* 4: the theme of territorial autochthony conveyed by the ode precludes this interpretation, proposed by Kirchberg 1965, 53–55; also we should not forget that the clod that comes to ground at Thera is of Libyan

origin! On the Spartan perspective on the legend as recounted by Herodotus, see Malkin 1994, 197–200.

123. The system of chronological calculation employed by Herodotus is analyzed by H. Strasburger, "Herodots Zeitrechnung," *Historia* 5 (1956): 129–62, a study taken up in W. Marg (ed.), *Herodot* (Darmstadt 1965), 688–736; by W. den Boer, "Herodot und die Systeme der Chronologie," *Mnemosyne* 3rd ser. 20 (1964), 30–60; and by Darbo-Peschanski 1987, 25–32; see also the remarks of J. Cobet, "Herodot und die mündliche Ueberlieferung," in von Ungern-Sternberg and Reinau (eds.) 1988, 226–33. For an illusory attempt to accord the chronology of the Herodotean narrative with that of the narrative of *Pythian* 4 by making Theras the founder of Cyrene in the fourth generation, see Büsing 1978, 62–66.

Concerning the succession of generations as a chronological principle of historiography, cf. Ricoeur 1985, 160–72 (Eng. transl. 1988, 109–17). On Athenian chronology in particular, see the references given *supra* n. 9.

124. Note that the scholiast to Pind. *Pyth.* 4 *Inscr.* b (vol. 2, p. 93 Drachmann), in commenting on this passage of Herodotus, makes "Battos" the name given by the Pythia to a hero who was earlier called Aristoteles; on this latter name of the founding hero, cf. *infra* n. 127.

125. See *supra* nn. 18 and 84. Aristarchus, cited by the sch. *ad Pyth.* 4.76b (vol. 2, p. 182 Drachmann), perfectly understood the civilizing action attached to the effect of Battus' voice, whatever other interpretation one might attach to it: cf. sch. *ad Pyth.* 4.78a, 80a and 83 (vol. 2, pp. 181–82 Drachmann). The onomatopoeic origin of the anthroponym *Báttos*, which surely refers to stammering, has been studied by Masson 1976. For Dougherty 1993, 105–7, it serves to expose the echoes of the Pindaric text in the text of Herodotus.

126. Paus. 10.5.7; cf. also sch. Call. *Ap.* 65 (vol. 2, p. 51 Pfeiffer); far from constituting a version of the origin of the city, as Burton 1962, 145, supposes, this version surely represents a later development: the displacement of Battus' fear of the wild beasts is only a "rationalization" of the legend. Cf. Acesandr. *FGrHist.* 469 F 4 (cf. *supra* n. 84) and 6; this second fr. is cited by the sch. Pind. *Pyth.* 4 *Inscr.* b (vol. 2, p. 93 Drachmann). The basic character of the transformation Battus undergoes in the process of his heroization has been explained by Giangiulio 1981, 2–7. On the transfer to Libya of the struggle of Cyrene against the lion, see C. Parisi Presicce, "Le raffigurazioni della ninfa *Kurana* e l'identità della comunità cirenea," in *op. cit.* n. 110, vol. 1, 247–58.

127. Call. *Ap.* 76; the sch. *ad loc.* (vol. 2, p. 52 Pfeiffer) gives the sense "healthy in terms of language" for *oûlos*; see the commentary of Williams 1978, 69–70. For the double name of Battus-Aristoteles, cf. Leschhorn 1984, 61 n. 2. See also Plut. *Pyth. Or.* 405b. *Pythian* 4 is, in this regard, without ambiguity: the oracular questioning concerning the awkwardness of the voice emerges into the institution of a royalty that is still prosperous in the eighth generation; cf. *supra* § 2.1. It should be noted that in a late version of the legends relating to the Athenian Thesmophoria (Ael. fr. 44 Hercher), Battus is said to have been emasculated because he had seen and heard what was not to be seen or heard: cf. Detienne and Vernant 1979, 184–209 (Eng. transl. 1989, 129–44). We should

leave to psychoanalytic critics exegesis of the impotence of the stammering hero: see on this Cosi 1983, 132–38 (Eng. transl. 1987, 123–29).

128. Medon: see *infra* n. 137; Cypselus: Hdt. 5.92b (cf. *infra* n. 130); Sparta: Plut. *Pyth. Or.* 399b–c, *Ages.* 3.30, and Paus. 3.8.9; on Battus III and the Mantinean legislator Demonax, cf. Hdt. 4.161 and Chamoux 1952, 138–42. This group was recognized by J.-P. Vernant, "Le tyran boiteux: d'Oedipe à Périandre," *Le Temps de la réflexion* 2 (1981): 235–55, who began with the most complex, but also in this sense the most marginal, case: that of Oedipus; on Oedipus, see P. Pucci, *Oedipus and the Fabrication of the Father* (Baltimore and London 1992), 66–78, and also my own study "Le nom d'Oedipe," in B. Gentili and R. Pretagostini (eds.), *Edipo. Il teatro greco e la cultura europea* (Rome 1986), 395–403; Segal 1986, 145–50, has also noted that Battus represents an inverse figure of the tyrant Oedipus; and on Periander, see C. Sourvinou-Inwood, *'Reading' Greek Culture. Texts and Images, Rituals and Myths* (Oxford 1991), 244–84. The defects attributed to Battus do not reveal the least of an anti-Battiad tradition that the many scholars listed by Giangiulio 1981, 10 n. 33, seem to believe existed. Brelich 1958, 316–20, is a bit swift in attributing these traits to the figure of the hero in general.

On Penthilus, cf. Paus. 2.18.6 and 3.2.1, along with Alc. fr. 70.16ff. Voigt. In addition, the destiny the Cyrenaean legend assigns to the mother of Battus curiously evokes that of the mother of Agamemnon: a Cretan and the granddaughter of Minos II, she is rejected by her son and, confined in Nauplia, is sold to a stranger before marrying the Atreid Pleisthenes at Argos; see Eur. *Cressae*, pp. 501f. Nauck (2nd ed.) and Apoll. 3.2.2.

129. Diod. Sic. 8.17.1f.; cf. Schmid 1947, 116–24, Malkin 1987, 43–47, and Giangiulio 1981 and also 1989, 134–38, who compares this narrative of foundation with those of Cyrene; see also D. Suarez de la Torre, "Gli oracoli relativi alla colonizzazione della Sicilia e della Magna Grecia," *Quad. Urb. Cult. Class.* 77 (1994): 7–37. As far as Herodotus is concerned, this type of oracular response — one not pertinent to the question posed — is only found in the narratives of the foundation of Cyrene; it is, however, to be found in the foundation narrative of Gela as told by Aristaen. *FGrHist.* 771 F 1: cf. Bérard 1957, 25–29. The famous response given to Oedipus, who was inquiring about his origin, is also in this category: Soph. *OT* 791ff. and 994ff., *Arg.* IV Aesch. *Sept.* (p. 7.15ff. Smith); other examples are cited by Fontenrose 1978, 122.

130. Croton: Antioch. *FGrHist.* 555 F 10 = Strab. 6.1.12 (cf. Malkin 1987, 43–47); Cyrene: Pind. *Pyth.* 4.60 (cf. *supra* n. 23) and *SEG* IX 3.25 ff. (cf. *infra* n. 143); these parallels are noted by Giangiulio 1981, 4–5, who adds to these the spontaneous responses from the Pythia received by Eetion, the Bacchiad father of Cypselus of Corinth (Hdt. 5.92b; see Nagy 1990, 182–85), and Lycurgus, the redactor of the Spartan constitution (Hdt. 1.62.2 f.); in both cases, the consultant is at the origin of a new political regime (tyrannical or constitutional) in his city. The sense of the verb used to designate these "spontaneous" responses is explored by H. W. Parke, "A Note on *automatizo* in Connection with Prophecy," *Journ. Hell. Stud.* 82 (1962): 145–46, who with reason connects the use of this word in the *Agreement of the Founders* with the Cyrenaean version of the oracle given to Battus.

131. Hdt. 2.13.2 f. Mentioned by Pindar, *Pyth.* 4.294, as noted above, the celebrated spring of Apollo that forms the geographical center of Cyrene (cf. *supra* n. 83) receives in Call. *Ap.* 88 the speaking name *Kúre*; cf. Steph. Byz. *s. v. Kuréne* (p. 396 Meineke), who mentions the etymology repeated by modern scholars; see on this subject Chamoux 1952, 126–27, and Williams 1978, 77, who notes the double etymological play on the name of the colony in which Callimachus engages. For the sense of "pierced sky," see already Pind. *Pyth.* 4.52, and the commentary of H. Stein, *Herodotos*, vol. 2, 2nd ed. (Berlin 1893), 42.

132. Arr. *Ind.* 43.13; Strab. 17.3.21; Hdt. 4.198f.; see Miller 1997, 32–35. On the various geographical locations of the Golden Age, see J. S. Romm, *The Edges of the Earth in Ancient Thought. Geography, Exploration, and Fiction* (Princeton 1992), 50–61, 125–27, and 162–65.

133. Heracl. Lemb. *Resp.* 25, Strab. 6.1.6 citing especially Antioch. *FGrHist.* 555 F 9, Diod. Sic. 8.23.2: cf. Vallet 1958, 67–71, along with Dougherty 1993, 73–76. Several colonial operations may have had at their origin a decimation (*dekáteusis*): cf. H. S. Versnell, "Apollo and Mars One Hundred Years after Roscher," *Visible Religion* 4 (1986): 134–72 (especially 141–43).

134. Hom. *Od.* 9.105ff. with the remarks on this subject of Vidal-Naquet 1983, 50–53 (English translation 1986, 18–22). The description of this island as *euktiméne* refers to its development and exploitation through civilization: cf. Casevitz 1985, 21–30. The obligatory passage through an island or a coastal town is frequently attested in legends of colonization; references are collected by Schmidt 1947, 172–73.

135. Menecl. *FGrHist.* 270 F 6; the interpretative controversy surrounding this version of the oracle is discussed by Malkin 1987, 66–68. The text of the oracle is unfortunately corrupt: cf. H. W. Parke and D.E.W. Wormell, "Notes on Delphic Oracles," *Class. Quart.* 43 (1949): 138–40. For the sense of the term *apoikía*, see *supra* n. 25.

136. Plat. *Leg.* 707e ff.; Parker 1983, 257–80, gives a series of examples of narratives in which a curse that falls on a city is lifted through the expulsion of *pharmakoí*; see also the study of C. Dougherty, "It's Murder to Found a Colony," in C. Dougherty and L. Kurke (eds.), *Cultural Poetics in Archaic Greece* (Cambridge 1993), 178–98.

137. Tlepolemus on Rhodes: cf. *supra* n. 101. Archias: Plut. *Amat. narr.* 772a ff.; cf. Bérard 1957, 116–19. Medon: Paus. 7.2.1; cf. Sakellariou 1958, 39–76, Prinz 1979, 347–55, and Carlier 1984, 360–63. Partheniae: Antioch. *FGrHist.* 555 F 13 and Eph. *FGrHist.* 70 F 216 (cited by Strab. 6.3.2 and 3); see *supra* § 5.3 with n. 119, and Vidal-Naquet 1983, 278–82 (Eng. transl. 1986, 212–14). Other narratives with the same plot are mentioned by Burkert 1977, 141–42 (Eng. transl. 1985, 83–84).

138. The oracles mentioned by Herodotus are compiled by Kirchberg 1965 and Lachenaud 1978, 271–75; for the Delphic oracles, one can of course look to the catalogue of Parke and Wormell 1956, vol. 2, 1–69. An estimation of the role played by the oracle at Delphi in the political conduct of Greek cities in the fifth century is presented by Defradas 1972, 229–257; for colonial enterprises in particular, see Malkin 1987, 17–91, and Miller 1997, 88–144.

139. Hdt. 5.42. Lachenaud 1978, 278–305, reasonably refutes the thesis of Crahay 1956, 21, who wishes to attribute the decrease of citations of oracles in the works of Thucydides and Xenophon to the temporal proximity of the enunciators of these texts to the historical events they recount. Lachenaud, however, while showing that the oracle "permet d'abolir la distance qui sépare passé, présent et avenir," underestimates the impact of the oracles in the purely narrative movement of the text, in order to connect their frequent occurrence to the problem of Herodotus' religion; an analogous position is taken by Darbo-Peschanski 1987, 74–83.

On the other hand, the motivating force of the oracles in the narrative action of Herodotus' text has been explored by Kirchberg 1965, 116–20, and by Crahay himself, 1956, 116–33; according to the latter, all the oracles appearing in Herodotus have been created *ex eventu*. See also now P. Pucci, *Enigma, segreto, oracolo* (Pisa and Rome 1996), 152–65, who insists on the enunciative coincidence between Apollo's voice and Herodotus himself, and F. Hartog, "'Myth into *Logos*.' The Case of Croesus or the Historian at Work," in Buxton (ed.) 1999, 183–95. Fontenrose 1978, 120–23, has again expressed the greatest reserve concerning the historical authenticity of the various oracular responses cited by Herodotus in his narrative of the foundation of Cyrene; it hardly stands in his way that Herodotus may well have heard (or read) the narratives that he recounts at Delphi itself! It should be noted that there exists in Classical iconography a parallel movement of Apolline sagacity: cf. J.-M. Moret, "L' 'apollinisation' de l'imagerie légendaire à Athènes dans la seconde moitié du Ve siècle," *Rev. Arch.* 1 (1982): 109–36.

140. Thuc. 1.22.4; the Thucydidean references to oracles are enumerated by Crahay 1956, 18–19. Motivations of actions as Thucydides conceives them are analyzed in the classic study of H. Strasburger, "Die Entdeckung der politischen Geschichte durch Thukydides," *Saeculum* 5 (1954): 395–428, reprinted in H. Herter (ed.), *Thukydides* (Darmstadt 1968), 412–76; note also the warnings of N. Loraux, "Thucydide n'est pas un collègue," *Quad. Stor.* 12 (1980): 55–81.

141. On the epic and poetic character of the narrative of Herodotus, see my own reflections presented in 1986, 70–81 (Eng. transl. 1995, 86–96), and those of Nagy 1990, 221–33. The "Homeric" design of Herodotus' work also influences his manner of recounting his material: cf. H. Erbse, *Studien zum Verständnis Herodots* (Berlin and New York 1992), 122–32.

142. This is the hypothesis formulated by Studniczka 1890, 87 and 100: see also Schmid 1947, 115–16, and Giangiulio 1981, 3 n. 6, who also posed quite well the problem of the origin of the narrative of the foundation of Croton and its relationship with the Delphic oracle in 1989, 131–48.

143. *SEG* IX 3.11 and 27f.; commentary in Jeffery 1961, particularly on the term *arkhegétes*, and in C. Calame, "La refondation d'une cité coloniale grecque. Espace et temps," in P. Azara, R. Mar, E. Riu, and E. Subías (eds.), *La fundación de la ciudad. Mitos y ritos en el mundo antiguo* (Barcelona 2000), 91–98; see also R. Osborne, *Greece in the Making, 1200–479 B.C.* (London and New York 1996), 8–17, and C. Dobias-Lalou, "*SEG* IX, 3. Un document composite ou inclassable?" *Verbum* 3/4 (1994): 243–56; I will come back to this important epigraphical text in *Time in Ancient Greece* (chap. IV). Cf. also

SEG IX 72.22 = 115 A 22 Sokolowski, with the remarks of Leschhorn 1984, 67–72 and 180–85 (especially on the same term); Casevitz 1985, 245–50; and Malkin 1987, 241–50.

144. Pind. *Pyth.* 5.93 (cf. *supra* n. 107) with the sch. *ad* 5.127a (vol. 2, p. 189 Drachmann) along with the sch. Aristoph. *Plut.* 925a (vol. 3.4a, p. 152 Chantry). The problem of the archaeological identification of the tomb of Battus is mentioned *supra* n. 110. Concerning the purificatory role shared by Apollo and by the founder Battus, see *SEG* IX 72, with the commentary of Chamoux 1952, 286, Defradas 1972, 254–57 (misleading), and Parker 1983, 336–39; the cultic association between Apollo Archegetes and Battus the oecist has been proposed by Leschhorn 1984, 63 and 68–70, who relies on the numerous epigraphic documents. The heroic cult of the oecist in general is studied by Malkin 1987, 189–203; see also Detienne 1998, 110–14.

145. The judgment of Aristarchus is transmitted by the sch. Pind. *Pyth.* 5.76b (vol. 2, p. 181 Drachmann). On the reforms of Demonax, cf. Hdt. 4.161.2 and Hermippus *FGrHist.* 1026 F 3, 197–205, with the commentary of H. Schaefer, "Die verfassungsgeschichtliche Entwicklung Kyrenes im ersten Jahrhundert nach seiner Begründung," *Rhein. Mus.* 95 (1952): 135–70, and Jähne 1988, 160–65.

146. The memorial function of the *Agreement* itself has been shown by Létoublon 1989, 109–13, in relation to the melting of wax *kollosoí* meant as a malediction on traitors.

147. *FGrHist.* 469 F 4 and 6: cf. *supra* n. 84. Note that here the historian has attempted to "rationalize" the legend by attributing the foundation of Thera directly to a descendant of Euphemus (Samos), not to an Aegid: F 5. See also Theochr. *FGrHist.* 761 F 1 a as well as the sch. Pind. *Pyth.* 4.88b (vol. 2, p. 110 Drachmann); there is an echo of another "historicization" of the legend in Strab. 17.3.21.

148. On the festival of the Carneia as well as the characteristics of *arkhegétes* and founder attributed to Apollo Carneius assimilated as a ram, see the references given *supra* nn. 105 and 106. As Williams 1978, 67, suggests, it is possible to see in the term *patróïos*, used to qualify the relationship between the narrator and the god in line 71, an explicit reference to the "Aegid" origin that Pindar claims for himself in *Pyth.* 5.76.

149. Cf. sch. Call. *Ap.* 27 (vol. 2, p. 50 Pfeiffer). This question has been discussed by A. P. Smotrytsch, "Le allusioni politiche nel II inno di Callimaco e la sua datazione," *Helikon* 1 (1961): 661–67, and by Williams 1978, 1–2, 36, and 65; there is a new biographical hypothesis by Corsano 1991, 14–72. For other Callimachean allusions to Cyrene and its foundation, see the study of L. Lehnus, "Antichità cirenaiche in Callimaco," *Eikasmos* 5 (1994): 189–207.

150. This poem should thus be included among those *Hymns* of Callimachus labeled "mimetic"; on this see especially M. R. Falivene, "La mimesi in Callimaco: *Inni* II, IV, V, e VI," *Quad. Urb. Cult. Class.* 65 (1990): 103–28, and M. Depew, "Mimesis and Aetiology in Callimachus' Hymns," in M. A. Harder, R. F. Regtuit, and G. C. Wakker (eds.), *Callimachus. Hellenistica Groningana,* vol. 1 (Groningen 1993), 57–77.

151. References to the Cyre spring are cited *supra* n. 131; for the spring of poetic inspiration, cf. already *Pyth.* 4.294 and 299, along with the references

mentioned *supra* n. 28. On the details of this particular narrative of foundation, see my own discussion in 1992, 54–66.

Chapter III

1. On the situation of enunciation in the three *Pythians* of Pindar, see the references given *supra* chap. II n. 3; the oracular and epic design of the work of Herodotus is discussed in the studies cited in nn. 139 and 141.

2. Strabo 1.2.6–9, with comment, *à propos* the geographical reality of the voyage of Odysseus, by Romm, *op. cit.* chap. II n. 132, 183–96 (with additional bibliography cited in n. 45); on Strabo's approach to myth, see *supra* chap. I, § 3.5 and n. 59, and also Veyne 1983, 72 and 119 (Eng. transl. 1988, 62 and 109), and F. Hartog, *Mémoire d'Ulysse. Récits sur la frontière en Grèce ancienne* (Paris 1996), 113–15; Plut. *Pyth. orac.* 406e.

3. Porph. *Antr.* 36; see on this subject the study of J. Pépin, "Porphyre exégète d'Homère," in *Porphyre. Entretiens sur l'Antiquité classique XII* (Vandœuvres and Geneva 1966), 229–66. Note that for the rhetor Theon, *Progymn.* 3 (vol. 2, p. 472 Spengel), living in the imperial period, *mûthos* is defined as "a fictional discourse (*lógos pseudés*) that represents truth"!

4. Plat. *Tim.* 21d–22c and 23a–b; according to Clement of Alexandria, *Strom.* 1.21.102, Plato here repeats the narrative of the birth of the first man and woman that the logographer Acousilaos described in his *Genealogies* (*FGrHist.* 2 F 23); cf. *supra* chap. I, § 3.4.

5. Plat. *Tim.* 23c–25d. In turn C. Gill, "The Genre of the Atlantis Story," *Class. Philol.* 72 (1977): 335–60, and Vidal-Naquet 1983, 335–60, have demystified and "demythified" the story of Atlantis by returning it to its historical context; see also C. Rowe, "Myth, History, and Dialectic in Plato's *Republic* and *Timaeus-Critias*," in Buxton (ed.) 1999, 263–78. On the long history of the successive creations of the myth of Atlantis, see the definitive contribution of P. Vidal-Naquet published in *La démocratie grecque vue d'ailleurs* (Paris 1990), 139–59.

6. Plat. *Tim.* 26c–e (cf. *supra* chap. I, § 3.1 with n. 29), referring to 17c–19a, 20d–e and 29c–e; *Crit.* 108b–e. Detienne 1981, 163–66 (Eng. transl. 1986, 87–89) pertinently compares the "archaeological" status given the story of Atlantis with that of the *muthología* the narrative itself indicates as an *anazétesis tôn palaiôn* in order to define it as a necessary stage in the development of civilization (*Crit.* 110a; cf. *supra ibid.*). In "La double mythologie entre le *Timée* et le *Critias*," in Calame (ed.) 1988, 17–33, M. Detienne clarifies, among other things, the relationship of this new "mythology" with writing and historiography; see also Loraux 1993, 307–314 (Eng. transl. 1986, 296–304).

7. Brisson 1994, 23–31, insists on the role played by memory in this inquiry into *arkhaîa*, but in order to trace a sharp distinction between myth and history; on 184–95, a semantic analysis of Plato's use of the terms *muthologéo* and *muthología* shows not only that these words designate both the fabrication and the narration of *mûthoi*, but also that they probably refer to the technique of the rhapsodes: cf. G. Nagy, "Epic as Music. Rhapsodic Models of Homer in

Plato's *Timaeus* and *Critias*," in K. Reichl (ed.), *The Oral Epic. Performance and Music* (Berlin 2000): 41–68.

8. Plat. *Phaed.* 60d–61b; see also 60c, where the activity of Aesop is presented as *mûthon suntheînai*. Note on this subject two commentaries: D. Sabbatucci, "Aspetti del rapporto *mythos-logos* nella cultura greca," in B. Gentili and G. Paioni (eds.), *Il mito greco. Atti del Convegno Internazionale (Urbino 7–12 maggio 1973)* (Rome 1977), 57–62, and Brisson 1994, 54–59. Both interpret the use of *lógos* in this context as referring to "argumentative discourse"; we can only say for certain that the term here indicates that the discourse is not marked, that is to say it is without metrical rhythm (on this point, cf. *Phaedr.* 258d).

9. This is clearly asserted by M. Kilani in the course of his study on contemporary Tunisia, *La construction de la mémoire. Le lignage et la sainteté dans l'oasis d'El Ksar* (Geneva 1992), 297–98, in which he attempted, without success, to obtain from his informants the written foundation document that was in fact nonexistent, save for its pragmatic function: "Comme le mythe, l'histoire adapte le passé aux conditions du présent. Comme lui, elle n'est pas pure mémoire, mais un travail sur la mémoire."

Bibliography

1. On Myth, Mythology, and History

Affergan, F. *Exotisme et altérité. Essai sur les fondements d'une critique de l'anthropologie*. Paris: PUF, 1987.

Benveniste, E. *Problèmes de linguistique générale*. Vol. 2. Paris: Gallimard, 1974.

Bouvier, D., and C. Calame, eds. *Philosophes et historiens anciens face aux mythes*. Lausanne and Paris: Faculté des Lettres et Belles Lettres, 1998.

Bremmer, J., ed. *Interpretations of Greek Mythology*. London and Sydney: Croom Helm, 1987.

Brisson, L. *Platon, les mots et les mythes. Comment et pourquoi Platon nomme le mythe?* 2nd ed. Paris: La Découverte, 1994.

Buxton, R. *Imaginary Greece. The Contexts of Mythology*. Cambridge: Cambridge University Press, 1994.

———, ed. *From Myth to Reason? Studies in the Development of Greek Thought*. Oxford and New York: Oxford University Press, 1999.

Calame, C. *Le récit en Grèce ancienne. Enonciations et représentations de poètes*. Paris: Méridiens Klincksieck, 1986. (2nd ed.: Paris: Belin, 2000; Eng. transl.: *The Craft of Poetic Speech in Ancient Greece*. Trans. J. Orion. Ithaca, NY: Cornell University Press, 1995.)

———, ed. *Métamorphoses du mythe en Grèce antique*. Geneva: Labor & Fides, 1988.

———. *Thésée et l'imaginaire athénien. Légende et culte en Grèce antique*. 2nd ed. Lausanne: Payot, 1996.

———. *Poétique des mythes dans la Grèce antique*. Paris: Hachette, 2000.

Cerri, G. *Platone sociologo della comunicazione*. Milan: Mondadori, 1991.

Darbo-Peschanski, C. *Le discours du particulier. Essai sur l'enquête hérodotéenne*. Paris: Seuil, 1987.

Detienne, M. *L'invention de la mythologie*. Paris: Gallimard, 1981. (Eng. transl.: *The Creation of Mythology*. Trans. M. Cook. Chicago: University of Chicago Press, 1986.)

———, ed. *Transcrire les mythologies. Tradition, écriture, historicité*. Paris: Albin Michel, 1994.

Dowden, K. *The Uses of Greek Mythology*. London and New York: Routledge, 1992.

Dundes, A., ed. *Sacred Narrative. Readings in the Theory of Myth*. Berkeley: University of California Press, 1984.

Edmunds, L., ed. *Approaches to Greek Myth*. Baltimore and London: Johns Hopkins University Press, 1990.

Gentili, B. "Überlegungen zu Mythos und Dichtung im antiken Griechenland."

In H. Froning et al., eds., *Kotinos. Festschrift für Erika Simon*. Mainz: von Zabern, 1992.

Graf, F. *Greek Mythology. An Introduction*. Baltimore and London: Johns Hopkins University Press, 1993. (Orig. ed.: Munich and Zürich: Artemis, 1985.)

Hartog, F. *Le miroir d'Hérodote. Essai sur la représentation de l'autre*. 2nd ed. Paris: Gallimard, 1992.

Honko, L. "The Problem of Defining Myth." In H. Beizais, ed., *The Myth of the State*, 7–19. Stockholm: Scripta Instituti Donneriani Aboensis 6, 1972. (Repr. Dundes, ed. 1984, 41–52.)

Hunter, V. *Past and Process in Herodotus and Thucydides*. Princeton: Princeton University Press, 1982.

Jamme, C. *Einführung in die Philosophie des Mythos II. Neuzeit und Gegenwart*. Darmstadt: Wissenschaftliche Buchgesellschaft, 1991.

Kirk, G. S. *Myth. Its Meanings and Functions in Ancient and Other Cultures*. Berkeley, Los Angeles, and Cambridge: University of California Press, 1970.

Konstan, D. "What Is Greek about Greek Mythology?" *Kernos* 4 (1991): 11–30.

Lévi-Strauss, C. *Anthropologie structurale*. Paris: Plon, 1958.

Lincoln, B. *Theorizing Myth. Narrative, Ideology, and Scholarship*. Chicago and London: University of Chicago Press, 1999.

Loraux, N. *L'invention d'Athènes. Histoire de l'oraison funèbre dans la "cité classique."* 2nd ed. Paris: Payot, 1993. (Eng. transl.: *The Invention of Athens. The Funeral Oration in the Classical City*. Trans. A. Sheridan. Cambridge: Cambridge University Press, 1986.)

Morgan, K. A. *Myth and Philosophy from the Presocratics to Plato*. Cambridge: Cambridge University Press, 2000.

Nagy, G. *Pindar's Homer: The Lyric Possession of an Epic Past*. Baltimore and London: Johns Hopkins University Press, 1990.

Neschke, A. B. "Griechischer Mythos. Versuch einer idealtypischen Beschreibung." *Zeitschr. für philos. Forsch.* 37 (1983): 119–38.

Piérart, M. "L'historien ancien face aux mythes et aux légendes." *Ét. Class.* 51 (1983): 47–62.

Pottier, R. *Essai d'anthropologie du mythe*. Paris: Kimé, 1994.

Reichler, C., ed. *Essais sur l'interprétation des textes*. Paris: Minuit, 1988.

Ricoeur, P. *Temps et récit. Tome I*. Paris: Seuil, 1983. (Eng. transl.: *Time and Narration*. Trans. K. McLaughlin and D. Pellauer. Chicago: University of Chicago Press, 1984.)

———. *Temps et récit II. La configuration dans le récit de fiction*. Paris: Seuil, 1984. (Eng. transl.: *Time and Narrative II: The Configuration of Time in Fictional Narrative*. Trans. K. McLaughlin and D. Pellauer. Chicago: University of Chicago Press, 1985.)

———. *Temps et récit III. Le temps raconté*. Paris: Seuil, 1985. (Eng. transl.: *Time and Narrative III: Narrated Time*. Trans. K. McLaughlin and D. Pellauer. Chicago: University of Chicago Press, 1988.)

Saïd, S. *Approches de la mythologie grecque*. Paris: Nathan, 1993.

Smith, P. "Positions du mythe." *Le temps de la réflexion* 1 (1980): 61–81.

Thomas, R. *Oral Tradition and Written Record in Classical Athens.* Cambridge: Cambridge University Press, 1989.

Ungern-Sternberg, J. von, and H. Reinau, eds. *Vergangenheit in mündlicher Überlieferung.* Stuttgart: Teubner, 1988.

Vernant, J.-P. *Mythe et société en Grèce ancienne.* Paris: Maspero, 1974. (Eng. transl.: *Myth and Society in Ancient Greece.* Trans. J. Lloyd. Sussex: Harvester Press, 1980.)

Veyne, P. *Les Grecs ont-ils cru à leurs mythes?* Paris: Seuil, 1983. (Eng. transl.: *Did the Greeks Believe in Their Myths?* Trans. P. Wissing. Chicago: University of Chicago Press, 1988.)

Vidal-Naquet, P. *Le chasseur noir. Formes de pensée et formes de société dans le monde grec.* 2nd ed. Paris: La Découverte, 1983. (Eng. transl.: *The Black Hunter: Forms of Thought and Forms of Society in the Greek World.* Trans. A. Szegedy-Maszak. Baltimore and London: Johns Hopkins University Press, 1986.)

2. On Cyrene and Legends of Colonial Foundations

Angeli Bernardini, P. *Mito e attualità nelle odi di Pindaro. La* Nemea *4, l'*Olimpica *9, l'*Olimpica *7.* Rome: Ateneo, 1983.

Ballabriga, A. *Le Soleil et le Tartare. L'image mythique du monde en Grèce archaïque.* Paris: EHESS, 1986.

Bérard, J. *La colonisation grecque de l'Italie méridionale et de la Sicile dans l'Antiquité.* 2nd ed. Paris: PUF, 1957.

Braccesi, L. *La leggenda di Antenore da Troia a Padova.* Padova: Signum, 1984.
———. "Antenoridi, Veneti e Libyi." *Quad. Arch. Libya* 12 (1987): 7–14.

Braswell, B. K. *A Commentary on the Fourth Pythian Ode of Pindar.* Berlin and New York: de Gruyter, 1988.

Brelich, A. *Gli eroi greci. Un problema storico-religioso.* Rome: Ateneo, 1958.

Bremmer, J. "The Case of the Bodily Blemished King." In *Perennitas. Studi in onore di Angelo Brelich,* 67–76. Rome: Ateneo, 1980.

Brillante, C. "Gli Antenoridi a Cirene nella *Pitica* V di Pindaro." *Quad. Urb. Cult. Class.* 62 (1989): 7–16.

Brunel, J. "Les Anténorides à Cyrène et l'interprétation littérale de Pindare, *Pythique* V, v. 82–88." *Rev. Et. Anc.* 66 (1964): 5–21.

Burkert, W. *Griechische Religion der archaischen und klassischen Epoche.* Stuttgart: Kohlhammer, 1977. (Eng. transl.: *Greek Religion.* Trans. J. Raffan. Cambridge: Cambridge University Press, 1985.)

Burton, R.W.B. *Pindar's Pythian Odes.* Oxford: Oxford University Press, 1962.

Büsing, H. "Battos." In *Thiasos. Sieben archäologische Arbeiten,* 51–79. Amsterdam: Castrum Peregrini, 1978.

Calame, C. "Narration légendaire et programme poétique dans l'*Hymne à Apollon* de Callimaque." *Et. Lettres* 4 (1992): 41–66. (Eng. transl.: "Legendary Narration and Poetic Procedure in Callimachus' *Hymn to Apollo.*" In M. A. Harder, R. F. Regtuit, G. C. Wakker, eds. *Callimachus,* 37–55. Groningen: Egbert Forsten, 1993.)

Carey, C. *A Commentary on Five Odes of Pindar: Pythian 2, Pythian 9, Nemean 1, Nemean 7, Isthmian 8*. New York: Arno Press, 1981.

Carlier, P. *La royauté en Grèce avant Alexandre*. Strasbourg: AECR, 1984.

Carson, A. "Wedding at Noon in Pindar's *Ninth Pythian*." *Greek Rom. Byz. Stud.* 23 (1982): 121–28.

Casevitz, M. *Le vocabulaire de la colonisation en grec ancien. Etude lexicographique des familles de* ktizo *et de* oikeo-oikizo. Paris: Klincksieck, 1985.

Chamoux, F. "Les Anténorides à Cyrène." In *Mélanges d'archéologie et d'histoire Charles Picard*, 154–61. Paris: PUF, 1949.

———. *Cyrène sous la monarchie des Battiades*. Paris: de Boccard, 1952.

Colomba, M. "Erodoto e la fondazione di Cirene." *Arch. Stor. Sicil.* 6 (1980): 45–80.

Corcella, A., and S. M. Medaglia. *Erodoto. Le storie IV. Libro IV. La Scizia e la Libia*. Milan: Mondadori, 1993.

Corsano, M. "Il sogno di Eufemo e la fondazione di Cirene nelle *Argonautiche* di Apollonio Rodio." *Rudiae* 3 (1991): 54–72.

Cosi, D. M. "Comunicazione disturbata. Battos il fondatore di Cirene, balbuziente e castrato." In M. G. Ciani, ed., *Le regioni del silenzio. Studi sui disagi della comunicazione*, 127–52. Padova: Bloom, 1983. (Eng. transl.: *The Regions of Silence. Studies on the Difficulty of Communicating*, 115–44. Amsterdam: Gieben, 1987.)

Crahay, R. *La littérature oraculaire chez Hérodote*. Liège and Paris: Belles Lettres, 1956.

Crotty, K. *Song and Action. The Victory Odes of Pindar*. Baltimore and London: Johns Hopkins University Press, 1982.

Defradas, J. "Le culte des Anténorides à Cyrène." *Rev. Et. Gr.* 65 (1952): 289–301.

———. *Les thèmes de la propagande delphique*. 2nd ed. Paris: Belles Lettres, 1972.

Detienne, M. *Les Jardins d'Adonis. La mythologie des aromates en Grèce*. 2nd ed. Paris: Gallimard, 1989. (Eng. transl.: *The Gardens of Adonis. Spices in Greek Mythology*. Trans. J. Lloyd. Princeton: Princeton University Press, 1994.)

———. "Apollon Archégète. Un modèle politique de territorialisation." In M. Detienne, ed., *Tracés de fondation*, 301–11. Louvain and Paris: Peeters, 1990.

———. *Apollon la couteau à la main. Une approche expérimentale du polythéisme grec*. Paris: Gallimard, 1998.

Detienne, M., and J.-P. Vernant. *Les ruses de l'intelligence. La mètis des Grecs*. Paris: Flammarion, 1974. (Eng. transl.: *Cunning Intelligence in Greek Culture and Society*. Trans. J. Lloyd. Sussex: Harvester Press, 1978.)

———. *La cuisine du sacrifice en pays grec*. Paris: Gallimard, 1979. (Eng. transl.: *The Cuisine of Sacrifice among the Greeks*. Trans. P. Wissing. Chicago: University of Chicago Press, 1989.)

Dougherty, C. *The Poetics of Colonization. From City to Text in Archaic Greece*. New York and Oxford: Oxford University Press, 1993.

————. *The Raft of Odysseus. The Ethnographic Imagination of Homer's* Odyssey. Oxford: Oxford University Press, 2001.

Felson-Rubin, N. "Narrative Structure in Pindar's Ninth *Pythian.*" *Class. World* 71 (1978): 353–67.

Fontenrose, J. *The Delphic Oracle. Its Responses and Operations.* Berkeley and London: University of California Press, 1978.

Froidefond, C. *Lire Pindare.* Namur: Société des Etudes Classiques, 1989.

Gentili, B. *Poesia e pubblico nella Grecia antica da Omero al V secolo.* 2nd ed. Rome and Bari: Laterza, 1989. (Eng. transl.: *Poetry and Its Public in Ancient Greece: From Homer to the Fifth Century.* Trans. A. T. Cole. Baltimore and London: Johns Hopkins University Press, 1988.)

————, ed. *Cirene. Storia, mito, letteratura.* Urbino: Quattro Venti, 1990.

Gentili, B., P. Angeli Bernardini, E. Cingano, and P. Giannini. *Pindaro. Le Pitiche.* Milan: Mondadori, 1995.

Giangiulio, M. "Deformità eroiche e tradizioni di fondazione. Batto, Miscello e l'oracolo delfico." *Ann. Scuola Norm. Sup. Pisa* III.11 (1981): 1–24.

————. *Ricerche su Crotone arcaica.* Pisa: Scuola Normale Superiore, 1989.

Giannini, P. "Interpretazione della *Pitica* 4 di Pindaro." *Quad. Urb. Cult. Class.* 31 (1979): 35–63.

————. "Cirene nella poesia greca. Tra mito e storia." In B. Gentili, ed., *Cirene. Storia, mito, letteratura,* 51–95. Urbino: Quattro Venti, 1990.

Gianotti, G. F. *Per una poetica pindarica.* Turin: Paravia, 1975.

Gierth, L. *Griechische Gründungsgeschichten als Zeugnisse historischen Denkens vor dem Einsetzen der Geschichtsschreibung.* Freiburg i. B. (dissertation), 1971.

Goodchild, R. G. *Kyrene und Apollonia.* Zurich: Raggi, 1971.

Graham, A. J. "The Authenticity of the ORKION TON OIKISTERON of Cyrene." *Journ. Hell. Stud.* 80 (1960): 94–111.

Hubbard, Th. K. *The Pindaric Mind. A Study of Logical Structure in Early Greek Poetry.* Leiden: Brill, 1985.

Hunter, R. *The Argonautica of Apollonios: Literary Studies.* Cambridge: Cambridge University Press, 1993.

Hurst, A., ed. *Pindare. Entretiens sur l'Antiquité classique* XXXI. Vandœuvres and Geneva: Fondation Hardt, 1985.

Jähne, A. "Land und Gesellschaft in Cyrenes Frühzeit (7.–6. Jahrhundert v. u. Z.)." *Klio* 70 (1988): 145–66.

Jeffery, J. H. "The Pact of the First Settlers at Cyrene." *Historia* 10 (1961): 139–47.

Kirchberg, J. *Die Funktion der Orakel im Werke Herodots.* Göttingen: Vandenhoeck & Ruprecht, 1965.

Kirkwood, G. *Selections from Pindar.* Chico, Calif.: Scholars Press, 1982.

Köhnken, A. "'Meilichos orga.' Liebesthematik und aktueller Sieg in der neunten pythischen Ode Pindars." In A. Hurst, ed., *Pindare. Entretiens sur l'Antiquité classique XXXI,* 71–111. Vandœuvres and Geneva: Fondation Hardt, 1985.

Krummen, E. *Pursos humnon. Festliche und mythisch-rituelle Tradition als Vor-

aussetzungen einer Pindarinterpretation (Isthmie 4, Pythie 5, Olympie 1 und 3). Berlin and New York: de Gruyter, 1990.

Lachenaud, G. *Mythologies, religion, et philosophie de l'histoire dans Hérodote.* Lille and Paris: Champion, 1978.

Lefkowitz, M. R. "Pindar's *Pythian* V." In A. Hurst, ed., *Pindare. Entretiens sur l'Antiquité classique XXXI*, 33–63. Vandœuvres and Geneva: Fondation Hardt, 1985. (Repr. 1991, 169–90).

———. *First-Person Fictions. Pindar's Poetic "I."* Oxford: Clarendon Press, 1991.

Leschhorn, W. *"Gründer der Stadt." Studien zu einem politisch-religiösen Phänomen der Griechischen Geschichte.* Weisbaden and Stuttgart: Steiner, 1984.

Létoublon, F. "Le serment fondateur." *Mètis* 4 (1989): 101–15.

Loraux, N. *Les enfants d'Athéna. Idées athéniennes sur la citoyenneté et sur la division des sexes.* Paris: Maspero, 1981. (Eng. transl.: *The Children of Athena. Athenian Ideas about Citizenship and the Division between the Sexes.* Trans. C. Levine. Princeton: Princeton University Press, 1984.)

Malkin, I. *Religion and Colonization in Ancient Greece.* Leiden: Brill, 1987.

———. *Myth and Territory in the Spartan Mediterranean.* Cambridge: Cambridge University Press, 1994.

Malten, L. *Kyrene. Sagengeschichtliche und historische Untersuchungen.* Berlin: Weidmann, 1911.

Masson, O. "Le nom de Battos, fondateur de Cyrène, et un groupe de mots grecs apparentés." *Glotta* 54 (1976): 84–98.

Miller, Th. *Die griechische Kolonisation im Spiegel literarischer Zeugnisse.* Tübingen: Gunter Narr, 1997.

Motte, A. *Prairies et Jardins de la Grèce Antique. De la Religion à la Philosophie.* Brussels: Palais des Académies, 1973.

Musti, D., ed. *Le origini dei Greci. Dori e mondo egeo.* Rome and Bari: Laterza, 1985.

Nafissi, M. "A proposito degli Aigheidai. Grandi ghéne e emporia nei rapporti Sparta-Cirene." *Ann. Fac. Lett. Filos. Perugia* 18 (1980/1981): 183–213.

———. "Battiadi e Aigheidai. Per la storia dei rapporti tra Cirene e Sparta in età arcaica." In G. Barker et al., eds. *Cyrenaica in Antiquity*, 375–88. Oxford: B.A.R., 1985.

Parke, H. W., and D.E.W. Wormell. *The Delphic Oracle.* 2 vols. Oxford: Blackwell, 1956.

Parker, R. *Miasma. Pollution and Purification in Early Greek Religion.* Oxford: Clarendon Press, 1983.

Prinz, F. *Gründungsmythen und Sagenchronologie.* Munich: Beck, 1979.

Robbins, E. "Cyrene and Cheiron: The Myth of Pindar's Ninth *Pythian.*" *Phoenix* 32 (1978): 91–104.

Sakellariou, M. B. *La migration grecque en Ionie.* Athens: Institut français, 1958.

Schmid, B. *Studien zu Griechischen Ktisissagen.* Frieburg i. d. Schw.: Paulus Druckerei, 1947.

Segal, C. *Pindar's Mythmaking. The Fourth Pythian Ode.* Princeton: Princeton University Press, 1986.

Stucchi, S. *Architettura cirenaica.* Rome: "L'Erma" de Bretschneider, 1975.

Studniczka, F. *Kyrene. Eine altgriechische Göttin.* Leipzig: Brockhaus, 1890.

Suárez de la Torre, E. "El mito de Cirene y la victoria de Telesicrates (Pind. *Pyth.* IX)." *Est. Clas.* 26 (1984): 199–208.

Vallet, G. *Rhégion et Zancle. Histoire, commerce, et civilisation des cités chalcidiennes du détroit de Messine.* Paris: de Boccard, 1958.

Vannicelli, P. "Gli Egidi e la relazione tra Sparta e Cirene in età arcaica." *Quad. Urb. Cult. Class.* 70 (1992): 55–73.

———. *Erodoto e la storia dell'alto e medio arcaismo (Sparta-Tessaglia-Cirene).* Rome: GEI, 1993.

Vian, F. "Les Anténorides et les Carnéia." *Rev. Et. Gr.* 68 (1955): 307–11.

———. *Les origines de Thèbes. Cadmos et les Spartes.* Paris: Klincksieck, 1963.

Williams, F. *Callimachus. Hymn to Apollo.* Oxford: Clarendon Press, 1978.

Woodbury, L. "Cyrene and the *teleuta* of Marriage in Pindar's Ninth Pythian Ode." *Trans. Amer. Philol. Assoc.* 112 (1982): 245–58.

Index